MAMMALS OF FLORIDA

By
Larry N. Brown, Ph. D.

Writing of this manuscript was funded by

**Florida Game and Fresh Water Fish Commission
Nongame Wildlife Program**

Windward Publishing, Inc.
105 NE 25th St.   P. O. Box 371005   Miami, FL 33137

Cover photos: front, bobcat, L. N. Brown; *back,* gray foxes, J. Waters.

*This book is dedicated to my late grandfather, IVO B. BROWN,
of Fair Grove, Greene County, Missouri, who was a devoted
conservationist, and my first teacher of mammalian natural history.*

Also by the author:
**Dolphins & Whales Including Other Sea Mammals
and The Manatee** (formerly **Sea Mammals**)

Contents

Preface

Prior to the publication of this book, there was no comprehensive guide to all the species of mammals living in Florida and its adjacent waters. The general public has difficulty identifying or obtaining information on Florida species. This book provides descriptive information on the mammals of Florida and is a comprehensive reference to facts about their lives.

I have spent more than 35 years studying mammals throughout the United States and accumulating a wealth of information on their natural history and ecology. Twenty-five of those years were concentrated specifically on the Florida fauna while I was employed as a university professor and researcher, visiting all corners of our varied and interesting state in pursuit of mammals.

This book is designed to serve both the layperson interested in knowing Florida's mammals, as well as the professional wildlife biologist, mammalogist, or natural resource manager who is making faunal evaluations in the state of Florida. Descriptive terms used in the text are as nontechnical as possible. Where technical language is necessary, every attempt is made to make terminology clear.

It is my sincere hope that this book will stimulate an even greater interest in the mammalian fauna of Florida among individuals who may discover new knowledge concerning mammals, and encourage them to devise better measures for conserving this valuable resource. The present generation has the responsibility to preserve suitable habitat throughout the state to ensure that Florida's mammal heritage is passed intact to future generations.

I wish to give special thanks to my children, Kristopher, Laurel, Curtis, Caleb, and Wesley, for providing invaluable assistance in preparing and proofreading the extensive manuscript dealing with Florida's mammals.

Larry N. Brown, Ph.D.

Introduction

Human beings have more than a passing interest in mammals—we are part of that group, and thus share a kinship to all the warm-blooded furry creatures of the world. This group also contains the largest animals that have ever lived, encompasses most of our pets and domestic animals, and even includes a few species of ubiquitous pests. The ways of mammals provide us with a source of endless fascination, and studying them helps us understand the human species a great deal better.

Mammals are warm-blooded vertebrates (homeotherms), and the only animals that have mammary glands that secrete milk to nourish the young. The word mammal comes from the Latin word which means breast or mammary gland. Also, mammals are the only animals on earth that have evolved hair to cover the body. However, some mammals, like the whales and dolphins, have hair reduced to just a few bristles in the snout or mouth area of young individuals. Other characteristics of mammals include a four-chambered heart; rooted teeth of four types (incisors, canines, premolars, and molars); and a single bone (the dentary) comprising each half of the lower jaw. Mammals exhibit two sets of teeth during their lifetime. Young mammals have a temporary set of small deciduous or milk teeth that are replaced by a permanent set of larger adult teeth.

Florida has a surprisingly rich and varied mammal fauna considering its relatively isolated position, surrounded on three sides by water, and its low elevation, just above sea level. There are 96 mammal species in Florida, including 63 terrestrial forms (orders Marsupialia 1, Insectivora 5, Chiroptera 18, Edentata 1, Lagomorpha 3, Rodentia 22, Carnivora 12, Artiodactyla 3), and 31 marine species (orders Cetacea 28, Sirenia 1, Pinnipedia 2) living in the warm waters off Florida's coasts. Thus marine mammals make up one-third of Florida's total mammal species.

Of the 63 terrestrial species living in Florida, 53 are native mammals and ten species (about 16 percent) are introduced non-native forms, now permanently established in the state. Three mammals that were known to exist in Florida in early historic times are now extirpated (gone from the state). These species are the red wolf (Canis rufus), the West Indian monk seal (Monachus tropicalis), and the buffalo (Bison bison).

Because of Florida's proximity to the Caribbean region and tropical America, it might easily be assumed that many of the mammal species may have close affinities there. This is true for the marine mammals—about 80 percent of the species include the tropical oceans in their ranges. However, the geographical affinities of the terrestrial mammals are mainly in temperate North America and, to some extent, in Mexico or Central America. Only one Florida species of terrestrial mammal, Wagner's mastiff bat (Eumops glaucinus), appears to have invaded from the Caribbean region. Therefore, the water barriers to the south of Florida have effectively prevented island hopping and invasion of terrestrial mammal species from the tropics.

In a few cases, endemic species of mammals (i.e., those species found nowhere else) have evolved in Florida over the past several thousand years. The most notable examples are the round-tailed muskrat *(Neofiber alleni)*, which occurs only in Florida and extreme southeastern Georgia, and the Florida mouse *(Peromyscus floridanus)*, confined almost entirely to the Florida peninsula region. In addition to these two interesting rodents, numerous endemic subspecies or races are found in Florida. These various endemics have evolved primarily on coastal islands or isolated islands of habitat on the mainland.

Several factors unique to Florida's geography have contributed to the unusual nature of our terrestrial mammal fauna. For example, the long narrow shape of the peninsula helps isolate one population from another and restrict the interchange of genes between populations. Also, the low elevation of the Florida land mass has subjected mammal populations to periodic inundation and isolation as sea levels fluctuated extensively. During past geological periods, sea levels have risen or dropped more than 100 feet from the current level. The presence of long coastlines and the development of barrier islands off Florida's shorelines likewise have contributed to the isolation of populations and development of genetic variation in mammals.

The Florida peninsula, with its warm temperate to subtropical climate, has served as a refugium for mammalian species during times of cooler ice age climates farther north. These mammals were able to survive in Florida, and in some cases, no doubt recolonized northward after the ice ages passed. There is also a great variety in the soil types and vegetative communities in Florida. This clearly reflects the complex geological and climatic history of the area, as well as drainage patterns, topography, susceptibility to fire, and the periodic effects of strong tropical hurricanes. These factors have contributed to a rather broad spectrum of ecological habitats occupied by numerous divergent mammalian species.

Geographical range maps are included for all terrestrial mammal species that do not have statewide distribution in Florida. The range of the species within the state is indicated by the dark areas or by asterisks. No range maps are shown for the wide-ranging marine mammals found along or off the Atlantic and Gulf coasts of the state.

Major Types of
Habitats in Florida

Mammals often are adapted or restricted to specific types of plant communities or habitats. A brief characterization of the major types of terrestrial and wetland habitats located in Florida will be helpful in understanding mammal distribution patterns. The terminology used is a somewhat modified version of that originally developed by John H. Davis of the University of Florida, Gainesville.

1. Pine Flatwoods

In these habitats the dominant tree is one or more species of pine, including slash pine, longleaf pine, or pond pine, combined with various understory plants such as wiregrass, palmettos, scrubby oaks, rusty lyonia, and blueberries. Flatwoods sites tend to be sandy with some organic matter present, and they are level and poorly drained. There is normally an acid, organic hardpan developed 1-4 feet beneath the surface of the soil. Pine flatwoods have a low species diversity of plants, partially due to lack of moisture during the annual dry season. Periodic fires are a natural and predictable aspect of the ecology of pine flatwoods. The pines are fire adapted and usually survive a fire, but hardwoods are killed or suppressed.

2. Longleaf Pine-Turkey Oak Woodlands

These habitats are often referred to as sandhill communities, and develop on well drained, yellowish to whitish sands. Longleaf pines and turkey oaks are the dominant trees, but other species such as bluejack oak, persimmon, wild cherry, southern red oak, and sand live oak are also often present. The understory plants include palmettos, wiregrass, partridge pea, milk pea, foxglove, and beggar's tick. In the central and southern areas of the Florida peninsula, slash pine often joins or replaces longleaf pine as the dominant overstory species associated with turkey oak. The sands where this habitat occurs are usually deep and sterile, but contain more organic matter than the soils of sand pine scrub. Fire is a dominant force in the ecology of the longleaf pine-turkey oak communities as it is in sand pine scrub. The pine trees are fire adapted and usually survive the periodic burns. Hardwoods are killed or suppressed by fire which clears the understory and favors the dominance of grasses and forbs. Burrowing animals play an important role in cycling nutrients in sandhill communities.

Habitats   7

pine flatwoods with saw palmetto-grass understory

pine-turkey oak woodlands; gopher mounds in foreground

sand pine scrub habitat; white sands visible

live oak-cabbage palm forest

Habitats

southern mixed hardwood forest in
north Florida

tropical hardwood forest

coastal strand vegetation

upland wet prairie

Habitats

3. Sand Pine Scrubs

These habitats are found only in Florida and are the most xeric type of plant community present in the state. They are dominated by a short-needle pine called sand pine and several scrubby hardwoods, including sand live oak, dwarf oak, Chapman's oak, myrtle oak, scrub hickory, and scrub holly. The habitat develops only on the highly sorted, sterile, white sands of old beach dunes. Such dunes of deep sand develop along present or former marine shorelines. The soil is extremely low in organic matter and the community is adapted to and controlled by periodic catastrophic fires. The cones of burned and dead sand pines open and release seeds after the fire. This results in the growth of even-aged new stands of sand pine following a fire. Many endemic plants and animals have evolved in the Florida sand pine scrubs.

4. Live Oak-Cabbage Palm Forests

These habitats are often called mesic hammocks and constitute the climax vegetation for much of central and northern Florida. The dominant tree species are live oak, water oak, laurel oak, southern magnolia, American holly, hophornbeam, blue beech, and cabbage palm. The understory is usually open because the dense canopy favors only shade-tolerant species. The mesic hammock tends to develop on rich sandy soils having a good organic content near the surface. For the climax community to be reached in plant succession, periodic fires must be excluded. The plant diversity in this habitat is high. Epiphytes such as Spanish moss, orchids, resurrection ferns, and bromeliads are usually present on the large old trees of this habitat. Either the live oaks or the cabbage palms may dominate certain areas alone.

5. Southern Mixed Hardwood Forests

These habitats are characterized by high species diversity, and constitute the climax vegetation on the clay-based soils of northern Florida. The dominant trees include American beech, southern magnolia, white oak, laurel oak, Shumard oak, basket oak, live oak, sweetgum, pignut hickory, mockernut hickory, white ash, spruce pine, and basswood. The understory includes redbud, white dogwood, blue beech, hackberry, and mulberry. The early and mid-successional stages of this community may be primarily loblolly or shortleaf pine, but these are, with time, gradually replaced by mixed hardwoods. Fire is rare to absent in the mature stages of the community, and can retard plant succession and maintain a pine sub-climax if it occurs in the earlier successional stages.

6. Tropical Hardwood Forests

These habitats are also called tropical hammocks or tropical broadleaf evergreen forests, and they occur only in southern Florida. The tropical hardwood forest contains the most species of any Florida habitat. These forests occur on the limestone ridge running along the Atlantic coast in southeastern Florida and on rocklands throughout much of the Florida Keys. Isolated islands of tropical hammock also dot the Everglades and southwestern coast of Florida.

10   Habitats

The dominant trees include gumbo limbo, West Indian mahogany, poisonwood, strangler fig, Jamaican dogwood, manchineel, stopper, wild mastic, pigeon plum, sapote, lancewood, bustic, and royal palm. Lignum vitae, thatch palm, Sargent's palm, coconut palm, tamarind, and torchwood also occur in some areas of the Florida Keys. Vines, epiphytic orchids, bromeliads and ferns are also abundant. Tropical hardwood forest is the climax community for the uplands in southern Florida, assuming fire does not set back succession and favor southern slash pines or pioneer communities.

7. Coastal Strand Communities
These communities develop along beaches bordering the ocean and include the zones of vegetation that begin at the dune and extend inland. Coastal strand vegetation normally is best developed where there is a strong surf and onshore winds. The flora of the beach and foredune include only those pioneer species that can establish themselves in shifting sands. They include railroad vine, sea oats, sand pea, and beach morning glory. Inland from the crest of the dune the dominant species include saw palmetto, yuccas, prickly pear, saltbush, wax myrtle, dwarf oaks, and cabbage palms. In warmer areas sea grape, buttonwood, and cocoplum also can be found. From the backdune inland, the vegetation becomes progressively woodier, taller, and less sheared by wind and salt spray. Progressing inland, there usually is a series of older dunes, each with larger and more mature scrub oaks, palmettos, sand pines, and cabbage palms. Coastal strand vegetation is stressed by the saline environment, by high onshore winds, and by moving sands. Salt spray plays a role analogous to fire, especially near the ocean, by retarding plant succession and helping to maintain pioneer stages.

8. Upland Prairies
These habitats are dominated by various grasses, including broomsedges, wiregrass, sedges, dropseed, and carpet grasses. They occur in an intermediate position between marshes or wet prairies and the forested uplands. Upland prairies are often subjected to seasonal saturation or temporary flooding during the wet season as water tables rise. This helps protect grassy areas from the germination of seeds of mesic trees. Saw palmettos, blueberries, dewberries, fetterbush, and staggerbush are common shrubby plants found in the upland prairies. In most areas north and west of Lake Okeechobee, where vast native prairies once occurred, the habitat has been converted to permanent pasture or improved pasture by the planting of introduced grasses.

9. Old-field Communities
A sequence of weedy-grassy plant communities develop on old cropland or fallow fields after cessation of agricultural activities. This community development involves the invasion of annual and perennial grasses and herbs, such as sandspur, nettle, chickweed, dropseed, foxtail, broomsedge, dog fennel, and ragweed. Bare, open soil gradually disappears under a carpet of weeds and grasses. Eventually, various invader tree seeds germinate, such as wax myrtle,

old-field early successional stage

freshwater marsh with heavy emergent vegetation

coastal salt marsh

mangrove swamp showing aerial prop-roots of trees

Habitats

cypress swamp with many air plants

black gum swamp showing enlarged
tree bases

floodplain forest

pines, sassafras, juniper, persimmon, wild cherry, wild plum, and scrub oaks. Over a period of years, the weedy-grassy field will become a thicket of vines, briars, and invading trees. Several species of small mammals are adapted to life in these varied and rapidly changing seral stages of secondary succession called the old-field communities.

10. Freshwater Marshes

These habitats consist of aquatic herbaceous plant communities that develop where the soil is completely saturated or covered with fresh water for an extended period each growing season. The plants consist of emergent, floating, and submergent vegetation, and the dominant species vary according to local conditions and the area of the state. Some of the subtypes of freshwater marshes include wet prairies, sawgrass marshes, cattail marshes, bullrush marshes, maidencane prairies, arrowhead-pickerelweed marshes, spikerush marshes, sedge marshes, and switchgrass marshes. Fire during the dry season is important in recycling nutrients and in maintaining the herbaceous nature by killing woody plants that have germinated.

11. Coastal Salt Marshes

These habitats develop along marine coasts, estuaries, and river mouths where the wave action is low and daily tides occur. Many salt marshes are dominated almost completely by one species such as saltgrass, blackrush, cord grass, glasswort, or saltwort. The species that dominates depends on the type of substrate present and the degree of inundation by tidal flow. Tides provide food and remove waste for the animals and plants adapted to live in salt marshes. In the warmer regions of coastal Florida, mangroves are interspersed with salt marshes or replace them entirely.

12. Mangrove Swamps

These saline habitats develop along warmer marine coasts, estuaries, and the mouths of rivers where the wave action is low. Three different species of mangrove habitats occur in movement inland from the ocean. The first encountered is the red mangrove zone, with prominent stilt roots bracing the trees against wave action. The second zone inland is dominated by black mangroves. At high tide the black mangrove roots are usually covered with water. The third and innermost zone is only inundated occasionally and is dominated by white mangroves and buttonwood trees. Leaf fall from the trees provides organic material that fuels the food chains of many organisms living in the water of mangrove swamps.

13. Cypress Swamps

Cypress swamp habitats develop along water courses, lake borders, and ponds where water stands above ground level for much of the year. The soils are generally sandy and acidic. The dominant tree is bald cypress which characteristically develops a buttressed trunk and numerous spike-like "knees" that grow upward from the root system, terminating above the water level. Other plants present include red maple, black gum, sweetbay, buttonbush, waterlocust, pop ash, and willow. Ground cover is sparse, but royal ferns, poison ivy, and greenbrier are common. Epiphytes include Spanish moss, bromeliads, orchids, and ferns. Bald cypress drops its needles during the winter months, and the swamp is much more open and barren looking than during the growing season.

14. Bay/Gum Swamps

These habitats are dominated by broadleaf evergreen trees that grow in saturated soils or standing water. The soils are very peaty and acidic. Three species of bay trees occur, either singly or in mixed stands, in these swamps: loblolly bay, sweet bay, and red bay. The three bays also often grow with black gum, and the latter sometimes forms almost pure stands. Other plants that are also often present include willow, buttonbush, pop ash, red maple, and sweetgum. Epiphytes are not common, but vines and ground ferns are abundant at the edges of bay/gum swamps. When stands of bay trees occur in isolated, pond-like depressions surrounded by drier habitats, they are usually called bayheads.

15. Floodplain Forests

Floodplain forests are also called hydric hardwood forests and develop in the floodplains of rivers and lake basins. The soils are rich in organic matter and saturated with water or actually inundated during floods. Surface water normally recedes fairly quickly, and during the dry season the humic soils dry out somewhat. A wide variety of trees from a dense overstory including water oak, sweetgum, water hickory, overcup oak, cabbage palm, red maple, pop ash, chestnut oak, spruce pine, and laurel oak. Epiphytes are abundant on the older trees and the understory is rather open and easy to walk through. Seasonal flooding is a dominant force in the ecology of this ecosystem. If periodic flooding is eliminated (such as by stream channelization or flood control projects), then more mesic forests will develop on floodplain sites.

Species Accounts

ORDER MARSUPIALIA
Pouched Mammals

Members of this group differ from other mammals by the presence of a pouch on the abdomen of the female, where the young are sheltered while they suckle. The order Marsupialia is very primitive, with the skeleton showing certain affinities to reptiles.

Most species of pouched mammals or marsupials inhabit Australia and nearby islands. These include kangaroos, wallabies, wombats, bandicoots, koalas, Tasmanian devils, marsupial moles, and marsupial wolves. Several species also occur in South and Central America. Only one species, the Virginia opossum, is found north of Mexico. The gestation period is very short and the young are poorly developed and very small at birth or parturition. They complete their development over several weeks after attaching to a nipple in the pouch. There is often considerable mortality of the poorly developed offspring at the time of birth, before they reach the pouch (or marsupium) and attach to a mammary gland. Young marsupials are also vulnerable to predation after they develop and finally leave the safety of the pouch to live on their own.

Marsupials are generally at a competitive disadvantage when compared to the more advanced placental mammals. They are sluggish, slow, and possess a low order of intelligence. Also, reproductive processes are inefficient (only a primitive placenta develops) and they are subject to higher mortality than advanced mammals.

Virginia Opossum *(Didelphis virginiana)*
Description: Florida's 'possum is about the size of a house cat, has a long, naked, grasping (prehensile) tail, and small leaf-like ears. The feet are shaped somewhat like human hands with a thumb-like inner toe. The fur color of Florida specimens is variable and ranges from the common gray form to an almost all white or all black coloration. Females have a fur-lined pouch on the abdomen, but males lack pouches and are heavier and larger. The skull is identified by a prominent median ridge on top, small brain size, and 50 teeth present in the jaws. No other Florida land mammal has more than 44 teeth.

Geographical Range: The opossum occurs throughout the state and in virtually all habitats. It also occurs throughout most of the United States except for a few western and northern states. Its range has been expanding northward and westward in historic times, aided greatly by human activities such as farming, ranching, lumbering, and outright releases of opossums into new areas.

Habitat Preference: Opossums show no clear-cut habitat preference and can be found virtually anywhere there are trees. They are excellent climbers and often seek safety in treetops. In some Florida residential and suburban areas, opossums are surprisingly abundant, nesting in yard trees or outbuildings.

Life History and Reproduction: Opossums forage extensively on the ground as well as in trees. They are mainly nocturnal, and have a slow, ambling gait. They are probably the most common roadkill victim found on Florida highways.

When cornered, opossums are slow witted and nonaggressive. They often open their mouths and hiss or growl at an offender, but rarely attack. If tormented extensively they sometimes feign death in a behavioral pattern commonly called "playing 'possum." When handled in this condition, they are limp and appear

Virginia opossum, 27-33 in. (68-85 cm) overall, tail 11-14 in. (29-35 cm)

dead. However, they quickly regain consciousness and escape after the molester has lost interest.

The breeding season is long, extending from December to midsummer in Florida. Each female usually produces two litters per year and the gestation period is an incredibly short 13 days. As many as 18-25 young may be born at one time, but the 13 milk-producing teats in the pouch limit the maximum number of young that can complete development. The actual number of young leaving the pouch averages 6-7 in Florida. When young opossums finally leave the pouch, they are about the size of a small rat and 70-80 days old. For a time they hang onto the mother's back or tail and are carried about as she forages. They are on their own for the first time when about three months old, and some breed when only six months of age.

The opossum is omnivorous and eats almost any animal or vegetable food available. In residential areas they often are found foraging in garbage cans if they can gain access to them.

The maximum longevity of opossums in the wild is not known; in captivity they have lived as long as 8-10 years. Population turnover in native Florida populations appears to occur every 4-6 years. They are prey for many carnivores, including dogs, domestic cats, foxes, bobcats, owls, and humans.

Economic Importance and Remarks: In Florida, opossums are sometimes hunted for food but are not considered an important game animal. The pelt is sometimes sold; however, it is of very low fur value in southern localities. Opossums cause some agricultural damage in certain truck gardening operations, but are not a major economic problem to most farming.

The forked penis of male opossums is sometimes a subject of interest, leading to the myth that opossums copulate via the female's nose. Instead, the bifurcate penis enters the paired lateral vaginae of the female to deposit sperm.

Although the opossum possesses a low order of intelligence, its lifestyle is adaptable to most ecological situations found in Florida. This may account for the opossum remaining essentially unchanged by evolution since the Eocene geological period. Its omnivorous food habits coupled with a high reproductive rate make it one of the most common Florida mammals.

ORDER INSECTIVORA
Insectivores

The insectivores are so named because insects often form the bulk of their food; however, these mammals also consume a wide variety of other small animals. They all possess long, pointed, flexible snouts that are sensitive organs of touch and smell. The bead-like eyes are tiny, and in some species are permanently closed. The leaf-like ears are buried in the head fur and not clearly visible.

This order includes the smallest mammals alive on earth, the shrews. One species, the pygmy shrew, has a body weight of 1/10 of an ounce or less. Insectivores, especially the shrews, also have a high metabolic rate and may consume nearly twice their body weight in food each day. Since most members of the order do not hibernate, they must have a constant and dependable supply of invertebrates available to feed upon. Insectivores have a reputation for being aggressive foragers, and sometimes they kill and consume prey somewhat larger than themselves. One group, the moles, have poorly developed or vestigial eyes and can only distinguish light and dark.

Most insectivores have a short life span and a rather high reproductive rate. Mortality is also high and populations turn over rapidly.

Insectivores are relatively primitive and considered the evolutionary stem group from which the more advanced mammals derived. The order has a worldwide distribution except Australia and part of South America. They include hedgehogs, solenodons, tenrecs, shrews, and moles. Five species of insectivores live in Florida.

Southeastern Shrew *(Sorex longirostris)*

Description: The southeastern shrew is Florida's smallest mammal and the only long-tailed shrew living in the state. It weighs only about 1/10 of an ounce (approximately the same as a penny) and is around two inches long. The fur is reddish brown and the tail reaches at least a half-inch beyond the length of an extended back leg. The skull is identified by its small size and the third unicusp being smaller than the fourth unicusp (small teeth near the front of the upper tooth row).

Geographical Range: This shrew is recorded only from the northern two-thirds of Florida. See map on page 200. The southernmost records are from Highlands County in the southcentral portion of the peninsula. Nationally, the range of the southeastern shrew fits approximately the southeastern quadrant of the country.

Habitat Preference: Most of the Florida records are from moist woodlands and floodplain forests. In many localities it has been identified in drier upland habitats.

Life History and Reproduction: The life history of this shrew in Florida is very poorly known because it is rarely captured. This apparent rareness of the shrew generally reflects nothing more than its reluctance to enter standard mammal traps. It can be taken in pitfall traps or sunken cans placed in the

C. BROWN

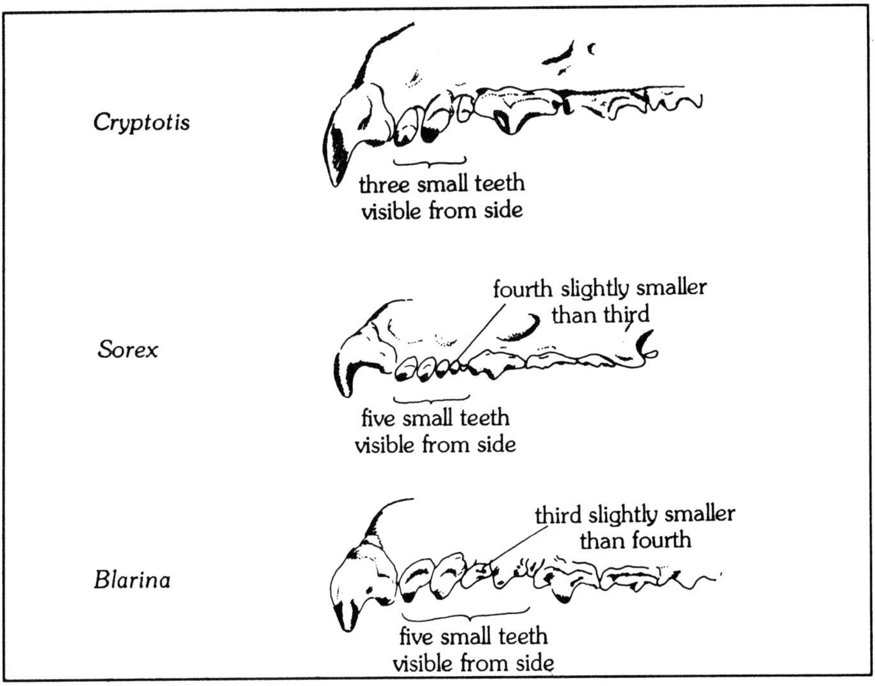

Cryptotis
three small teeth
visible from side

Sorex
fourth slightly smaller
than third
five small teeth
visible from side

Blarina
third slightly smaller
than fourth
five small teeth
visible from side

tooth arrangement in three genera of shrews

T. FRENCH

southeastern shrew, 3-3.6 in. (76-92 mm) overall, tail 1-1.3 in. (26-34 mm)

ground, but such methods are seldom used because of the hard work involved in setting the traps.

The shrews spend most of their time under the leaf litter of the forest floor and in subterranean tunnels. Nests are bulky and are made of leaf litter lined with fine grasses or fibers. They are often located in or under logs, stumps, and tree roots.

Analysis of stomach contents reveals they feed primarily on spiders, lepidoptera larvae, snails, centipedes, and slugs.

Southeastern shrews are known to breed during the spring and summer months when arthropods are most abundant, and produce 4-6 young per litter. The length of gestation or length of maternal care is unknown.

Economic Importance and Remarks: The southeastern shrew has little or no economic importance, except as a voracious consumer of arthropods living in the leaf litter of the forest floor.

This species is sometimes taken by owls, opossums, snakes, and domestic cats. All shrews have strong musk glands and sometimes they are killed by predators and not eaten.

Those populations of the southeastern shrew found in the Homosassa Springs area are listed as a "species of special concern" by the Florida Game and Fresh Water Fish Commission.

Southern Short-Tailed Shrew *(Blarina carolinensis)*

Description: The southern short-tailed shrew is slightly smaller than a mouse and has velvet-like, slate-gray fur. The tail is short and barely reaches beyond the extended hind foot. The gray coloration is only slightly darker on

20   Insectivores

the back than on the belly. The summer pelage is a bit lighter and browner than winter pelage, indicating there are two molts a year.

Geographical Range: This species ranges throughout Florida, except for the Keys. The range in the United States includes the southeastern quadrant of the country.

Habitat Preference: The southern short-tailed shrew is most common in wooded localities, but sometimes it is found in old fields, weedy or brushy areas, and openings in the forest. It is often found associated with the runways and tunnels of mice and moles.

Life History and Reproduction: All shrews, including this common Florida species, have a high metabolic rate and spend most of their time actively foraging for food. They have a heart rate of 160 beats per minute and respiration is around 150 breaths per minute.

L. N. BROWN

short-tailed shrew, 3.1-4.7 in. (78-120 mm) overall, tail 0.6-1.1 in. (14-28 mm)

J. F. PARNELL

least shrew, 2.8-3.6 in. (70-92 mm) overall, tail 0.4-0.9 in. (12-24 mm)

The diet of short-tailed shrews consists of mice, small snakes, snails, slugs, centipedes, millipedes, insects, spiders, and earthworms. This species is considered one of the most pugnacious of all shrews, and it will attack and kill prey much larger than itself. They accomplish this partly through the presence of a poison-producing, submaxillary salivary gland. The poison in the shrew's saliva enters a bitten animal, causing the victim's breathing and heart rate to slow while it is being subdued by this pint-sized predator.

The nest is a bulky ball composed of dried grasses and leaves, usually placed in a stump, log, or underground. It is 6-8 inches in diameter and may have several openings.

Short-tailed shrews breed primarily from early spring to late fall, but sporadic breeding is also reported during the winter. Two or three litters are produced annually comprised of 2-8 young (average 5.5) each. The gestation period is about 21 days long. The young are weaned at an age of just over one month and they can breed when three months old.

Economic Importance and Remarks: Short-tailed shrews are of some economic benefit because they often kill rodents and consume large numbers of insects and other arthropods.

Few animals feed on the short-tailed shrew because it has strong musk glands located in the flank area, which give it a pungent smell. Owls, however, take them regularly, and domestic cats frequently kill shrews but seldom eat them. Cats very often deposit them at the back door of the house to be disposed of by the owner.

The vocalization of short-tailed shrews consists of a series of high-pitched squeaks and clicks, some of which are above the audible range of hearing for humans. Some researchers believe these sounds are part of a system of echolocation used by shrews to find food and detect objects in their path. Shrews do possess small, weak eyes and an echolocation system would be useful to a small, foraging predator in dark tunnels or nocturnal conditions. Further research is needed to verify whether shrews use more than just keen senses of smell, hearing, and touch to locate food.

Short-tailed shrews kept in captivity are gregarious and get along well together if well fed. Fighting and cannibalism will occur, however, if the food supply is short.

As a result of several morphological and chromosomal studies published in recent years, the southern short-tailed shrew is now regarded as a separate species from the northern short-tailed shrew *(Blarina brevicauda)*. The two forms are very similar in general appearance, but the southern shrews are smaller in overall body size.

The Florida Game and Fresh Water Fish Commission lists the central west coast populations of the short-tailed shrew as a "species of special concern."

Least Shrew *(Cryptotis parva)*

Description: The least shrew is the second smallest mammal in Florida; only the southeastern shrew is smaller. The pelage is grayish brown on the upper

Insectivores

parts and distinctly paler on the underside. The feet are white or light gray and the tail is short, only slightly longer than the extended hind leg.

Geographical Range: In Florida, the least shrew has statewide distribution, except for the Keys. Its national range includes all of the eastern two-thirds of the United States south of the Great Lakes.

Habitat Preference: This species is found most often in dry grassy areas, fallow fields, and brushy, weedy sites. Occasionally they are in marshy habitats and woodlands as well. They often use the runways and tunnels of mice and moles.

Life History and Reproduction: The diet of the least shrew is very similar to that of the short-tailed shrew except that smaller prey are taken. The major food items are insects, spiders, centipedes, millipedes, snails, slugs, and earthworms. Preferred insects include beetles, lepidoptera, crickets, and grasshoppers. They actively forage both day and night to supply their very high metabolic needs. In captivity, least shrews consume their body weight in food each day. The species is gregarious and sociable; thus several can be housed together as long as plenty of food is available. If food runs short, cannibalism occurs.

Least shrews make a globular nest of dried grasses and leaves about 4-5 inches in diameter, lined with finely shredded grass. Males and females nest together and cooperate in caring for the young.

In Florida, least shrews can breed any month of the year and produce several litters per year. The size of the litter varies from 2-8, with 5 being the average size. The gestation period in more northern populations has been reported to be 21-23 days. The young are naked and helpless at birth, but are fully furred with open eyes at two weeks of age. They are weaned at three weeks of age and reach adult size when one month old. In captivity, I have observed breeding of individuals at five weeks of age. Females can come into estrus and breed again on the day they give birth.

Economic Importance and Remarks: Like the other Florida shrews, least shrews consume many insects. Occasionally they also enter commercial bee hives to feed on the larvae and pupae, which results in some damage to honey production. They can be controlled by using small mammal traps.

The major predators of the least shrew are owls, hawks, snakes, skunks, weasels, and cats. They have the musky, pungent odor characteristic of all shrews; therefore, least shrews are sometimes killed and not eaten by mammalian predators.

Eastern Mole (Scalopus aquaticus)

Description: The Florida form of the eastern mole is a pint-sized version of the species, being only about half the size of its northern form. Moles are extremely specialized anatomically for living under the ground (called a fossorial lifestyle). These specializations include broad, shovel-like front paws with large digging claws, and a long, flexible snout for probing in the soil. Moles are several times larger than shrews and are covered with velvety, silvery, gray-brown fur.

eastern mole, 4.5-5.3 in. (115-135 mm) overall, tail 0.6-1.0 in. (14-25 mm)

The tiny degenerate eyes have sealed eyelids and can only distinguish light from dark. Skin glands on the belly sometimes stain the fur a bright orange color in that area. They molt twice a year, in the spring and fall. The tail is short,nearly naked and functions as an important organ of touch in the underground world.

A mole's skull can be identified by its flat, triangular shape; narrow, delicate cheekbones; and teeth that lack the chestnut-brown staining found in the shrews.

Geographical Range: This mole occurs statewide except for the Keys. Nationally, the eastern mole is found in the eastern two-thirds of the United States, from the Great Lakes south.

Habitat Preference: The eastern mole is present in virtually all types of soil and in all terrestrial habitats from forest to grassland. It is often absent from saturated muck or peat soils and also missing in extremely sterile sandy soils in parts of Florida.

Life History and Reproduction: Moles spend their entire lives under the ground, living in labyrinthine tunnels that they excavate. The tunnels are of two different types. One tunnel is a pushed-up, elevated ridge that marks the mole's passage just beneath the surface of the ground. These are temporary, foraging tunnels (1 - 1½ inches in diameter) and are used only for a few days. The other type is located several inches to two feet beneath the surface and is more permanent in nature. When constructing the deep tunnels, the mole sometimes opens vertical shafts to the surface, through which it pushes up excess dirt into mounds. In sandy Florida soils, the mole builds these mounds much less frequently than it does in northern localities. Often in Florida, it merely redistributes the excavated soil beneath the surface into older sections of its tunnel system rather than making surface mounds. The small linear, elevated foraging tunnels are the usual evidence of the presence of moles in Florida.

Insectivores

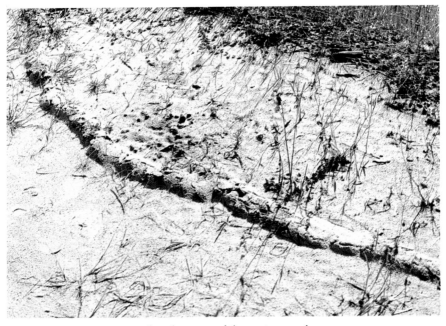

surface burrows of the eastern mole

star-nosed mole, 7.2-8.3 in. (183-210 mm) overall, tail 2.6-3.3 in. (65-83 mm)

Insectivores

25

Moles can dig rapidly and have been observed to excavate surface tunnels in sandy soil at a rate of more than 1½ feet per minute. Deeper tunnels proceed at a slower rate because of the need to redistribute excavated dirt. The mole's nest chamber is always constructed in one of the deeper tunnels of the system and is four to eight inches in diameter with multiple entrances. The bottom of this spherical cavity is normally lined with a thick bed of fine grasses and leaves.

Moles produce only one litter per year, born during the spring months. The litter size ranges from 2-5 and averages three. Breeding in Florida moles usually takes place in January or February. The exact length of gestation is disputed, but falls between 4-6 weeks. Young moles are naked and blind at birth, but grow rapidly and are able to fend for themselves when about four weeks old.

Moles are active both day and night and during all seasons of the year. Activity peaks in the early morning and late evening hours. Moles live a solitary life style and are antisocial except at the time of breeding. Normally, if two moles are placed together in a terrarium of dirt, they will fight almost continuously until one is dead.

The diet is variable, depending on habitat and season of the year, but consists of insects, earthworms, and many other kinds of soil organisms. The eastern mole has a voracious appetite, and each day consumes a sizeable percentage of its body weight in food.

Moles are probably fairly long-lived, especially for an insectivore. Their low annual breeding output would suggest they live several years, but very little information is available on their actual longevity.

Economic Importance and Remarks: The tunnel systems of Florida moles often cause damage to lawns, flower beds, agricultural crops, and golf courses. There are also instances where moles have caused extensive losses in Florida earthworm farms. Damage to plant bulbs and roots usually results from foraging by mice and rats that invade and utilize the extensive mole tunnel systems.

Moles are better controlled by traps than poison. The poisons used are seldom, if ever, consumed by moles and many poisons used persist in the soil and are damaging to the environment. A special trap is needed to successfully trap moles. Ordinary rat or mammal box traps are useless. Three types of mole traps are available: the choker-loop trap, the harpoon or pitchfork trap, and the scissor-jaw trap. For Florida's small-bodied mole, the scissor-jaw trap is by far the most effective, but unfortunately is seldom available at retail outlets. The harpoon trap is widely marketed, but because it was designed for the large northern moles, its effectiveness is limited in Florida. The traps operate on the principle that a mole will return to repair damage to its surface feeding tunnel, which has been artificially closed by the trapper. Therefore, the traps must be placed astride freshly dug surface tunnels to increase the probability that a mole will return to forage and be caught.

Moles, because of their fossorial life style, have very few predators. They also possess strong musk glands that give them a pungent odor and make them less palatable to many carnivores. Some species of snakes occasionally take moles, as do owls, skunks, foxes, and cats.

Moles have a positive value in tilling and farming soil, and in distributing organic matter and nutrients to plants. They also feed on certain types of destructive insects such as beetle larvae and lepidoptera larvae and pupae.

Once there was a viable business in mole pelts in both Europe and America, but they are not sold today. During the 1700s and 1800s, they were highly sought after for making soft, plush linings in purses, hats, tobacco pouches, pockets, and other garments.

Moles normally have five toes on each foot, but I once caught an eastern mole in my backyard that, surprisingly, had *seven* complete and separate toes on its right hind foot. Each digit had a completely normal claw on it, and there was no abnormality except the number of digits. Such an aberration as extra toes is rare in mammals.

Star-nosed Mole *(Condylura cristata)*

Description: The star-nosed mole is probably the most easily identified small mammal in Florida—it has 22 fleshy pink appendages on the nose. These appendages are delicate touch (tactile) receptors that form a unique rosette or star around the nasal openings. The thick fur is black to blackish brown on the back and slightly paler on the belly. The front paws are longer than they are wide and equipped with long, heavy digging claws on the toes. This mole has functional eyes, but they are very small bead-like organs that suggest very weak eyesight. The tail is long, scaly, moderately haired, and serves as a fat storage organ (thus the tail's diameter is large). The tail also functions as a sensitive tactile organ at the rear end of the body, and as a rudder when the star-nosed mole is swimming.

The skull is more narrow, delicate, and elongated than that of the eastern mole. A weak, slender zygomatic arch (cheekbone) is present as in the eastern mole skull. However, the star-nosed mole has 44 teeth in the skull; the eastern mole has only 36 teeth.

Geographical Range: In Florida, this species has been recorded only at two locations in Leon County, one location in Alachua County, and from the Okefenokee Swamp area. All of these sites are found in the northern third of Florida, which suggests this mole might occur in scattered isolated pockets over the northern portion of the state. See map on page 200. The United States range of the star-nosed mole encompasses the Great Lakes area, the northeastern states, and several scattered and apparently isolated populations in the southeastern states.

Habitat Preference: Moist saturated soils are the preferred habitat of this semiaquatic mole. Its tunnels usually border streams, swamps, marshes, and some of the burrows lead directly into the water.

Life History and Reproduction: Star-nosed moles are excellent swimmers and frequently forage for food in the aquatic environment. They also travel above ground and forage in the leaf litter like shrews. They are active both night and day. The diet consists of aquatic and terrestrial insects, aquatic worms, crayfish, minnows, frogs, salamanders, snails, and various other invertebrates.

Only one litter is produced each spring or early summer, consisting of 3-7 young (average 5). The gestation period is about 45 days. Newborn moles are naked, helpless, blind, and pink in color. Hair first appears at about 10 days of age and the eyes open at two weeks. They first leave the nest to forage for themselves when about four weeks old. Reproductive maturity does not occur until the following spring when the moles are about 10 months old.

Star-nosed moles are often difficult to trap with standard mole traps. I once spent five days trying to catch a single animal using both scissors and pitchfork type mole traps. Every day the mole very delicately probed the traps with its sensitive fleshy nose, and usually dug its way around them without setting off the trap mechanisms. Twice a day I kept resetting the traps, using hair-trigger positions for the trap mechanisms. Finally, on the evening of the fifth day, I caught this wily star-nosed mole in a scissors trap at the edge of a small brook.

The list of carnivores that occasionally prey on this mole includes owls, hawks, foxes, cats, dogs, raccoons, minks, and skunks. They have even been found in the stomachs of large game fish such as bass, pike, and trout.

Economic Importance and Remarks: The star-nosed mole has been recorded infrequently (from accidental encounters) in only a few scattered locations in northern Florida. An intensive survey is needed to determine if the species is possibly more widespread than presently indicated. The absence of a suitable sampling method is the principal drawback.

ORDER CHIROPTERA
Bats

Bats are the only mammals with the ability to fly. They have mouse-sized bodies with the forelimbs modified into large wings covered with a soft, membranous skin. A broad tail membrane is also present and serves as an effective rudder to change direction in the air. Some species also use the tail membrane to capture insects. Nearly every specialized feature of a bat's anatomy is related to its ability to fly. For example, all the bones are thin-walled, hollow, and tubular in structure to make the skeleton lighter. The chest or pectoral muscles are massive and well vascularized to provide the strong wingbeat necessary to fly.

Bats can reduce their metabolism and hibernate on a day-to-day or seasonal basis depending on the ambient temperatures and relative availability of food. Nearly all bats have a finely tuned echolocation or biological radar system for locating food and avoiding objects in their path. They emit supersonic squeaks and clicks from the mouth that bounce off objects. Their extremely sensitive ears then pick up the sound pulses that bounce back.

This large order has worldwide distribution, but by far the greatest number of species occurs in the tropics rather than in the temperate zones. Florida is blessed with a total of 16 species of bats, all of which feed exclusively on insects. They are extremely beneficial since they consume hordes of nocturnally flying insects in every corner of the state.

Bats and bat skulls are very difficult for the casual observer to identify and should always be examined by an expert in mammalogy to determine species.

If bat colonies occur in buildings and become a nuisance, the best control method is to seal the colony entrance in the late evening after the bats have left the roost to forage, or after the colony has left for the winter. If colony entrances are sealed during the daytime, the bats will die and decompose, causing serious sanitation and odor problems. In problem colonies where the entrance cannot be sealed, sprinkling paradichlorobenzene crystals or naphthalene (mothballs) in the roosts will sometimes repel bats without killing them. The installation of bright lights is even more effective.

Humans, due to unwarranted fear and misunderstanding, are the most serious enemy of bats. Their destruction of many colonies each year is unfortunate since bats are so beneficial in consuming hordes of insects.

Little Brown Bat *(Myotis lucifugus)*

Description: This species has glossy, olive-brown fur with a slight metallic or burnished tint to the hair on the back. The ears are fairly narrow and naked

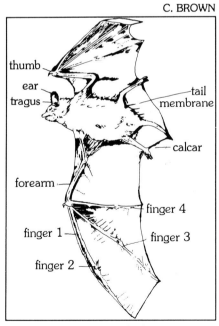

C. BROWN

body parts of a bat

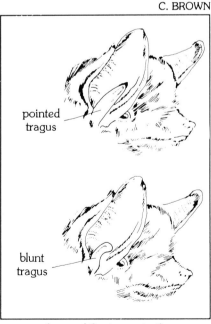

C. BROWN

shape of the tragus in the ears of Florida bats

with bluntly rounded tips. When the ears are laid forward, they just barely extend beyond the nostrils. The tragus, a leaf-like spike projecting upward in the ear, is pointed and is only about one-half of the ear length. The tail membrane (interfemoral membrane) is not furred and the calcar (the ankle bone supporting the tail membrane) is not keeled.

Geographical Range: In Florida, the little brown bat occurs only along the northern border of the state. It is presently known from only one Florida specimen taken near Niceville, in Okaloosa County. See map on page 200. This species has a broad distribution in North America and is found throughout the United States, including Alaska.

Habitat Preference: In many parts of its range, the little brown bat shows a preference for caves during winter and attics of houses during summer, if they are located in forested areas. They also roost during the daytime in hollow trees, under loose tree bark, and in other dark locations, often near a stream, lake, or river where foraging for insects is favorable.

Life History and Reproduction: During the spring and summer months, females with their young form sizeable nursery colonies, living apart from the males. The males are either solitary or live in small bachelor groups during the warmer months of the year. In the fall and winter the sexes live together in large hibernating colonies, often in a cave. When hibernating, they hang upside down from the ceiling by their back feet in closely packed groups numbering several dozen to several hundred individuals.

Mating occurs in the fall just before hibernation begins and sometimes again in the spring when they become active once more. The female ovulates one egg in the spring shortly after arousal from hibernation. The sperm present in her reproductive tract from the preceding fall remain viable all winter and are capable

C. BROWN

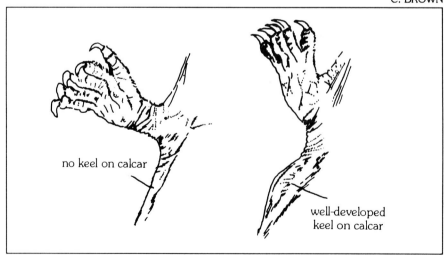

no keel on calcar

well-developed keel on calcar

calcar (ankle bone) with and without keel or flange

of fertilizing the egg released in the spring (delayed fertilization). The time female bats store sperm in their reproductive tract is the longest known for a mammal.

The gestation period in the little brown bat ranges from 50-60 days, and each female produces one offspring per year. Most young are born in late May or early June. Young bats are quite large when born, being one-fifth to one-fourth the size of their mother. They are naked and the eyes are closed at birth, but the eyes open when they are two days old. When the mother bat departs the nursery colony to feed each evening, she leaves the baby hanging at the roost. When the mothers return, they search diligently through the young until they unerringly locate their own baby for nursing. Each baby bat apparently has a slightly different scent or produces a squeak that the mother can identify.

Young little brown bats can fly when three weeks old, but are not weaned until six weeks of age. When two months old, they reach adult size. Some young females breed their first fall, but most males don't mature sexually until they are one year old.

Analysis of the stomach contents of foraging little brown bats reveals a preference for beetles, moths, flies, and wasps.

Economic Importance and Remarks: Little brown bats eat large quantities of nocturnal flying insects, a very beneficial function. Studies show that a bat can catch up to 500 insects in an hour, locating each one with its biological radar system (echolocation). This system is based on the emission of supersonic squeaks from the bat's mouth that bounce off the prey and return to be picked up by the bat's ears. The bat accordingly adjusts its flight path to either close in on and capture the insect or to avoid a larger object in its path. A large colony of bats can account for the removal of tons of potentially harmful insects each year.

On the negative side, little brown bats are found to transmit diseases in some parts of the country. Histoplasmosis and rabies are two diseases that have been associated with this species in the Midwest and Northeast. However, the vast majority of little brown bats examined have been found to be healthy.

The life span of the little brown bat has been studied extensively using tiny numbered aluminum bands placed on the wings. They exhibit remarkable longevity for so small a mammal, with several individuals known to have lived longer than 20 years, including one bat that survived 25 years. It is quite common for bats to live 10-12 years and longer. Owls, snakes, raccoons, and cats occasionally prey on little brown bats.

Gray Bat *(Myotis grisescens)*

Description: In this species the upper pelage is a uniform grayish-brown and the hairs, when parted at the back, are the same color all the way to the roots. (Other similar bats have hair darker at the roots than the tips.) The body size is slightly larger than other *Myotis* and it is the only bat in this group in which the wing membrane is attached at the ankle rather than at the base of the toes. The calcar of the ankle is not keeled and the tragus of the ear is narrow and pointed.

Geographical Range: The gray bat is rare in Florida and found only in a

little brown bat, 3.1-3.7 in. (80-95 mm) overall, tail 1.2-1.6 in. (30-41 mm)

few caves in the Panhandle (near Marianna in Jackson County). See map on page 200. Its range in the United States occupies the mid-Mississippi Valley and some areas of the Deep South.

Habitat Preference: The gray bat is exclusively a cave-dwelling species. It shows a distinct preference for large, moist caves in limestone strata, where large colonies frequently are found.

Life History and Reproduction: The females and offspring form maternity colonies during the late spring and early summer. They select large caves containing streams for the nursery colonies. Males form bachelor colonies in separate caves at this time of year. During the winter months, both sexes

(ASM)—R. K. LaVAL

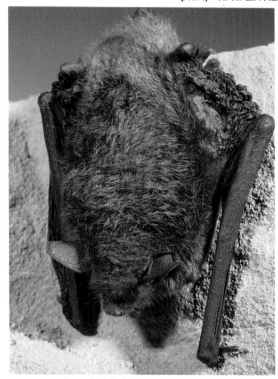

gray bat, 3.1-3.8 in. (80-96 mm) overall, tail 1.2-1.7 in. (30-44 mm)

Bats

reassemble in large hibernating colonies, often selecting inaccessible caves that have vertical, shaft-like entrances and relatively constant humidity.

Gray bats emerge from the caves at dusk and usually forage over bodies of water and nearby forested areas. They show a dietary preference for the flying aquatic insects such as mosquitoes, mayflies, stoneflies, caddisflies, and beetles.

Mating takes place in the hibernation colony in the fall. Each female ovulates one egg the following March or April after she becomes active from hibernation, and the sperm that overwintered in her reproductive tract fertilize the egg. Gestation is 50-60 days after fertilization, and each pregnant female gives birth to a single offspring in late May or early June. The young grow rapidly in the large nursery colonies and some can fly when 25 days old. After weaning, the nursery colonies disperse, and individuals may wander over considerable distances before returning to a particular hibernation cave in the fall. Young gray bats become sexually mature in their second year, in contrast to the little brown bat.

Economic Importance and Remarks: This species is beneficial because of the large number of mosquitoes and other aquatic insects consumed. Because gray bats roost in only a few selected caves, they are extremely vulnerable to decimation by humans. The popularity of cave exploration by humans over the past few decades has apparently contributed to a marked decline in populations of gray bats in many areas of their range. The state and federal governments have officially classified the gray bat as endangered. Since adult female bats produce only one young per year, the recovery potential in a partially decimated gray bat population is painfully slow even under ideal conditions. It is probably advisable to close all caves containing nursery colonies of gray bats to the public, to save this unique species from extinction.

Today it is estimated that less than 10,000 gray bats remain in the few maternity caves present in the Panhandle of Florida. Several former nursery caves have been bulldozed shut or sealed with concrete, and developers threaten some of the remaining ones. These caves represent critical habitat for this endangered species, and one has been purchased by the Florida Game and Fresh Water Fish Commission as a preserve for the gray bat and other cave dwellers.

Keen's Bat *(Myotis keenii)*

Description: Keen's bat is very similar to the other *Myotis* species. Its fur is light reddish brown or olive brown above and buffy gray below. The fur on the back is dark at the roots when parted, in contrast to the gray bat. The fur is shorter and less glossy than that of the little brown bat, and the ankle calcar is slightly keeled. The tragus is long, narrow, and pointed. The ears are large and when laid forward, extend well beyond (3/16 to 1/4 inch) the nose.

Geographical Range: This bat has a peripheral range in Florida, known only from a few caves in the Panhandle. See map on pg. 200. The range in the U.S. spans most of the northern three-fourths of the country east of the Rocky Mountains, as well as some disjunct populations in the Pacific Northwest.

Habitat Preference: Keen's bat is primarily a cave dweller in winter, but in summer it may be found in hollow trees, under loose bark, in attics and barns,

Keen's bat, 3.1-3.5 in. (80-88 mm) overall, tail 1.4-1.7 in. (36-44 mm)

and under the eaves of houses, as well as in caves. It prefers cooler hibernation sites than most species of bats.

Life History and Reproduction: Females form small maternity colonies during the late spring and summer, but individuals tend to live a solitary existence during the rest of the year. Very little is known about the reproductive cycle, but it is apparently very similar to other members of the genus. Females annually give birth to a single offspring in June or July.

Like other hibernators, Keen's bat accumulates considerable body fat during late summer. Copulation has been observed in caves, just before hibernation takes place in September or October in the northern part of its range.

During hibernation, Keen's bat roosts singly or in groups of two or three, often seeking deep crevices in the ceiling to spend the winter months. A hibernation cave may contain up to 500 bats dispersed in this manner, but most colonies are much smaller.

Economic Importance and Remarks: These bats tend to forage in forests beneath the crowns of trees and are beneficial because they consume many insects. Their semi-solitary habits make them much less vulnerable to decimation by humans than most cave-dwelling species. Like most hibernating species of bats, Keen's bat is long-lived. One specimen banded in a field study in the Midwest lived 18.5 years.

Southeastern Bat *(Myotis austroriparius)*

Description: This bat has back fur that is a dull grayish brown, or very rarely a dull reddish brown. The parted hair is slightly darker at the roots than the tips. The underparts vary in color from grayish white to tan. The southeastern bat

Bats

is very similar to the little brown bat and difficult to identify, but it exhibits a much duller coloration and shorter fur on the back. The ears are short and when bent forward, extend only as far as the tip of the nose. The tragus is fairly short, slender and pointed; the calcar is not keeled.

Geographical Range: The southeastern bat is found throughout the northern two-thirds of Florida. See map on page 201. It is very rare or absent from the Everglades and southern tip of the state. The range in the United States is confined to the lower Mississippi Valley, Ohio Valley, and adjacent areas, as well as the Deep South.

Habitat Preference: In Florida this species prefers limestone caves, hollow trees, attics of buildings, crevices of bridges, concrete storm sewers, and other dark man-made structures. The colonies are adaptable to a variety of locations and physical conditions. They are sometimes found in association with other species—Brazilian free-tailed bats, evening bats, gray bats, or Indiana bats.

Life History and Reproduction: In the northern part of its range, the southeastern bat hibernates in colonies from October to late February or early March. However, in Florida the colonies are active during much of the winter and only hibernate for short periods during cold spells when the nighttime temperatures fall to 45 degrees F. or below.

Females breed in the spring and normally produce twins 50-60 days later. This is the only *Myotis* that commonly produces more than one young per pregnancy. The mothers and offspring form large maternity colonies sometimes numbering many thousands, and often a few adult males are also present. Births

M. TUTTLE

southeastern bat, 3.3-3.8 in. (84-96 mm) overall, tail 1.5-1.8 in. (37-45 mm)

occur from late April to the end of May, with the peak birthing usually occurring in early May. The young can fly when about five weeks of age.

Predators include owls, rat snakes, corn snakes, opossums, and skunks.

Economic Importance and Remarks: Since southeastern bats usually occur in large groups, they can help control excessive insect populations within the foraging range of the colony. This species is so adaptable to man-made structures that many Florida populations appear to be holding their own. However, the bats sometimes become a nuisance when they form large colonies in home attics. Also, a fungal disease, histoplasmosis, is sometimes associated with the roosts of southeastern bats.

Indiana Bat *(Myotis sodalis)*

Description: The Indiana bat's upper fur is a dull grayish brown or pinkish brown, and when parted is distinctly darker at the roots. The underside is pinkish white or gray. The ears, when laid forward, barely project beyond the nose. The wing membrane joins at the base of the toes, and the calcar has a distinct keel. The tragus is short, narrow, and pointed.

Geographical Range: The Indiana bat has a peripheral range in Florida, occurring only in a few caves in the Panhandle. Its range in the United States includes the middlewestern and northeastern states south of the Great Lakes, plus Alabama, northwestern Georgia, and northwestern Florida.

Habitat Preference: This species spends the winter in just a few large, cool, moist limestone caves scattered throughout its range. In the spring and summer, Indiana bats disperse widely throughout the forest forming small colonies under loose bark of dead trees, in small caves, and in other crevices.

Life History and Reproduction: The Indiana bats form extremely large wintering colonies that, like the gray bat, make them especially vulnerable to repeated disturbance and decimation by humans. This has occurred extensively over the past few decades and their overall populations have declined sharply.

These bats enter hibernation in the fall and copulation occurs just prior to the winter torpor. During the winter months, they often gather in large tightly packed clumps and hang from the ceiling near the entrance of the caves, where the air is coldest. It is not unusual to find a few little brown bats and gray bats in among the clumps of Indiana bats. The Indiana bats wake from hibernation and leave the caves in March or April in more northern locations. They prefer moths to other food items, but also take flies, beetles, and various aquatic insects from various riparian and floodplain forest habitats.

Breeding occurs in the caves in fall, and females ovulate the following spring. Only one offspring is produced per year by each mother, usually in late June or early July. The mother and young live in small maternity colonies widely scattered through their woodland habitats. Banding studies in the Midwest reveal that the maximum longevity of the Indiana bat exceeds 20 years.

Economic Importance and Remarks: This is another highly beneficial bat species that consumes large quantities of insects within flying range of each colony. Because of its vulnerability and declining numbers, the Indiana bat is listed as an endangered species by both the federal government and state of Florida. The large colonies must be protected from disturbance or the Indiana bat may eventually become extinct.

Silver-haired Bat *(Lasionycteris noctivagans)*

Description: The color of the silver-haired bat's back and belly fur is brownish black washed with silvery white at the tips of the hair. The frosted coloration is most conspicuous on the back. The wing and tail membranes are black, with the upper surface of the latter being well furred near the body. The ears are short and rounded and contain a broad, blunt tragus. The wing membrane attaches to the foot at the base of the toes, and the calcar is unkeeled.

Geographical Range: Florida is on the periphery of the range of this species. It is presently known from only one specimen taken in northern Santa Rosa County of the western Panhandle. It is probably rare in Florida, possibly represented only by wandering or migrating individuals from farther north. See map on page 200. In October, 1992, a silver-haired bat was captured at the Ft. Lauderdale-Hollywood (Florida) International Airport. It is probable that this specimen hitched a ride on a southbound plane, since it was so far south of its known range. The range in the United States extends from coast to coast, with records in every state.

Habitat Preference: The silver-haired bat is a forest dweller and roosts in dense foliage, under loose bark, in hollow trees, in rock crevices, and in cabins and sheds. They like to forage along wooded streams and lake borders.

Life History and Reproduction: The silver-haired bat is a migratory species that moves north in the spring and south in the fall. Most of them winter in the southern states, but a few enter caves and hibernate all winter. Others have been taken on islands, including Bermuda, or have landed on ships off the east coast of the United States. It is something of a mystery where these oceanic bats are migrating for the winter. During migration, silver-haired bats sometimes fly during the daytime as well as at night.

Males are always solitary but females are more gregarious, especially during the summer, when they form small roosting and nursery colonies. Mating occurs in the fall, but females don't ovulate until spring. The gestation period is 50-60 days long. A female normally gives birth to two young (range 1-3) in late June or early July. The babies grow rapidly and can fly when about three weeks of age. They are weaned at about 36 days of age and breed their first fall.

Economic Importance and Remarks: Beetles comprise the main dietary item for silver-haired bats, but they also eat moths and other sizeable nocturnal insects. Since many beetles and moths are forest pests, these bats are beneficial in helping to control harmful species.

Some silver-haired bats appear to be nonmigratory and hibernate from November to March in buildings, mines, and other protected locations. Little is known about the overall biology of the silver-haired bat because it is so difficult to locate and study in numbers.

Bats

Indiana bat, 3.0-3.6 in. (78-90 mm) overall, tail 1.2-1.6 in. (30-40 mm)   silver-haired bat, 3.1-4.5 in. (95-115 mm) overall, tail 1.5-1.8 in. (37-46 mm)

Eastern Pipistrelle *(Pipistrellus subflavus)*

Description: The eastern pipistrelle is Florida's smallest bat, and has pale yellowish-brown or yellowish-gray upper fur. The hairs, when parted by blowing into the fur, are dark at the root. The belly fur is yellowish brown. This is the only Florida bat that has black wing membranes combined with burnt-orange skin covering the arm bones. The ears are large for a small bat; when bent forward, they extend slightly beyond the tip of the nose. The tragus is fairly long, narrow, and pointed. The calcar is not keeled and the tail membrane is slightly haired only where it joins the body.

Geographic Range: The eastern pipistrelle occurs throughout the state of Florida in many different forested habitats. Range in the U.S. is the eastern half of the country. It also occurs in eastern Mexico and northern Central America.

Habitat Preference: In the northern part of their range, eastern pipistrelles hibernate singly in caves. In Florida, they also hibernate during the winter when night temperatures are cool. During summer they roost in attics, cabins, hollow trees, crevices, stumps, culverts, bridges, and other dark places in forested areas.

Life History and Reproduction: During the spring and summer months, females form small nursery colonies away from the males. Mating has been observed in the fall, winter, and spring. Sperm are viable after overwintering in the female's reproductive tract. Each year, females give birth to a single litter of 1-3 (normally two) offspring from mid-May to mid-July. Although the babies grow rapidly and can fly when they are about four weeks of age, pipistrelles do not reach sexual maturity until they are about one year old.

Eastern pipistrelles have a weak, erratic, fluttering type of flight that is somewhat reminiscent of a moth. They are easy to distinguish on the wing from other bats because of this characteristically slow flight style. The species feeds on tiny nocturnal insects such as flies, moths, beetles, caddisflies, and mayflies. They prefer to forage over bodies of water and take many flying aquatic insects.

Economic Importance and Remarks: Like other bats, they are insect eaters. However, because of their small size and semi-solitary lifestyle, they may have less impact on insect numbers than most colonial species of bats.

Pipistrelles probably hibernate more deeply than other bats and are less easily aroused by disturbances than the other species. They usually stay in one spot for weeks during the winter hibernation period. In caves it is also common to find a layer of tiny water droplets condensed on the surface of the pipistrelle's fur. The beam of a flashlight hitting the water droplets makes them appear shimmering white or crystalline hanging from the ceiling. Studies of banded animals in several areas to the north of Florida have revealed a maximum longevity of about 15 years for the pipistrelle.

Rafinesque's Big-eared Bat *(Plecotus rafinesquii)*

Description: Also known as the eastern big-eared bat, it is easily identified by its huge ears, which are 1¼ inches long, and by the prominent lumps on the

B. MANSELL   M. TUTTLE

eastern pipistrelle, 3.1-3.6 in. (80-90 mm) overall, tail 1.4-1.8 in. (35-45 mm)   big-eared bat, 3.8-4.3 in. (96-110 mm) overall, tail 1.7-2.0 in. (42-52 mm)

Bats   39

nose. The ears are slightly coiled like a ram's horn and reach the middle of the body when laid back. The fur is buffy brown above and whitish below. The tragus is also very long (half the ear length) and pointed. Also, the hairs on the feet of the big-eared bat are so long that they project beyond the ends of the toes.

Geographical Range: In Florida this species occurs over all except the extreme southern tip of the state. An eastern big-eared bat was found roosting in an abandoned cabin in the Big Cypress Swamp area in Collier County in October, 1992. This extended the known range of the species southward by 150 miles. See map on page 201. The range in the United States is confined to the southeastern quadrant of the country.

Habitat Preference: This species roosts in hollow trees, under bark, in cabins and barns, and in culverts and attics throughout forested areas. It shows a particular preference for old, abandoned or dilapidated houses and shacks in rural areas of Florida.

Natural History and Reproduction: Rafinesque's big-eared bat flies late, well after dark, so it is seldom observed on the wing. In Florida it is most often taken in mature, open, pine flatwoods, so presumably that is one of its favorite foraging areas.

Copulation apparently takes place in the autumn and winter, but the exact length of gestation is not known. Small groups of females form nursery colonies in the spring and early summer months. Each female gives birth to one young per year, usually born in May or early June. The babies grow rapidly and can fly in about three weeks, but are not weaned until two months old. Young big-eared bats molt from juvenile to adult pelage when about three months old.

In Florida, this bat is active year-round when the nights are warm enough for insects to be flying. Farther north they enter caves or crevices and hibernate all winter. Studies of banded big-eared bats indicate a maximum life span of more than 10 years. Known predators include rat snakes, rattlesnakes, pine snakes, raccoons, opossums, cats, and owls.

Economic Importance and Remarks: The main food items of big-eared bats are moths. They undoubtedly reduce the numbers of several forest pest species in their nocturnal foraging activities. These bats are very swift fliers and extremely agile in changing directions to pursue their quarry.

Big Brown Bat *(Eptesicus fuscus)*

Description: The big brown bat is fairly large and has rich chestnut-brown fur that is rather long and glossy. The underparts are cinnamon, and the wing membranes are black. The ears are not large and the tragus is short and rounded at the tip. The calcar is keeled and the tail membrane is devoid of hair.

Geographical Range: In Florida, the big brown bat ranges over the entire state, except the Keys. In the United States, it occurs throughout the country from coast to coast. The big brown bat also occurs on most of the larger Caribbean and Bahama islands.

Habitat Preference: This bat in attics, hollow trees, chimneys, caves, outbuildings, storm sewers, bridges, and many other man-made structures.

Life History and Reproduction: In the northern part of its range, the big brown bat hibernates during the winter, but in Florida it is probably active any time the night temperatures are not low. When in caves, they usually select a place near the entrance and may roost in partial daylight.

Hibernation has been extensively studied. The body temperature falls to that of the environment, and they can survive as low as 30 degrees F. When they arouse and the metabolism returns to normal, the body temperature is around 99 degrees F. In hibernation, big brown bats may go 4-8 minutes without taking a breath; when active they may breathe at a rate of 200 times per minute.

Compared to other bats, this species is very sedentary. Banding studies show that most live their lives within 10 miles of their birth place. Like many other bat species, females form nursery colonies in the spring apart from the males. These colonies break up by midsummer and males and females roost together again.

Mating takes place in the fall, winter, and again in the spring. The females may ovulate 2-7 eggs in the spring, but normally only two young complete development. Babies are usually born in May or early June after a gestation period of about 60 days. Brown bats are naked at birth, and their eyes open when two days old. The offspring remain at the roost when the mother leaves to forage each night. She only carries the young when flying to a new roosting location. Young big brown bats can fly when three weeks old and most reach maturity and breed their first autumn.

Economic Importance and Remarks: Big brown bats eat mainly beetles, including tree borers and other pests. They consume large quantities of insects each year, especially where the colonies are large. They are relatively slow, straight fliers, and do not veer about erratically like many bat species. Their large body size enables big brown bats to capture even large beetles, moths, and other large flying insects.

Maximum longevity is around 10-12 years, based on banding studies conducted in the northeastern states. Big brown bats occasionally carry rabies; one study revealed a 10 percent infection rate in certain populations.

Hoary Bat *(Lasiurus cinereus)*

Description: The hoary bat is one of Florida's largest bat species (wing span 12-14 inches) and probably the most attractive. The fur on the back is a beautiful mixture of deep browns and yellows tipped with a heavy white frosting. The underparts are mostly yellow and buff with slight white frosting. There is an yellowish-white shoulder patch that usually continues across the chest. The wing and tail membranes are brownish black, and the latter is heavily furred and frosted on the upperside. The ears are small, broad, rounded, and contain a short, blunt tragus. The calcar is keeled.

Geographical Range: In Florida, the hoary bat ranges across the northern third of the state. See map on page 201. In the United States, this bat occurs in every state from coast to coast. There is also a population of hoary bats in Hawaii, and the species lives throughout most of Mexico, Central America, and South America.

big brown bat, 4.1-5 in. (105-128 mm)   hoary bat, 4.9-5.7 in. (125-145 mm)
overall, tail 1.7-2 in. (42-52 mm)   overall, tail 2-2.6 in. (50-66 mm)

Habitat Preference: The hoary bat prefers mature pine forests and mixed hardwood-pine forests in Florida. It is a strong, high flier, and is often seen foraging well above the canopy. In the northern states it is also associated with coniferous forests.

Life History and Reproduction: Hoary bats are solitary forest dwellers and rarely seek shelter in caves or buildings. During the daytime, they roost in deep foliage, under bark, and in clumps of Spanish moss.

Hoary bats are highly migratory and most spend their winters in the southern states or Mexico, actively foraging on warm nights. They then migrate northward in the spring to a summer range.

Breeding takes place in the fall and winter, and females are pregnant when they head northward in the spring. The litter size is usually two (range 1-4), and the offspring are born from late May to early June in the summer range. The babies are often carried from roost to roost attached to the mother's ventral side. Young hoary bats are able to fly when they are about four weeks old.

Hoary bats feed mainly on moths, but also consume dragonflies, beetles, wasps, large flies, mosquitoes, and other sizeable insects.

Economic Importance and Remarks: The large body size of this bat makes it an especially valuable insect consumer in the mature forest. Since they do not form colonies in buildings, they are never a nuisance to man.

The hoary bat usually ventures forth just before dark and is seldom noticed by the casual observer. However, during the winter months across the southern states, it may forage in the late afternoon or early evening when temperatures are warm enough for insects to be flying. They are often overlooked by casual observers who take them for swallows, nighthawks, or other insect-eating birds.

Hoary bats are sometimes preyed upon by hawks, owls, and rat snakes, but have few other predators. Rabies is sometimes carried by this species; in some populations, as high as 25 percent have tested positive for the disease.

Red Bat *(Lasiurus borealis)*

Description: The red bat is the most brightly colored Florida bat, and one of the few which is sexually dimorphic. In males the upper pelage is brick red, while in females it is dull red with pronounced white frosting on the tips of the fur. The ears are small, broad, and rounded and the tragus is short and blunt at the tip. There is an yellowish-white patch on each shoulder at the base of the wing. The underparts are paler than the back and usually frosted white. The tail membrane is heavily furred over the entire upper surface and the calcar is keeled.

Geographical Range: This species ranges over the northern two-thirds of Florida. See map on page 201. It has not been taken in the southern part of the Peninsula or in the Keys. In the United States, the red bat is found in nearly every region except the Rocky Mountains and Great Basin. It also ranges throughout Mexico, Central America, and South America.

Habitat Preference: The red bat is strictly a tree dweller and does not roost in caves or buildings. It sleeps in dense foliage, under loose bark, in hollow trees, and in clumps of Spanish moss during the daytime. Hardwood forests seem to be preferred over pine or cypress. The red bat often hangs upside down by one foot from a limb, resembling a dead leaf.

Life History and Reproduction: Red bats, like the hoary bat, are extremely migratory, spending the winters in the southern states and Mexico, returning north in the spring to a distinct summer range. They lead largely solitary lives and do not form nursery colonies; however, they are sometimes observed migrating in small unisexual groups. A few red bats remain in the north year-round, hibernating in well sheltered locations such as large hollow trees, crevices, or caves.

Red bats mate in the late summer and fall (often while flying) before they migrate southward. The females store the sperm over the winter months and ovulate in early spring. Copulation in spring has also been reported. The gestation period is 80-90 days and usually two (range 1-4) young are born in late May or June, after the females arrive in the summer range. The babies are naked and blind at birth, but their eyes open when three days old. They start flying when about four weeks of age, but remain with the female until weaned at around six weeks. Females are frequently captured with one or more

red bat, 3.9-4.5 in. (98-115 mm) overall, tail 1.8-2.1 in. (45-54 mm)

Bats

43

nearly full-grown young attached to them. The combined load is sometimes too heavy for the mother to support when she tries to carry the young from one roost to another. There is considerable mortality in red bats at this time of the year. This species puts on a heavy layer of fat prior to both fall and spring migrations.

Red bats consume many types of flying insects including moths, flies, beetles, true bugs, crickets, cicadas, and wasps. They forage at low levels among the trees, over meadows, and along water courses. The flight speed is fairly slow but very erratic, as they veer this way and that to capture insects. They sometimes even land on the vegetation to capture a choice insect and then resume flight.

Economic Importance and Remarks: Like all insectivorous bats, this species is a valued consumer of many flying pests. On the negative side, red bats are occasionally found to carry rabies. Any bat, regardless of species, should be avoided if found fluttering about in the daytime or if it appears sick.

A red bat shows a tendency to return to the same spot to forage. The same individual often can be seen, repeatedly, catching insects at a streetlight or security light each night. I have captured the same banded red bat on successive nights with a long-handled insect net as the animal whirled about a night light.

This species has great tolerance to cold weather and is occasionally observed foraging during the afternoon and evening on cold winter days. Due to the red bat's habit of roosting in trees, its major predators are owls, hawks, blue jays, crows, rat snakes, raccoons, opossums, and other arboreal carnivores.

Seminole Bat *(Lasiurus seminolus)*

Description: The Seminole bat is a sibling species to the red bat and its characteristics are very similar. Instead of brick red on the upper parts, however, the Seminole bat is a rich mahogany or reddish brown. It is sometimes called the mahogany bat for that reason. The females tend to have the upper fur frosted white, and the males less so. Like the red bat, they have small rounded ears, a short blunt tragus, and a fully-furred tail membrane. The belly fur is paler and there are white patches at the shoulder.

Geographical Range: In Florida, the Seminole bat has a statewide distribution except for the Keys. In the United States, its range is confined to the Gulf Coast and Atlantic Coast as far north as New York.

Habitat Preference: The Seminole bat prefers cypress forests and other hydric woodlands, bordering streams and lakes. It roosts in clumps of Spanish moss, in dense tree foliage, and occasionally under tree bark.

Life History and Reproduction: Seminole bats leave the roost at early twilight to forage at treetop levels. They sometimes feed lower, especially when they are over water. Their flight is swift and not as erratic as that of the red bat.

Seasonal movements occur, but not the long-distance north-south migration characteristic of the red bat. They are active on a year-round basis when the air temperature is 70 degrees F. or higher.

Very little is known about reproduction in Seminole bats, but it appears to be similar to the red bat. The average litter size is two (range 1-4), and the offspring are born from May through mid-June. I have, on one occasion, seen Seminole bats copulating in mid-August. On 15 August 1979, I found a pair of Seminole bats locked together *in copulo* on the ground under a streetlight at 2:00 A.M., near I-75 in Hamilton County, Florida. Sperm apparently remains viable in the female reproductive tract until the following spring, when ovulation occurs. Young Seminole bats grow rapidly and first fly when about four weeks of age.

Economic Importance and Remarks: This species feeds on a variety of insects that occur in the tree canopy including small moths, beetles, flies, mosquitoes, and true bugs. Since they are often numerous along lake borders, residents of lakeshore homes benefit from the bats' insect diet.

The predators that take Seminole bats in their exposed tree roost locations are generally the same as those listed for the red bat.

Previously, some mammalogists have speculated that the Seminole bat is a southern color form of the red bat, but this appears not to be the case. No intermediate forms or mixed-color litters have ever been found where both bats occur in the same region. Also, there are some consistent, minor differences in skull and body morphologies that separate the two bats. Behaviorally, they forage in somewhat different locations and have differing flight patterns. For these reasons they are considered valid and distinctly separate species.

Yellow Bat *(Lasiurus intermedius)*

Description: The yellow bat is only slightly smaller than the hoary bat, so it is one of the largest bats in Florida. The upper side is yellowish tan or grayish yellow and the underside is slightly paler. The wings are dark brown, and the anterior half of the tail membrane is furred on its upper side. The ears are small, broad, and rounded, and the tragus is short and blunt as in other members of this group of bats.

Geographical Range: The yellow bat has been recorded throughout Florida except for the Keys. The range in the United States is restricted to the Gulf Coastal Plain from Mexico northward, and the Atlantic Coastal Plain from Florida north to Virginia. The yellow bat is also a resident of Cuba, but no populations have been recorded in the Florida Keys thus far. The species also ranges southward through Mexico into northern Central America.

Habitat Preference: Yellow bats can be found—at least sparingly—in most Florida habitats having trees. They are most abundant in upland oak hammocks and open pine-oak woodlands; they are also numerous in residential areas. Most yellow bats roost in Spanish moss or among the hanging dead fronds of palm trees.

Life History and Reproduction: Yellow bats start flying in the evening well before dark and are one of the most visible Florida bats. They are slow, straight fliers, are of large size, and move back and forth over the same course repeatedly. They are common foragers in the backyards and on the streets of quiet residential neighborhoods.

Yellow bats are active year-round, providing it is warm enough at night for flying insects. These bats take a wide variety of large and medium-sized insects, including moths, beetles, true bugs, wasps, and dragonflies.

The reproductive cycle of yellow bats is not well known, but it is probably similar to other members of the group. The number of young in a litter averages

Bats   45

Seminole bat, 4-4.5 in. (100-115 mm)
overall, tail 1.8-2.1 in. (45-54 mm)

yellow bat, 4.5-5.1 in. (115-130 mm)
overall, tail 1.9-2.3 in. (48-58 mm)

three (range 1-4), and they are usually born in late May or June. Mating has been observed in the fall, and ovulation takes place the following spring. Young yellow bats can fly by 3-4 weeks of age. Foraging females leave the young at the roost.

Most yellow bats live a solitary existence, but small unisexual groups are sometimes found roosting together in the fronds of a palm tree or other sheltered areas.

Economic Importance and Remarks: Like other Florida bats, this species accounts for the consumption of many insects. On the negative side, yellow bats carry rabies fairly consistently. Over a 15-year period, approximately 20 percent of all yellow bats tested, using the fluorescent antibody test, were positive for rabies in the Tampa, Florida area. This does not indicate that one-fifth of the yellow bat population carries rabies—bats that are caught for evaluation have a high probability of being sick. However, it does suggest that yellow bat populations in Florida may be a natural reservoir for rabies.

Predators known to eat yellow bats on occasion include rat snakes, owls, hawks, raccoons, opossums, and foxes.

Evening Bat *(Nycticeius humeralis)*

Description: The evening bat is most likely to be confused with bats of the genus *Myotis*, which are in its size range and similarly colored. The upper parts are a rich chocolate brown and the underparts are paler and more buffy. The fur on the back, when parted, is dark at the roots. Evening bats have short, narrow wings and the wing membranes are black. The tail membrane is unfurred

Bats

and the wing membrane joins the foot at the base of the toes. The calcar is not keeled.

The diagnostic features that identify this species are small black ears containing a short blunt-tipped tragus that is less than half of the ear length.

Geographical Range: This species occurs throughout Florida except for the Keys. The range in the United States occupies the southeastern quadrant of the country from Kansas eastward to the Atlantic Coast and from Michigan southward through Florida.

Habitat Preference: The evening bat forms colonies that roost in hollow trees, attics, abandoned buildings, barns, old bridges, culverts, and even Spanish moss. They prefer mature forest areas with many old hollow trees.

Life History and Reproduction: This species leaves the roost at early twilight to forage, so they are sometimes observed in flight. Mating occurs in the fall, winter, and sometimes again in the spring. The females normally form nursery colonies separate from the males, and average two young (range 1-4), born in late May or early June. The babies are blind and naked at birth, but by the ninth day, they are fully furred. Their eyes open 18-21 hours after birth. During the first 10 days of life, the baby bats squeak and chirp almost constantly, and it appears that in this species, individualized vocalization permit mothers to locate their own young unerringly when they return to the nursery colony. Young evening bats can fly when three weeks old, but they continue to nurse until about eight weeks of age.

Economic Importance and Remarks: Since evening bats often form colonies in human dwellings and other buildings, they sometimes are a nuisance.

Documented predators of the evening bat include domestic cats, raccoons, hawks, owls, and rat snakes. Study of banded animals indicates maximum longevity in the species is around 10 years.

R. W. BARBOUR

evening bat, 3.1-3.9 in. (80-99 mm) overall, tail 1.2-1.6 in. (30-41 mm)

Brazilian Free-tailed Bat *(Tadarida brasiliensis)*

Description: The tail of this bat continues beyond the tail membrane for half its length (1 - 1¼ in.), thus the free-tailed name. The upper and lower pelage varies from blackish brown to brown mixed with charcoal gray. The funnel-like ears are broad and short. When laid forward, the ears do not reach the tip of the nose. Numerous hairs, as long as the foot itself, grow from the tips of the toes. Free-tailed bats have small, narrow, black wings and a short tail membrane.

Geographical Range: Brazilian free-tailed bats are found statewide in Florida except for the Keys. The range in the United States encompasses the entire southern half of the country. The species also ranges through Mexico, Central America, and South America.

Habitat Preference: Free-tailed bats live in colonies year-round in a wide variety of locations including attics, tile roofs, caves, palm trees, bridges, culverts, storm sewers, and outbuildings. They reside in most types of habitat available including forests and open, nonforested areas. They are a common bat of the inner city as well as the suburbs.

Life History and Reproduction: This is one of the most gregarious bats in Florida. In some western caves single colonies will number in the millions, but in Florida the colonies number a few hundred to a few thousand bats each. In western colonies the sexes tend to segregate and occupy different areas, but this has not been observed in Florida. The nightly foraging flights begin shortly after sunset and the bats fly forth from the entrance in a steady stream until the roost is empty. On cold nights some bats remain at home and those that leave may return within a couple of hours. On warm nights they usually continue to fly until around 4:00 A.M. before returning to the roost.

Florida free-tailed bats are sedentary and usually remain in the same general area permanently. In the western states, however, the species often migrates several hundred miles from a summer range to a warmer winter range. In Florida, free-tailed bats have several colony locations in the same area, and they may move from one roost to another, especially if they are disturbed by humans.

Breeding is synchronized and occurs during a short span of a few days in March. Females ovulate right after copulation, and one offspring is born after a gestation period of 75-85 days. Babies are born from early to mid-June, but two-thirds are produced within a five-day period, indicating the high degree of breeding synchrony. Babies are blind and naked at birth. Free-tailed bats do not fly until they reach about five weeks of age, later than the twilight bats.

Free-tailed bats have a penetrating, musky odor that can be detected at some distance from the colony. The musky scent apparently emanates from powerful skin glands.

These bats feed extensively on small moths and other nocturnal insects of comparable size, including winged ants, small beetles, midges, chalcid wasps, and mosquitoes. Free-tailed bats are considered to be the most rapid fliers of American bats; their flight pattern is very erratic and hard to follow with the eye.

Economic Importance and Remarks: These bats are important economically because the colony consumes tons of insects per year. Each bat is estimated to eat three grams of insects per night. A large bat colony thus makes a great impact on the local insect populations. Some western free-tailed bat colonies also generate large quantities of guano (droppings) on the floor of the cave. This is a rich nitrate fertilizer, which is mined and sold in some areas.

The maximum longevity for the species, based on banding studies, is about 15 years. Most of the population probably only lives 8-10 years, however. Free-tailed bats sometimes carry rabies, but the incidence of the disease is low in most areas of the United States.

Predators include hawks, owls, snakes, foxes, coyotes, raccoons, and skunks.

During the early 1900s, several hundred Brazilian free-tailed bats were brought to the Florida Keys and introduced in a desperate attempt to control the hordes of mosquitoes found there. Unfortunately, the bats quickly disappeared. Since we now know that free-tailed bats feed almost totally on small moths, the effort would have been fruitless even had the bats stayed in the Keys. The lesson learned, of course, is to study the ecology and life history of a species thoroughly before introductions are ever contemplated. Also, most bats probably cannot live in the Keys because there is a general absence of fresh water for them to drink.

Wagner's Mastiff Bat *(Eumops glaucinus)*

Description: This species, sometimes called the Florida mastiff bat, is by far the largest bat living in Florida. It looks much like the Brazilian free-tailed bat but is several times larger. The upper fur is grayish brown and the belly is gray. The ears are broad, short, funnel shaped, and when laid forward, do not reach the tip of the nose. The wing and tail membranes are small and narrow, dark brown in color, and naked. The tail extends beyond the tail membrane for half its length (1¼ to 1½ inches). The toes also have long hairs extending from them.

Geographical Range: Wagner's mastiff bat is known only from the southern part of Florida. See map on page 202. It has been captured as far north as Fort Lauderdale, Broward County, and across the peninsula at Punta Gorda in Charlotte County. The species does not occur elsewhere in the United States, but does live in Cuba, Jamaica, southern Mexico, Central America, and parts of South America.

Habitat Preference: This tropical bat prefers to roost among the fronds of tall palms, under the Spanish tiles of roofs, in the upper reaches of tall buildings, and in tree hollows.

Life History and Reproduction: Wagner's mastiff bat is considered a rare species throughout its range, but since it forages late and at high levels, it may be just difficult to collect. It was first reported in the United States from a single specimen taken in 1936. At that time it was thought to have been accidentally imported on a banana boat. However, since then, more than 50 other specimens have been taken, so there is certainly a well established population in southern Florida, regardless of the source. The species has also been found in fossil deposits from eastern Florida, so it is possible that a relic population could have survived in southern Florida. It is also conceivable that a hurricane could have blown a founding population of these strong, fast fliers to our shores from Cuba (a distance of less than ninety miles). At their flight speed,

J. F. PARNELL   R. W. BARBOUR

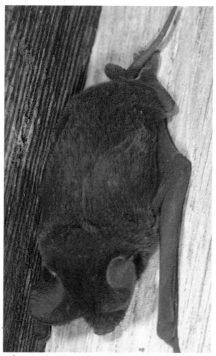

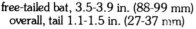

free-tailed bat, 3.5-3.9 in. (88-99 mm)   mastiff bat, 4.7-5.5 in. (120-140 mm)
overall, tail 1.1-1.5 in. (27-37 mm)   overall, tail 1.2-2.2 in. (44-55 mm)

the bats could make the flight across the Florida Straits in well less than two hours, even without a tailwind. Since there are no records of this bat living in Florida before the second third of the 20th century, colonization by storm-blown refugees from Cuba seems most plausible.

Very little is known about the life history of Wagner's mastiff bat. In Panama, they have been found roosting in small colonies of 10-12 individuals in the attics of houses. In September, 1979, a small colony of eight Wagner's mastiff bats (seven females and one male) was found living in an old woodpecker nest cavity in a longleaf pine tree near Punta Gorda, Florida. Five of these females were post-lactational and one was pregnant with a single fetus, two inches long. In Cuba, the species is polyestrous and breeds throughout the year, so in southern Florida its reproduction is probably similar. The sex ratio of the Punta Gorda colony suggests that this group may have represented a male and his harem. In Cuba, however, males and females have been found roosting together through-out the year in tree hollows, in groups of as many as 32 individuals. Litter sizes of both one and two young have been recorded.

Economic Importance and Remarks: Due to its limited geographical range in Florida and apparent rarity, this bat has little economic impact despite its large size. Analysis of fecal pellets of the species reveals that, by volume, the diet was 55 percent beetles, 15 percent flies, and 10 percent true bugs. Mastiff bats are thus very beneficial as insect consumers.

Mastiff bats make a characteristic high-pitched call as they fly overhead at night. This vocalization is being used by wildlife biologists to locate colonies of these rare creatures. The Florida Game and Fresh Water Fish Commission has listed Wagner's mastiff bat as endangered since it has been recorded only twice in the last 15 years.

Little Mastiff Bat (*Molossus molossus*)

Description: This species is similar to the Brazilian free-tailed bat, but slightly larger in body size. There are two color phases: one with short velvety hair of uniform color throughout, and one with longer fur and bicolor banded hairs. The pelage is variable in color from chestnut brown to rusty dark brown to blackish. The base of each ear joins in the middle of the forehead. The skull has one upper premolar on each side in the upper jaw, which distinguishes it from the Brazilian free-tail, which has two upper incisors on each side.

Geographical Range: The little mastiff bat was recently recorded for the first time in the United States in the lower and middle Florida Keys (Boca Chica, Key West, Stock Island, and Marathon). See map on pg. 202. This species ranges throughout Central America, South America, and many islands of the Caribbean, including Cuba.

Habitat Preference: This bat is found in moist tropical broadleaf forests and dry tropical deciduous forests.

Life History and Reproduction: At the start of the summer rainy season, females congregate in nursery colonies in hollow trees, buildings, caves, or palm fronds. The colonies in the Florida Keys are often found in the roofs of buildings. While foraging for insects at dusk, these bats fly very rapidly and veer from side to side a great deal, much in the manner of swifts. They appear to feed on most types of flying insects, but especially moths and beetles.

In Puerto Rico, *M. molossus* mates in February or March and gives birth to a single young in June, then mates again and produces a second offspring in September or October. The young suckle for about six weeks and are left at the roost in a cluster during foraging. Young are on their own at about 65 days old.

(ASM)--P. V. AUGUST

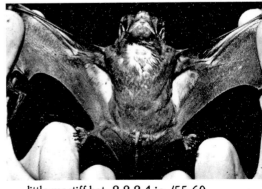

Economic Importance and Remarks: The little mastiff bat has probably been an overlooked resident of the Florida Keys for some years, because the colonies discovered there appear to be well established, ranging in size from 50-300

little mastiff bat, 2.2-2.4 in. (55-60 mm) overall, tail 1.4-1.6 in. (35-40 mm)

individuals. Since there are large hords of flying insects throughout the Keys, this bat should be beneficial in reducing their numbers.

Antillean Fruit Bat *(Artibeus jamaicensis)*

Description: Also known as the Jamaican fruit bat, this is a large brown bat with no tail and is the only bat in the eastern United States with a nose leaf. It is also the only fruit bat found in the eastern United States, and it lives only in the Florida Keys. The upper parts are various shades of brown; the underparts are often grayish and somewhat paler than the back. White facial markings are usually present. The skull is large and broad, with a slightly elevated brain case, and there are 30 teeth in the upper and lower jaws.

Geographical Range: In the U.S., this bat has been reported only from the southern Keys. See map on pg. 202. This species ranges throughout many islands of the Caribbean Sea, including Cuba, Jamaica, Puerto Rico, Hispaniola, and the Lesser Antilles. It also occurs in Mexico, Central America, and parts of South America.

Habitat Preference: In the tropics, this species lives in a wide range of forest habitats. It roosts in caves, hollow trees, tents of folded leaves made by biting the midribs, and in buildings.

Life History and Reproduction: This species is mainly frugivorous and feeds primarily on figs. However, it also feeds on pollen, nectar, flower parts, and occasional insects. Preferred fruits besides figs are mangos, avocados, and bananas. Food can pass through the digestive tract in as little as 15 minutes, and fecal material usually has the odor of the food being eaten.

The reproductive period of this species is tied closely to maximum abundance of figs. In Panama, births peak in Mar.-Apr. There is a post-partum estrus followed by a second birthing peak in July-Aug. This is followed by estrus, fertilization, and implantation, but the implanted embryos remain dormant from

P. V. AUGUST

Antillean fruit bat 3.0-3.3 in. (75-83 mm) overall, no tail present

Sept.-Nov. Development then proceeds normally until birth occurs in April. The species is polygynous; males accumulate harems of up to 25 females. A single young is born to each female, although occasionally twins are born. Females have a daytime roost and leave their young during each nightly feeding foray.

Economic Importance and Remarks: Antillean fruit bats often forage in small groups and they are much less active on bright moonlit nights. Besides harems, this species also forms groups of bachelor males or non-breeding females. Individual fruit bats have been known to live 8-10 years. Owls, snakes, and bat falcons are known predators.

ORDER EDENTATA
Sloths, Anteaters, and Armadillos

Edentates are a bizarre-looking group of mammals that includes sloths, anteaters, and armadillos. All are characterized by having reduced, degenerate teeth or no teeth at all—the word edentate means without teeth. The armadillos and anteaters feed mainly on insects using a long, mucous-covered tongue to secure ants, termites, and other arthropods. The prey is swallowed whole so no teeth are needed. Sloths are sluggish tree dwellers that feed on leaves, and have degenerate but functional teeth that chew up the food.

The three families (sloths, anteaters, and armadillos) are placed in a common order primarily because of skeletal similarities, but they do not resemble each other externally. Some experts think they are not too closely related, and the skeletons may be similar because of convergence in their evolution from unrelated ancestors.

Some edentates, such as the giant anteaters of South America, are more than six feet long. The giant armadillo found in northern South America weighs up to 120 pounds. Most edentates, however, are medium to small animals less than two feet long and weighing only a few pounds. The largest edentates that ever lived were the giant ground sloths, some of which were almost as large as an elephant. Their fossilized bones have been found in Florida.

Only one kind of edentate, the armadillo, occurs in the United States, but a variety of species is found in Mexico, Central America, and South America.

Nine-banded Armadillo *(Dasypus novemcinctus)*

Description: This strange-looking mammal is nearly hairless and covered with armor plates, and is about the size of an opossum. Along the back, some of the armor is arranged into nine connected movable rings which account for the nine-banded part of its name. The nine flexible bands extend from a broad shoulder shield to a slightly smaller hip shield. The head and snout are small, tapered, and narrow. The tail is also long, tapered, and encased in twelve bony rings. All the feet are armed with long, white claws specialized for digging. The color of the armor plates is brownish black and white hairs are sparsely scattered over the thinner skin on the belly. The head, sides, and tail have ivory-yellow spots on the armor plates. The ears look like two bare leathery funnels that nearly join one another at the midline of the head.

Geographical Range: Armadillos are not native to Florida, but were introduced by man several times during the early 1900s. They are now widely established over most of Florida. In the United States, the nine-banded armadillo ranges across the southern third of the country, as far west as Texas and New Mexico. It also lives in much of Mexico, Central America, and South America.

Habitat Preference: Armadillos prefer both forested and semi-open habitats on deep sandy soils. They like areas with dense ground cover and a loose-textured soil that makes digging easy. There are few armadillos in areas with heavy clay or rocky soils, or in regions dominated by marshes and swamps.

Life History and Reproduction: Armadillos are burrowing mammals and dig a series of dens scattered throughout their home range. They often place the entrances at the bases of trees, stumps, palmettos, brush piles, or other protected locations. At the end of a downward-sloping tunnel, they make a slightly enlarged nest chamber containing a mass of leaves or grass. Armadillos occasionally make massive above-ground nests consisting of leaves and grass. Many animals such as snakes, lizards, rabbits, frogs, toads, mice, rats, opossums, and skunks also use armadillo burrows for homes or refuge. Armadillo burrows usually have two or more entrances to provide added escape routes.

An armadillo, when pursued, can dig a burrow and disappear underground in just a few seconds, and is very difficult to pull out of a partially completed burrow when grasped by the tail. They cannot roll themselves up into a ball as is alleged; a small South American armadillo is capable of doing this, however.

Armadillos breed in July or August. Ovulation follows insemination and fertilization of an egg then takes place. However, implantation of embryos in the uterus is delayed until late November or early December. The gestation period averages about 120 days. Generally a litter of identical quadruplets (all of the same sex) is produced. This occurs because each litter of four results from the splitting of a single egg after fertilization. I have also collected females in Florida with embryo counts of three and six. Presumably a litter of three results when resorption of one embryo occurs early in gestation. An embryo count of six is a little more complicated, but might be explained by the simultaneous ovulation of two eggs, before splitting of both into four individuals, then followed by a loss of two of the eight. A single fertilized egg could possibly result in eight individuals under conditions of excessive splitting.

Birth of the young usually occurs in late March or April, but some are also born in May. The offspring are precocial, the eyes open within a few hours, and the babies can walk and follow their mother on their first day.

Armadillos do not hibernate during cold weather and this probably restricts their northward range expansion. Even if they failed to freeze during a long cold spell, starvation probably would occur. They consume all kinds of insects and

L. N. BROWN

armadillo, 27.6-32.3 in. (70-82 cm) overall, tail 11.8-15.7 in. (30-40 cm)

Armadillos

other invertebrates, as well as some plant material. One study found that beetles and beetle larvae composed 45 percent of the armadillo's diet.

Armadillos are mainly nocturnal foragers, but on cloudy days they are often seen probing the ground along roadsides or heard scratching about in the palmettos. They have very poor eyesight but keen ears, so they can often be approached and captured with a hand net, if no sounds give the stalker away.

These mammals are sedentary and often remain in the same general area for long periods. They forage over a home range only a few acres in size. Their life span in the field is not known, but in captivity they have lived as long as 10 years.

Economic Importance and Remarks: Armadillos are beneficial in consuming certain destructive insects such as termites, ants, and ground-dwelling beetles and their grubs. On the negative side, their prodigious diggings can damage lawns, golf courses, peanut fields, corn, cantaloupes, and other truck garden crops. They occasionally eat the eggs of ground-nesting birds such as sparrows and quail, but this is a very minor fraction of their diet.

They are used extensively for biomedical and genetic research, because of their unique characteristic of bearing identical quadruplets.

The habit of digging multiple dens provides homesites for a long list of other vertebrates and many invertebrates. There is also some concern that foraging armadillos may reduce populations of certain native endangered or threatened species in Florida. The remains of sand skinks, worm lizards, rat snakes, and scrub lizards have been found in the stomachs of armadillos.

Some states consider the armadillo a game animal and encourage hunters to take and eat them. Most people remain unconvinced of its palatability, however. Armadillo hides are sometimes made into baskets and handbags for the tourist trade in parts of the United States.

Armadillos are apparently the second commonest animal killed on Florida's highways, after the opossum. This is partly explained by their unwary nature and tendency to forage on grassy road shoulders. They also have a peculiar reflex that causes them to jump straight up into the air when startled. This causes many more to be killed by cars that might otherwise pass right over them without injury.

Predators other than man include a variety of carnivores such as dogs, bobcats, coyotes, black bears, panthers, and foxes. Hawks and owls may occasionally take young armadillos.

Horses, cattle, and sheep sometimes break their legs when they step into armadillo burrows. Such burrows and foraging holes are also a nuisance along road shoulders, and can weaken dikes or canal banks in some parts of Florida. Also, a small percentage of some armadillo populations have been shown to carry the bacterial disease, leprosy. It is used as a research animal by medical institutions to study this crippling disease of humans.

ORDER LAGOMORPHA
Rabbits and Hares

Rabbits and hares resemble rodents rather closely and were once considered a subgroup of that order. Like rodents, they have a pair of large chisel-shaped upper incisors but differ from them by the presence of a second smaller pair right behind the first pair. Rabbits and hares also have very large hind feet compared to the front feet, and their ears are very large and elongated. The males lack a baculum or penis bone, which is present in rodents. The tail is always short and covered with fluffy cotton-like hairs. Rabbits and hares eat only vegetable matter. Lagomorphs and rodents are no longer considered close relatives, and their superficial resemblance is probably due to their similar herbivorous adaptations.

Lagomorphs are unusual in that they produce two types of fecal pellets from the digestive tract. One is a soft, green pellet that is only partially digested. These are re-eaten, passed through the digestive tract a second time, and virtually all remaining nutrients are removed. The second type is a dry, brownish pellet that is the true feces. This whole process of re-ingestion is called pseudorumination, because it is functionally analogous to the method used by cattle to extract more nutrition from grass, which involves regurgitation, chewing of the cud, and swallowing the food a second time.

Three species of rabbits and hares occur in Florida. Rabbits and hares now have virtually a worldwide distribution because of introductions by man. They were once absent from Australia, but were introduced by the English colonists and are now a considerable pest. All rabbits exhibit a hopping or saltatorial type of locomotion.

Eastern Cottontail *(Sylvilagus floridanus)*

Description: This species is slightly smaller than a cat and its upper parts are grayish to reddish brown sprinkled with black. The nape of the neck is rusty red, as are the forelegs. There is a cream-colored ring around the eye and usually a white star or blaze on the forehead. The underparts are white except for a brown throat patch. The tail hair forms a cotton-like tuft, which gives its name.

The skull is identified by the presence of a supraorbital process that is only partially fused to the cranium, leaving a slit-like opening when viewed from above.

Geographical Range: The eastern cottontail occurs throughout Florida except for the Keys and coastal marshes. It can be found throughout the eastern two-thirds of the United States.

Habitat Preference: This rabbit is highly adaptable and lives in virtually all upland Florida communities except dense forest. It is most abundant in fallow, weedy fields, brushlands with grassy openings, and fairly open forest edge. The cottontail is usually absent from wetter habitats occupied by the marsh rabbit.

Life History and Reproduction: The eastern cottontail is primarily nocturnal, but often it is seen actively feeding at dawn and dusk, as well as on cloudy days. The rabbits rest in a shallow depression or form, concealed in a dense clump of grass. It consists of nothing more that a well worn or slightly scratched-out depression. They eat the leaves of a wide variety of plants but prefer legumes, grasses, and various broad-leafed weeds.

In Florida there is a year-round breeding season, but in more northern locations they exhibit seasonal breeding that coincides closely with the growing seasons. Most litters are born between February and October. Eastern cottontail rabbits are noted for their high reproductive output. The litter size varies from 1-8 and averages 3-4 in Florida. The gestation period averages 28 days (range 26-32), and females can potentially produce as many as 12 litters per year, but average 5-6 litters.

Dominant-subordinate interactions have been reported during the reproductive season. Male hierarchies prevent fighting over females at the time of breeding. Dominant male cottontails inseminate more females than do subordinate males.

The nest is a shallow saucer-like depression in the ground, lined with fine grass and soft fur plucked from the female's breast with her teeth. She also covers the young with a top layer of grass and hair when she leaves the nest to forage. The babies are altricial, i.e., naked, blind, and helpless at birth.

Immediately after giving birth, the mother again comes into estrus and is bred. An adult female cottontail is pregnant and nursing young much of the time. Baby rabbits grow rapidly; their eyes open and they are fully furred in a week. At the end of 3-4 weeks, they leave the nest and are weaned, and the female is frequently ready to deliver another litter. Young cottontails have been known to breed when as young as 3-4 months of age, and females can produce several litters their first year of life.

Mortality is high in juvenile cottontails, with only about 55 percent surviving to reach the age of one month. They are preyed upon by virtually every terrestrial carnivore big enough to catch them. These include foxes, dogs, cats, coyotes, snakes, owls, hawks, crows, weasels, and bobcats. The maximum potential life span of the eastern cottontail is about 10 years. However, in natural populations few live more than two years. Home range size varies from 1-10 acres, depending on the quality and density of the plant cover.

Economic Importance and Remarks: Cottontail rabbits are among the most important small game animals in the United States. They are not hunted as extensively in Florida as farther north, but are still a valuable small game mammal. Cottontails are also a vital link in the food chain of many predators.

Cottontails occasionally are infected with the disease tularemia. This is a bacterial disease that can be contracted through a break in the skin while skinning and handling an infected animal. If the disease is not diagnosed and not treated with antibiotics, it can do serious damage to the human nervous system. Ticks are the primary transmitters of the disease between rabbits. Thorough cooking of a wild rabbit before eating eliminates any danger of contracting tularemia from the meat.

Cottontails frequently cause damage to garden vegetables and commercial agricultural crops in Florida. They are best controlled by trapping or shooting in such situations, or by elimination of nearby rabbit cover if direct removal is not feasible.

Marsh Rabbit *(Sylvilagus palustris)*

Description: The marsh rabbit is slightly smaller and somewhat darker colored than the eastern cottontail. The gray-brown tail is small and lacks a white powder-puff appearance. The back is dark reddish brown sprinkled with black hairs. The nape of the neck is rufous brown and the underparts are gray to buff.

The skull is identified by its small size and a posterior supraorbital process that is completely fused to the cranium, leaving no slit-like openings when viewed

eastern cottontail, 11.8-19.7 in. (30-50 cm) overall, tail 1.6-2.0 in. (4-5 cm)

marsh rabbit, 15.7-17.7 in. (40-45 cm) overall, tail 1.2-1.6 in. (3-4 cm)

Rabbits and Hares

from above. The ears and tail are smaller and darker than those of the eastern cottontail.

Geographical Range: This species occurs throughout the state of Florida and is the only rabbit found in the Keys. In the United States, it ranges across the Atlantic and Gulf coastal plains from Virginia to Alabama. It is replaced by a sibling species, the swamp rabbit *(Sylvilagus aquaticus),* on the western fringe of its range. They differ very little except that the marsh rabbit is smaller, and some experts believe they should both be considered a single species.

Habitat Preference: As the common name implies, these rabbits are found in both freshwater and brackish marshy areas. They are seldom found far from standing water and occur in most Florida floodplain habitats and in wet brushy areas as well. In southern Florida, they occur in sawgrass marshes, wet prairies, canal banks, salt marshes, mangrove swamps, cypress stands, tropical hammocks, sugarcane fields, and fallow fields of truck gardening areas. Marsh rabbits swim readily and for considerable distances. They are semiaquatic in their habits, and there are records of them swimming strongly as far as one-fourth mile from the nearest shoreline.

Natural History and Reproduction: The resting place is located in thickets, under stumps, in logs, and various other slightly elevated, sheltered locations. They often make runways through dense vegetation and habitually travel a network of paths or trails running throughout their home ranges.

The breeding season extends year-round in most of Florida. However, breeding peaks from December through June, after which it slows. In northern Florida there appears to be very little breeding from November to February, perhaps related to the colder weather. Litter size averages just under three young and ranges from 1-6. The gestation period is not known but probably is identical to that of the swamp rabbit, which averages 37 days (range 35-40).

The nest, like that of the eastern cottontail, is a cup-shaped depression in the ground lined with grass and breast fur. Babies are born well furred but their eyes are closed until two days old. They leave the nest when two weeks of age but remain with their mother to nurse until about four weeks old.

Adult females often come into estrus at the time they give birth and breed again. Thus, mother marsh rabbits have a high fecundity, and potentially could produce 8-10 litters per year. Most females, however, appear to become reproductively inactive from time to time, so it is doubtful that such maximum numbers are ever achieved. Females in southern Florida were found to average seven litters per year in one study. Marsh rabbits are capable of first breeding when 5-6 months old.

Marsh rabbits eat a wide variety of emergent aquatic vegetation and wetland plants including grasses, sedges, maidencane, broad-leafed herbs, and weeds. Most foraging occurs at night, but they are also active at dawn and dusk, as well as almost anytime on cloudy days. Home range size varies from 1-6 acres, depending on the density of the cover and location.

Economic Importance and Remarks: Marsh rabbits are not hunted as extensively as the eastern cottontail, but they are a valuable small game mammal in Florida. They sometimes cause damage to sugarcane and truck garden crops in southern Florida, and to home gardens situated adjacent to wetlands. With the continued draining, filling, and conversion to other uses of many of Florida's wetlands, marsh rabbits are losing thousands of acres of habitat yearly. They can still coexist with many agricultural uses, however.

Predators of the marsh rabbit include the same extensive list that take the eastern cottontail. Another mortality factor is flooding of their habitat by heavy rains, which is especially destructive to young rabbits and nestlings. Hurricanes sometimes eliminate entire populations from wide expanses of coastal marshes. For example, hurricane Donna in 1960 is said to have wiped out marsh rabbit populations in parts of the Keys and in southwestern Florida.

In 1990, the Florida Game and Fresh Water Fish Commission and the U.S. Fish and Wildlife Service added the lower Keys subspecies of the marsh rabbit to the endangered species list, primarily because of its restricted range and encroaching development in the Florida Keys.

Black-tailed Jackrabbit *(Lepus californicus)*

Description: This is a large, robust rabbit with extremely long ears and large hind limbs. The dorsal pelage of the black-tailed jackrabbit is grayish brown or grayish buff with wavy black markings. There is a dense, whitish underfur. A black area extends from the rump onto the entire upper surface of a short fluffy tail. The outer borders and undersurface of the tail are pure white. The tops of the ears are tipped in black, the inside of each ear is buffy, and the back of each ear is whitish. The underparts are generally white with a buff band across the neck and chest. A small white star or blaze is frequently present on the forehead.

The skull is about twice the size that of an eastern cottontail or marsh rabbit.

Geographical Range: The black-tailed jackrabbit was introduced and became established in the Miami area in the 1930s and 1940s. See map on page 202. It was repeatedly released to train greyhounds and many escaped into the surrounding countryside. Black-tailed jackrabbits also were released near the Tampa Dog Track in the 1960s, and I observed a few of them on the University of South Florida campus, in north Tampa, in 1968 and 1969. A perma-

(ASM)—R. H. BARRETT

black-tailed jackrabbit, 18.1-25.6 in. (46-65 cm) overall, tail 2.0-2.7 in. (5-7 cm)

Rabbits and Hares

nent population, however, did not become established in west-central Florida. The southeast Florida population still exists in a small area, but is not expanding its range, probably because of barriers to dispersal. The natural range of the black-tailed jackrabbit is confined to the western half of the United States.

Habitat Preference: The jackrabbit prefers grassy open areas and does not do well in any forested location. Due to extensive urbanization in the Miami area, today it is found mainly in the grassy areas bordering runways at Miami International Airport and in open areas and fields nearby.

Life History and Reproduction: Little is known about the life history in Florida of this exotic species. Jackrabbits spend most of the day resting in a shallow form or bare area scratched out in a clump of grass. They become active at dusk and forage nocturnally, but can be out and about anytime on cloudy days. They consume a wide variety of herbs and grasses, in addition to a long list of cultivated crops and vegetables.

Breeding occurs year-round in the southern part of the black-tailed jackrabbit's range in the western states, but is most intense from January to September. The gestation period averages 43 days and ranges from 41-47 days. Females can produce 1-8 young but average three in a litter. Females are sometimes both pregnant and nursing young at the height of the breeding season.

The young are precocial and born well furred and with their eyes open. They can hop about the first day, but usually stay in or near the nest during the first 3-4 days. Juvenile jackrabbits are weaned and on their own at about three weeks of age. A few breed late in the first year of their birth, but most wait until the next year to reproduce.

Economic Importance and Remarks: Foraging jackrabbits consume large amounts of vegetation and can damage gardens and row-crops extensively. However, they have such a restricted range in southeastern Florida that any impact is presently minor. If they were to become established in the vast truck garden areas around Homestead, Florida, considerable damage would occur.

Like all rabbits, this species can transmit tularemia. Precautions should be taken to protect hands with gloves when skinning or handling wild rabbits.

ORDER RODENTIA
Gnawing Mammals

Rodents are one of the largest groups of mammals found in Florida, both in number of species and in population. They are quite diverse, ranging from the tiny harvest mouse weighing only a few ounces to the large beaver, which may weigh more than 80 pounds. The skeletal characteristic shared by all rodents is one pair of large, chisel-like incisors located in the upper and lower jaws at the front of the mouth that are adapted for gnawing plant material. Canine teeth are absent, leaving a wide gap (the diastema) between incisors and cheek teeth. Incisors continue to grow throughout the rodent's life and are worn down during use. In some species the incisors grow as rapidly as one inch per month.

Most rodents are capable of reproducing profusely. Many species are specialized to produce large litters of offspring and to breed several times a year. Rodents have several reproductive functions that are rather advanced and specialized. These include induced ovulation, induced estrus, and post-birth pregnancies. Induced ovulation is the release of eggs in the female stimulated by the act of copulation. The presence of the male also induces estrus in the female of some rodents. And, in many species, females come into estrus, breed, and become pregnant again immediately after birth of a litter. These reproductive specializations and other adaptive features make the rodents one of the most successful mammalian groups on earth.

Rodents have a worldwide distribution and occur in virtually every terrestrial habitat that supports plant growth. Rodents comprise the largest group of mammals in the world with approximately 2,000 living species. A total of 22 rodent species live in Florida.

Eastern Chipmunk *(Tamias striatus)*

Description: The eastern chipmunk is a small ground-dwelling squirrel that has conspicuous lengthwise stripes on the back and face. The back fur is reddish brown with five dark stripes alternating with two light buffy stripes, ending at a rusty red rump patch. The belly and sides are buff to white and the feet are tan.

J. F. PARNELL

eastern chipmunk, 8.7-10.2 in. (22-26 cm) overall, tail 2.7-3.9 in. (7-10 cm)

The tail is blackish above and rusty below, with a narrow fringe of white or yellow hairs. The ears are short, rounded, and held erect.

The skull looks like that of a small squirrel, with a broad interorbital area. Only four cheek teeth are present on each side and the two cheek tooth rows converge slightly toward the rear of the palate. In contrast to the flying squirrel, no notch is present in the bone at the upper rim of the eye socket.

Geographical Range: The range of the eastern chipmunk penetrates the western portion of the Florida Panhandle. It has been recorded from Holmes County westward to Escambia County. See map on page 202. In the United States, the range occupies the eastern half of the country, exclusive of nearly all the southeastern coastal plain.

Habitat Preference: In Florida, the eastern chipmunk frequents the banks of streams and gullies covered with beech, oak, holly, magnolia, and ferns. It also occurs on drier sites dominated by oak, hickory, and pine. In more northern regions the chipmunk occurs in rocky, wooded ravines with limestone outcrops and in brushy woodlands having numerous fallen logs, woodpiles, and rocks. They are primarily ground dwellers but will climb trees occasionally to forage.

Natural History and Reproduction: Chipmunks are solitary animals that are active in the daytime, mostly in the early morning and late afternoon. They live in burrow systems that are fairly extensive and complex, usually constructed under a tree, rock, bank, or other protected locations. There are normally 2-3 burrow entrances, and the nest, containing dried leaves, is an enlarged chamber about 10 inches in diameter. Other special chambers are dug to provide for storage of nuts and seeds—usually acorns, pecans, beech seeds, pine seeds, and hickory nuts in Florida. They also eat considerable numbers of insects, including grasshoppers, katydids, large beetles, and cicadas. On some occasions they also eat young mice, frogs, salamanders, small snakes, mushrooms, berries, and bird eggs.

Chipmunks have cheek pouches located inside the mouth (internal cheek pouches), that can be crammed with food while foraging to be carried back to the burrow. When the cheek pouches are full of seeds and nuts, the face bulges so much that the chipmunk appears to have the mumps. Besides storing food in several underground chambers, they also cache food in shallow excavations on the forest floor like tree squirrels. During periods of food scarcity, chipmunks use the various stores.

When alarmed or agitated, eastern chipmunks usually emit a trilling chip sound, which serves to warn others. During the winter months, they are less active above ground than normal, but they do not appear to hibernate in Florida. I have seen them out on warm balmy days of December and January, in the upper Yellow River area.

Two seasonal breeding peaks occur, one in the early spring and another in the summer. The first litter is usually born in April after a 31-day gestation period. The second litter follows in July or August. Litter size is 2-7 and averages 4-5 young. Some years, the females produce only one litter in the spring; if conditions are favorable, a second litter is produced in the summer. The young are naked and blind and they remain in the underground nest chamber for 5-6 weeks. Eyes do not open until the young chipmunks are 30 days old; they are weaned when two months of age. A few females born in the spring will breed later in the summer, but most do not breed until the following spring. All young males mature and produce sperm by their first summer.

Economic Importance and Remarks: Chipmunks are so restricted in their Florida range as to have no economic impact. They are, however, an attractive and easily observed small mammal with considerable aesthetic value. If indiscriminate or extensive development takes place along the Yellow River and its tributaries, they could easily be eliminated from the state.

Their habit of burying seeds at the surface promotes the dispersal and germination of several nut-bearing trees. Tunneling by chipmunks provides aeration and distributes organic matter through the soil.

Eastern chipmunks have lived as long as eight years in captivity, but maximum longevity in wild populations is rarely longer than three years. They are preyed upon by cats, dogs, foxes, weasels, bobcats, hawks, owls, and rat snakes. The long-tailed weasel and various rat snakes represent the greatest threat because these predators can enter tunnel systems and follow a chipmunk wherever it goes.

This species is currently listed as a "Species of Special Concern" by the Florida Game and Fresh Water Fish Commission because of its possibly tenuous position in the western Panhandle. It is a peripheral species in Florida.

Eastern Gray Squirrel *(Sciurus carolinensis)*

Description: This medium-sized, slender, tree squirrel has a long, flattened, bushy tail. In Florida, it is often called "cat squirrel," presumably because of its agile climbing abilities. The upper side is grayish brown and usually white or grayish white on the underside. A common variation has an orangish-yellow belly instead of white. Albinos are also fairly common, as are color variants known as blonds, which have a diluted whitish upper fur with a gray stripe down the middle of the back only. The ears are small, rounded, erect, and brown in color, often with a prominent patch of white hair on their back side. The tips of the tail hairs are also white or pale gray.

The skull is distinguished from the fox squirrel by its smaller size and the presence of five upper cheek teeth on each side instead of four.

Geographical Range: The gray squirrel has a statewide distribution in Florida, including the upper Keys, and is one of our most common mammals. In the United States, the natural range of the gray squirrel occupies the eastern half of the country. It is also introduced and established as "town squirrels" in some western cities.

Habitat Preference: Gray squirrels occur in all types of wooded habitats. They probably reach maximum numbers in the mature hardwood forest, considered the ecological climax forest for most of Florida. They also are abundant in all suburban and residential areas of cities, where many of their

Gnawing Mammals

natural predators are absent. Gray squirrels are amazingly adaptable and even occur in some urban areas that have only a few scattered trees and expanses of mowed lawn between widely separated buildings. They prefer to nest in tree hollows, but if these are not available, they build bulky leaf nests in the treetops and take refuge there.

J. WATERS

gray squirrel, 15.7-19.7 in. (40-50 cm) overall, tail 7.5-8.7 in. (19-22 cm)

Life History and Reproduction: Gray squirrels forage both in trees and on the ground. They habitually bury individual acorns and other nuts in numerous shallow pits scattered throughout the home range. They also eat various fruits, buds, mushrooms, berries, insects, and bird eggs. It has recently been found that they will even leave their normal home range and travel some distance to feed on an attractive nut crop such as pecans, which mature in the early fall. They appear to detect the nuts by the scent carried on the wind.

Eastern gray squirrels are strictly diurnal and forage mainly in the early morning and late afternoon hours. They do not hibernate and are active year-round. Population size varies directly in response to the abundance of food. In years of good acorn and nut crops (mast), mortality of young is low and populations increase. A poor mast crop in the fall will be followed by a population decline resulting from starvation and emigration of individuals in search of food.

The breeding season has two peaks: one in the late winter and early spring, and another in the late spring and summer. The gestation period is 44-45 days, and each adult female normally produces two litters per year of 2-6 young, each averaging three. The first litter is born during January-March, and the second during May-July in Florida. Newborn young are hairless, with eyes and ears tightly closed. The eyes finally open when they are 28 days old, and they are also well furred. Young squirrels may continue to suckle up to 3-4 months of age. When a new litter is due, the mother will leave the den to the juveniles and select a new site to bear the second litter. As the newly weaned young squirrels disperse and try to establish their own homes, a great deal of mortality occurs. Nearly all young squirrels breed the following year.

Gray squirrels are often vocal and will scold intruders with a barking chatter that can continue for some time. Such warning vocalizations are usually accompanied by vigorous pumping and wagging of the bushy tail. Males exhibit antagonism toward one another, especially during the mating season. Mating chases are common, with several males ardently following and quarreling over a female in heat.

Gnawing Mammals

Economic Importance and Remarks: The eastern gray squirrel is a very important small game species, harvested in large numbers by Florida hunters. Squirrels also have aesthetic value to humans in parks and backyards, where they often become so tame as to be hand fed. On the negative side, they also may bite the hand that feeds them and their abilities to steal food intended for birds is legendary. They can overcome most squirrel-proof bird feeders designed by man, and are so habitual about eating food put out for birds that they become notable pests. Nuisance individuals can be readily removed by live-trapping or shooting, however.

Gray squirrels sometimes nest in attics and outbuildings, doing damage by gnawing and accumulating fecal material. Occasionally, they damage the insulation on electrical wiring, and they can short out transformers in urban areas. Local power failures induced by electrocuted gray squirrels are common in Florida.

Beneficially, the caching of seeds and nuts by gray squirrels results in dispersal and germination of many oaks, hickories, pecans, and other hardwoods. This not only ensures that future generations of squirrels will have food and shelter, but also eventually provides timber for humans.

Heavy agricultural losses can occur when gray squirrels live near pecan groves, cornfields, or certain truck garden vegetables. I personally fight a battle every year with gray squirrels who harvest my crops of pecans, tomatoes, and peaches in the yard and garden. Squirrels invariably pick fruit or nuts when they are too green for human consumption.

Gray squirrels and the much larger fox squirrels rarely occur together in numbers in habitats suitable for both species. Usually one species or the other will dominate to the apparent exclusion of the other. This mutual exclusion could be caused by interspecific behavioral aggressiveness, but the actual reasons are not clear. Some Floridians believe that gray squirrels and fox squirrels can hybridize, but this is a myth. The two species never interbreed anywhere in their broadly overlapping ranges.

Fox Squirrel *(Sciurus niger)*

Description: This "giant" Florida squirrel is several times larger than any other species in the state. Fox squirrels have a robust squarish profile and are much heavier than the eastern gray squirrel. The Florida fox squirrel occurs in several color phases ranging from gray, tan, gray brown, and blackish brown dorsally to a totally black squirrel. The underside varies from white to creamy yellow, rusty orange, and black. Regardless of the color combination, Florida fox squirrels always have a white muzzle and forehead, and most also have white patches on the back sides of the ears. The tail is long, bushy, and variably colored depending on the color phase.

The skull is distinguished from the gray squirrel by its much greater size and the presence of four upper cheek teeth on each side rather than five.

Geographical Range: Fox squirrels have a statewide distribution in Florida, except for the Keys. However, it appears that populations once present in southeastern Florida (especially Dade and Broward counties) are now extinct because of urbanization, intensive agricultural development, and elimination of pinelands in recent decades. The United States range of the fox squirrel is nearly identical to that of the eastern gray squirrel, i.e., the eastern half of the country. Fox squirrels also have been introduced and become established in some western states where they are not native.

Habitat Preference: Throughout most of Florida, fox squirrels are animals of mature open pine flatwoods and open pine-oak forests. They forage extensively on the ground and don't do well where there is heavy ground cover. Periodic fires that kill hardwoods and promote grassy ground cover in the pinelands are absolutely necessary for fox squirrel populations to thrive. In southwestern Florida, fox squirrels occur not only in pinelands, but sparingly in cypress strands, mixed cypress-pine, and even tropical hammocks.

Life History and Reproduction: Fox squirrels spend much more their time foraging on the ground than do gray squirrels. They bury many acorns, nuts, and pine seeds as a hedge against low food supplies. They also eat mushrooms, bulbs, tubers, buds, fruits, berries, insects, and bird eggs. Adult males range over a large area that averages about 100 acres, but adult females range over an area that averages only about 40 acres.

Fox squirrels are strictly diurnal, but are later risers than gray squirrels. They usually forage in the mid-morning hours, again around noon, and then close with a late afternoon foraging period. Fox squirrels are active year-round and do not hibernate during cold weather.

Fox squirrel numbers in Florida have declined steadily over the last several decades, due primarily to fire suppression and habitat destruction. Two races (Sherman's fox squirrel in northeastern and central Florida, and the Everglades or Big Cypress fox squirrel in southern Florida) are already listed on threatened and endangered species lists. Their prospects for survival into the next century are not bright if current land use trends continue.

The reproduction season of the fox squirrel is similar to that of the gray squirrel. There are two breeding peaks, one in the late winter and early spring, and another in the summer. Older females usually produce two litters per year, but spring-born females usually produce only one litter the following year when they reach maturity. The litter size in Florida ranges from 1-6 and averages 2-3 offspring. The gestation period averages 45 days, and the young are naked and blind at birth. The ears and eyes open at about 28 days of age, by which time they are also fully furred. They do not leave the nest until they are about eight weeks old, and they are on their own at three months of age.

Fox squirrels prefer to nest in hollow pine, oak, or cypress, but also build large temporary leaf nests in the treetops. The scolding chatter of a fox squirrel is similar to that of gray squirrels, but is deeper and stronger.

Economic Importance and Remarks: The Florida fox squirrel is a small game species highly sought by hunters. Because of their impressive size, striking

fox squirrel, 23.6-39.4 in. (60-100 cm) overall, tail 11.4-13.4 in. (29-34 cm)

pelage coloration, and relative rarity, many fox squirrels end up as mounted trophies rather than on the table. With the continued downward trend in fox squirrel populations, fewer and fewer of the state's fox squirrels will be hunted in the future. Currently, fox squirrels are most abundant in northern Florida, and they are increasingly rare as one proceeds southward on the peninsula.

Fox squirrels seldom become as tame as gray squirrels when fed or subjected to repeated human contact. On rare occasions, they will become semi-tame in preserves, parks, or on golf courses. Like gray squirrels, they sometimes rob bird feeders, but they are not as agile at invading the squirrel-proof designs.

Fox squirrels are beneficial in dispersal and germination of oaks, pecans, hickories, pines, and various hardwoods found in their habitat. In northern Florida, they are sometimes numerous enough to reduce the pecan harvests or damage cornfields. Control methods include live-trapping or shooting pest individuals.

Mexican Red-bellied Squirrel *(Sciurus aureogaster)*

Description: This introduced species is slightly larger than the eastern gray squirrel and smaller than the eastern fox squirrel. The upper parts are light to dark gray frosted with white. The underparts are rich mahogany red which also extends high up on the sides in the midbody region, almost to the back. The ears are small, rounded, and erect with reddish brown on their back sides. The tail is large, bushy, and salt-and-pepper gray with white frosting on the tips of the hair. There is also a totally black color phase that is very common in the Florida populations. The skull is very similar to the gray squirrel and must be examined by an expert for positive identification.

Gnawing Mammals

Geographical Range: The red-bellied squirrel was introduced from Mexico to Elliott Key, Dade County, Florida in 1938 by a resident of the island. See map on page 202. Only two pairs were released, but the species thrived, gradually increased in numbers, and covered the entire eight-mile-long island. It does not occur on the mainland or on the other Florida Keys. The native range of the red-bellied squirrel occupies the southern half of Mexico and part of Guatemala.

After hurricane Andrew roared through south Florida on August 24, 1992, totally devastating the tropical forest on Elliott Key, it is not known how many of the red-bellied squirrels survived this catastrophe. The population was almost certainly decimated. Further study is needed to determine the current status of the red-bellied squirrel population.

Habitat Preference: In Florida the species is established in a dense second-growth tropical hammock type of forest, containing such trees as mahogany, stopper, gumbo limbo, strangler fig, mastic, poisonwood, Jamaica dogwood, manchineel, pigeon plum, and coconut palm. In Mexico the red-bellied squirrel is found in various lowland and foothill tropical forests.

Life History and Reproduction: Red-bellied squirrels spend most of their time in the tree canopy (an arboreal lifestyle), and rarely come down to the ground to forage. They are shy and very difficult to observe.

On Elliott Key, a live-trapping study in 1972 revealed a density of approximately one red-bellied squirrel per acre. It was also found that 50 percent of the squirrels were melanistic (all black) and the other half had the normal frosted gray and red pelage. The original introduction included one black phase squirrel, so

L. N. BROWN

Mexican red-bellied squirrel, 16.5-22.4 in. (42-57 cm) overall,
tail 7.9-12.2 in. (20-31 cm)

this coloration has been perpetuated. The black squirrels are much easier to see in the tropical vegetation, but the gray-red phase blends with the background so well that researchers virtually never saw them except in the live traps. There is a strong possibility that these color phases are sex linked, because 68 percent of the red-gray squirrels were males and only 36 percent of the black squirrels were males.

The home range size of male red-bellied squirrels on Elliott Key averages 5.9 acres; the female's home range averages less than half of that at 2.2 acres. In most mammals the home range size of males is significantly larger.

Red-bellied squirrels are frugivorous, feeding primarily on tropical fruits and seeds. In Mexico, they eat mangos, figs, jubo plums, tamarind pods, zapote, and maize. On Elliott Key, they consume the fruit and seeds of a wide variety of tropical trees, including sea grape, wild mastic, papaya, coconut palm, gumbo limbo, thatch palm, and Sargent's palm. During the dry season (late winter and spring) when fruit is scarce, the squirrels survive by browsing on the buds and twigs of mahogany, gumbo limbo, and sea grape. The huge nut of the coconut palm is heavily utilized, but it requires many hours of effort for the squirrels to cut through the thick outer husk and hard shell. Once the squirrel finally penetrates the shell, it will return repeatedly to feed, up to a week or so, until all the nut meat has been consumed.

Red-bellied squirrels are diurnally active, with most foraging taking place between one-half hour after sunrise and about 11:00 A.M. They are rarely active in the afternoon or evening except on cloudy days. Red-bellied squirrels make extensive use of temporary leaf nests constructed in the canopy as well as permanent nests constructed in tree hollows. Leaf nests are of a dome type consisting of a base of interwoven twigs supporting an inner cup of tightly packed leaves. The inner surface of the nest cup is sometimes lined with a thin layer of soft fibers stripped from the trunk of palm trees, papaya plants, or other tropical trees.

The breeding season extends throughout the year in the red-bellied squirrel. Meager data exist, but the litter size ranges from 1-4 and averages two. Adult females generally breed 2-3 times a year. Young squirrels do not become sexually active until they are about one year old.

Economic Importance and Remarks: Red-bellied squirrels have a beautiful pelage that has considerable aesthetic value to humans. In Mexico, they are often kept as cage pets because of their beauty.

In Florida they have no economic importance at present, and this should continue as long as they remain on the island eight miles from the mainland. However, since they are tropical frugivores (fruit eaters), there could be considerable impact on commercially grown and backyard fruit trees (especially mangos, papaya, avocados, and citrus), if they should ever reach the south Florida mainland.

There is little or no predation on the red-bellied squirrels of Elliott Key. Young squirrels may occasionally be taken by rat snakes, indigo snakes, hawks, and raccoons.

Southern Flying Squirrel *(Glaucomys volans)*

Description: This is Florida's pint-sized tree squirrel and the only one with a loose fold of skin (the gliding or alar membrane) running along the side of the body from wrist to ankle. When both front and hind legs are spread, the gliding membrane creates a wing-like surface as the squirrel soars from tree to tree. The flying squirrel is buffy brown to gray on the back, and the fur is exceptionally soft, dense, and silky feeling. The fur of the underside is completely white. The body is horizontally flattened and the tail is also very broad, flat, heavily furred, and serves as a rudder and stabilizer during flight.

The skull is very small for a squirrel and has five cheek teeth on either side of the upper jaw. There is also a deep notch in the frontal bone located at the upper rim of the eye socket.

Geographical Range: The southern flying squirrel occurs throughout Florida, except for the Keys. Its range in the United States is confined to the eastern half of the country. There are also several isolated populations scattered through the mountains of Mexico and Central America.

Habitat Preference: Flying squirrels occur in most of Florida's forested habitats, but they reach highest densities in mature pine-oak woodlands and mature oak hammocks. In all habitats, they need hollow, dead snags or hollow cavities in living trees for nest sites. They are largely dependent upon woodpeckers to provide such hollows.

Life History and Reproduction: The lovely little flying squirrel is seldom seen because it sleeps all day, becomes active at dusk (crepuscular), but forages during the nighttime. They are sometimes glimpsed gliding from tree to tree on a bright moonlit night or with a flashlight. Flying squirrels have large eyes that glow red in the light and are well adapted for night vision. The tail, serving as a rudder, enables them to execute sharp turns and maneuvers during each glide. Their forward momentum is checked by an upward swoop, just before they land at the base of a tree feet first and head up. Each glide is normally 30-50 feet in length, but extremely long ones of 100-200 feet have been reported.

Flying squirrels do very little foraging on the ground, concentrating on the treetops, trunks, and branches. Their favorite foods are hickory nuts, acorns, pecans, insects, bird eggs, bird nestlings, berries, fruits, buds, and seeds of many other trees. They eat more insects and other types of protein than any other squirrels. Flying squirrels occasionally even feed on carcasses of dead animals. They hoard and cache nuts and seeds in tree cavities to use when food supplies are short.

Flying squirrels are rather gregarious, especially in the colder months of the year (November-March). I have found as many as 28 sleeping together in a single large tree cavity, but a more normal number is 3-8. The nest is usually made of Spanish moss mixed with shredded nuts, bark, and leaves. During the warmer parts of the year, males and females are found as pairs in the nests. The male leaves before the young are born, and the female alone takes care of the babies. Male and female again form a pair after weaning of the offspring.

young southern flying squirrel, 8.3-9.8 in. (21-25 cm) overall,
tail 3.5-4.7 in. (9-12 cm)

Mating takes place twice a year, with litters produced in the spring and again in the fall. Mating for the first litter usually occurs in January or February, and the young are born in March or April. The gestation period is 39-40 days, and the average number of young is 2-3 (range 1-6). The babies are tiny, blind, and hairless at birth. They grow rapidly and in 14 days they are fully furred, but the eyes don't open until the squirrels are about 28 days old. They are weaned and able to fend for themselves by six weeks of age. Mating for the second litter takes place in August or September, and the young are born in October or November. Juveniles do not breed until one year old.

At night, flying squirrels can often be detected by the faint bird-like chirps and twitters that they make while foraging in the trees. They also sometimes utter a soft chattering noise similar to their larger relatives, the gray and fox squirrels.

Economic Importance and Remarks: Flying squirrels are often kept as pets. They are easily tamed, rather docile, and seldom bite unless handled roughly. They are one of the gentlest of all rodents. However, they sleep all day and frolic at night when people want to sleep.

Flying squirrels sometimes gain access to attics and become a nuisance because of the noise and accumulation of fecal pellets. The place of entry should be plugged at night when they are gone, or they also can be readily live-trapped and transported elsewhere.

This species will often use nest boxes provided for purple martins and other birds. In stands of timber lacking many hollow tree cavities, flying squirrels can actually be attracted and the population increased by placing artificial nest boxes on the tree trunks, 8-10 feet above the ground.

Gnawing Mammals

Flying squirrels are much too small to be hunted as a game species, but they are aesthetically pleasing to many for their appearance and interesting habits. Major predators include owls, cats, rat snakes, bobcats, raccoons, and weasels.

Southeastern Pocket Gopher *(Geomys pinetis)*

Description: The southeastern pocket gopher or "salamander", as some residents call it, is a peculiar looking rat-sized mammal with huge buck teeth at the front of the mouth, enlarged front feet with long claws, a stocky body, and a short, naked tail. The upper pelage is short and chestnut brown or cinnamon brown in color, and tan or buff below. The forelimbs are enlarged for digging and each of the five toes is armed with a large curved claw. The gopher's most distinctive characteristic is a pair of large fur-lined cheek pouches or pockets, which open by vertical slits on each side of the face, near the mouth. They extend backward as far as the shoulders and are used for carrying food and nest material.

The large, orange-bordered incisor teeth are always exposed because the furry lips close behind them. This allows pocket gophers to dig dirt and cut roots with these large teeth without getting soil inside the mouth. Pocket gophers have small, beady eyes and a limited range of vision. The ears are tiny, rounded, and fold shut to keep dirt out of the auditory canal. Large facial whiskers, called vibrissae, located around the snout are very sensitive organs of touch. A naked tail serves the same tactile function at the posterior end of the pocket gopher.

The skull is identified by very large upper incisors having two lengthwise grooves on the anterior surface of each. The skull also has a large rostrum and is broad and flattened.

B. MANSELL

Geographical Range: This gopher is restricted to portions of the northern two-thirds of Florida. See map on page 203. In the United States, it ranges only from central Alabama and central Georgia southward into Florida as far as Highlands County.

Habitat Preference: The southeastern pocket gopher prefers deep sandy soils. It is rare or absent from most hard clay or rocky soils as well as from saturated hydric or mucky soils. Pocket gophers are most abundant in pine-oak woodlands, open pine flatwoods, and open weedy or grassy fields with sandy soils.

pocket gopher, 9.1-12.2 in. (23-31 cm) overall, tail 2.7-3.5 in. (7-9 cm)

Life History and Reproduction: Like the much smaller moles, pocket gophers live under the ground (a fossorial lifestyle) in an extensive series of tunnels that are plugged from inside and lack an opening to the surface. They build two types of tunnels: a shallow feeding tunnel system located in the plant root zone within a foot or so of the surface; and, a deep tunnel system located 18-36 inches below the surface that contains a single nest chamber and several food storage areas. The southeastern pocket gopher normally builds a tightly spiraling ramp or "spiral staircase" connecting the surface feeding tunnels to the deep tunnel system. It is probable that a spiraling tunnel confuses predators (such as snakes and weasels) that enter the gopher's system and, if plugged by the pocket gopher, the sharply curving trail is difficult to follow and reopen.

While excavating a tunnel system, the pocket gopher generates a great deal of loose dirt that is pushed up a sloping tunnel to the surface to form large mounds. The large front paws and cheeks are used to thrust the dirt bulldozer-style along the tunnels and up to the surface, forming a flat fan-shaped mound in front of the tunnel entrance. The opening is eventually plugged at the entrance when the mound is nearing completion. Thus, the plugged tunnel leads away from one edge of each surface mound, rather than the center of the mound as moles construct them. A single pocket gopher usually produces a series of mounds in a line, marking the approximate course of its underground tunnel system. The surface mounds vary a great deal in size, but are large. Freshly constructed mounds are 12-18 inches across and 4-8 inches high. Rain and wind gradually erode them, but each mound scar usually persists for a year or more.

Pocket gophers are solitary, antisocial animals that will not tolerate one another except at breeding time. Only one individual lives in each tunnel system, except when females are nursing offspring. The southeastern pocket gopher can breed during any month of the year, but there are two peaks in Florida

L. N. BROWN

southeastern pocket gopher surface mounds in a lawn

Gnawing Mammals

(February-March and June-July), when most females are involved. The average litter size is slightly less than two and the range is 1-3 young. Gestation is about four weeks long. At birth, baby gophers are approximately two inches long, have hairless, pink, wrinkled skin, and their eyes are closed. They develop slowly and the eyes do not open until they are five weeks old. Weaning takes place when they are about six weeks old, at which time the young disperse and dig their own new tunnel system near their parent's home. They start breeding when about six months of age.

It is not clear how the highly territorial pocket gophers locate one another at the time of breeding. It appears that males may leave their tunnel systems and travel above ground in search of receptive females. It is possible that females also surface and emit a sex attractant chemical (called a pheromone) that is detected downwind by males, who then follow the scent to the female and copulate.

The southeastern pocket gopher feeds on a wide variety of roots, tubers, bulbs, and other plant parts. They especially like Bahia grass tubers in many Florida lawns and pastures. Food is cached in special storage chambers and used when supplies are short. The nest chamber usually contains only a shallow pad of grasses, plant fibers, or dried roots. Pocket gophers extend their tunnels less actively during the cooler months of the year than during the warm months, but they do not hibernate. They are active around the clock each day in the tunnel system, but foraging peaks during late evening and night. They are often taken by owls, indicating they spend some time above ground at night. Also, green plant cuttings from the surface are often abundant on the floor of tunnels.

Adult females produce an average of two litters per year in Florida. Pocket gophers have a low reproductive output because of small litter sizes, yet they are common in most habitats where they occur. This strongly suggests a high survival rate in the young. The closed tunnels protect pocket gophers from many predators. They are vulnerable mainly to snakes and weasels, the latter being rare in Florida. When on the surface or building dirt mounds, pocket gophers are sometimes taken by owls, hawks, cats, foxes, skunks, and dogs.

Economic Importance and Remarks: Pocket gophers are a considerable nuisance when they live in lawns, golf courses, parks, gardens, and certain agricultural crops. They are best controlled by trapping, since most poisons are largely ineffective and hazardous to the environment. Poisonous gases, such as automobile exhaust fumes, funneled into their tunnel system also are not effective because the gopher quickly plugs off the gassed tunnel. The most effective trap, the MacAbee gopher trap, is a small metal variety that fits inside a tunnel entrance. First the tunnel system must be opened with a shovel to set the trap. This requires digging beyond the dirt plug associated with the surface mound until the open subterranean tunnel is reached. The tunnel traps are especially effective because the pocket gophers will not tolerate a surface opening in their system and always respond by plugging it. The jaws of the trap are designed to catch the gopher as it pushes a load of dirt forward to plug the open end of the tunnel. These traps are almost 100 percent effective if properly placed and set.

The southeastern pocket gopher is a great soil mixer, beneficial in redistributing organic matter and surface nutrients in our sterile, sandy Florida soils. This churning of the earth is a useful and normal aspect of the ecology in the natural terrestrial communities. The tunnels of pocket gophers serve as homes for a wide variety of other creatures including snakes, lizards, frogs, toads, insects, spiders, and other invertebrates.

The name "salamander" which is used by native Floridians for the southeastern pocket gopher is probably derived as a corruption of "sandy mounder," describing their conspicuous surface mounds.

The maximum longevity of the southeastern pocket gopher in nature probably approaches five years. They do not do well in captivity and usually die within a few days of capture, apparently from stress-related causes. Thus, their maximum life span as determined by genetics is not known.

One race of the southern pocket gopher until recently was listed as endangered by the Florida Game and Fresh Water Fish Commission, but it is now declared extinct. It is called Goff's pocket gopher, known only from Pineda Ridge, bordering the Indian River in Brevard County, Florida. No mounds or specimens of Goff's pocket gopher have turned up for many years.

Beaver *(Castor canadensis)*

Description: The beaver is Florida's largest rodent and one of the most recognizable. Adults usually weigh 30-50 pounds, but individuals up to 85 pounds have been recorded. The dorsal fur is a rich glossy brown with a fine dense underfur that is grayish. The underside is grayish tan and the feet and tail are black or brownish black. The back feet are webbed for swimming and the tail is broad, flat, scaly, and used as a rudder and propeller when swimming. The two inner toes on the back feet have specialized double claws that are used for combing and grooming the fur.

The massive skull is easily distinguished by its large size and well developed incisor teeth, the front surfaces of which are pigmented deep orange.

Geographical Range: The beaver occurs throughout the Florida Panhandle and in the northwestern portion of the peninsula as far south at the mouth of the Suwannee River and adjacent streams. See map on page 203. In the United States, they occur nationwide where habitat is suitable. The beaver was extirpated from much of its former range well before the 1900s by excessive trapping for the early fur trade. Beginning in the late 1950s, conservation and management practices were initiated to reintroduce and restore the beaver to its former range using animals from the Great Lakes area. These efforts were very successful, and beavers have increased in number and invaded nearly all habitats where they can live successfully. In fact, the beaver populations in peninsular Florida apparently represent a southward expansion of the range beyond its historical limits when European explorers arrived. Originally, the beaver's southern range boundary ended in the Panhandle.

beaver 39.4-49.2 in. (100-125 cm) overall, tail 15.4-17.7 in. (39-45 cm)

Habitat Preference: Beavers are active nocturnally and can live in almost any stream, swamp, bayou, or lake having a suitable adjacent supply of trees available for food. They feed on the inner bark, twigs, and buds of a variety of trees in Florida including sweet gum, cottonwood, sweet bay, elm, loblolly pine, willow, tupelo gum, box elder, ironwood, yaupon, chinaberry, wax myrtle, and spruce pine. The preferred tree species depends on what is available at a given site and whether the trees are small enough to cut down. Beavers seldom cut down trees greater than 12 inches in diameter, and most are 1-6 inches across. Many larger trees are debarked and girdled, however.

Life History and Reproduction: Beavers are famous for their diligent dam-building and maintenance activities. The dams are made of limbs and branches from the trees they cut down with their large incisors. Hundreds of pieces are sectioned to workable size, floated or dragged to the dam, and interwoven with considerable engineering skill into an effective water retaining structure. Beavers tend the dam carefully each night and quickly set about repairing it whenever it is damaged.

In some areas of Florida, where the streams are fairly deep and maintain a good year-round flow, beavers do not build dams. Most Florida beavers also do not build the massive stick lodges in which to live, that we associate with more northern colonies. They occasionally construct such homes in the quiet water of lakes and marshes, but most beavers live in deep dens in the banks of streams. Entrances to dens are usually below water level, and the tunnel slopes up to a dry chamber above water level back in the bank.

Gnawing Mammals 77

beaver lodge

Beavers are social animals that live in family units which consist of the adult male and female and their offspring from two breeding seasons (called yearlings and kits). They are primarily nocturnal in their activity, but sometimes venture out during the day in protected or remote areas. They can remain under water for 10-15 minutes and have been known to swim nearly half a mile before coming up for air.

When felling a tree, the beaver stands on its hind feet propped by the tail and gnaws at a convenient height, removing large chips with the incisor teeth. They are not able to control the direction in which a tree falls. The tree snaps when the encircling cut reaches a critical depth, and the beaver scurries away to avoid being hit. On rare occasions, beavers are killed or pinned by a falling tree. A single beaver can cut down a willow tree five inches in diameter in as little as three minutes. Large trees often take more than one night to fell, and many times they are merely girdled and abandoned. Beaver colonies eventually "eat themselves out of house and home." When most of the suitable trees within 300 to 600 feet of the water's edge have been depleted, beavers usually abandon the site and move to a new location, generally upstream or downstream. Beavers do consume some non-woody vegetation including aquatic plants, water weeds, cattails, streamside shrubs, acorns, and even corn when available.

The main sound associated with beavers is a loud slap of the tail on the surface of the water just before they dive. It serves as a warning signal to other members of the colony that danger is near.

The reproductive season begins in December or January, and adults apparently pair for life. Usually one litter (rarely two) is produced per year, and the gestation period is about four months. The litter size ranges from 1-8 but usually numbers 2-4. The kits are precocial, born with a full coat of fur and open eyes, and weigh about one pound. They leave the den for the first time when about one month old and wean at six weeks of age. They live with the parents and work cooperatively on all family projects until two years old. They are then driven away by the parents just before the birth of a new third litter. They become transients for awhile and at this time most mortality occurs. Most eventually find a mate and start their own family in a new unoccupied location. The majority first breed in the early spring of their third year.

Economic Importance and Remarks: Beaver trapping was one of the main commercial inducements for the early exploration and settlement of the United States and Canada. Beaver pelts were manufactured into all types of fashionable coats, jackets, hats, etc. Indians and early explorers also used the beaver for food. They are still trapped and sold for pelts in northern states, but the market value is a fraction of its former worth.

L. N. BROWN

tree gnawed by beaver

Beavers have large castor glands (scent glands) located at the base of the tail. Beavers use them to mark scent posts, which signify the territorial boundaries of the family, to ward off beavers that are transients or members of adjacent families. These castor glands are also marketed by trappers because they form an important ingredient in high-quality perfumes. Today most castor glands are sent to France where they are processed into very expensive perfumes.

Beavers are legendary for their flood-control and pond-forming activities along streams. A series of beaver dams will often slow silt-laden floods and contribute to clearing of the waters. The creation of ponds also changes the water temperature and other conditions for fish and other aquatic organisms. Some species are benefitted and others are injured by beaver ponds.

In northern Florida, the flooding of low areas by beavers sometimes conflicts with forestry operations and farming activities. Cornfields and pine plantations are sometimes damaged extensively. The insertion of water control structures into beaver dams can be effective in preventing excessive flooding. Also, problem beavers can be controlled by trapping and relocation, but authorization or permits may be required by landowners and local or state authorities.

The beaver has few enemies other than man, although kits and yearlings in Florida are vulnerable to alligators and large carnivores. When dispersing, transients on land are sometimes killed by dogs, bobcats, and automobiles. Maximum longevity in the wild is about 15 years, although some in captivity have lived to the age of 20.

Eastern Woodrat *(Neotoma floridana)*

Description: This species is also called the "pack rat" because of its habit of building bulky stick nests. The eastern woodrat is a medium-sized rodent with large, rounded, leaf-like ears, bulging black eyes, long whiskers, and a moderately well-haired tail that is slightly shorter than the head and body combined. The tail is distinctly bicolored—blackish brown above and white below—and the feet are white. The woodrat's dorsal fur is brownish gray mixed with black and the ventral side is white.

The skull is identified by the presence of a slight depression on the top between the eye sockets, which is not present in other Florida rats. The cheek teeth also have looping enamel folds surrounding dentine.

Geographical Range: The eastern woodrat ranges over the northern two-thirds of Florida. See map on page 203. On the west coast, I have trapped the eastern woodrat at Port Charlotte, in Charlotte County, its southernmost locality on that side of the peninsula. On the east coast it occurs at least as far south as Vero Beach in Indian River County. There is also an isolated island population restricted to the northern end of Key Largo in Monroe County. This population is seriously threatened by developers and classified as endangered by both the state and federal governments. In an effort to save Key Largo woodrats, they were introduced to Lignum Vitae Key, Monroe County, in 1970 and are still thriving on that small island. In the U.S., the eastern woodrat ranges from Connecticut westward to eastern Colorado and southward to Florida and Texas.

L. N. BROWN

eastern woodrat, 13.4-16.9 in. (34-43 cm) overall, tail 6.3-7.9 in. (16-20 cm)

Gnawing Mammals

Habitat Preference: The eastern woodrat in Florida prefers mature flood-plain forest and is rare or absent in dry wooded uplands and all open habitats. On Key Largo, it occurs only in the older, mature stands of tropical hammock and is almost entirely absent from the early successional stands of hammock. In the Keys, woodrats build huge stick nests that are shaped like beaver lodges (some are four feet high and more than six feet in diameter), but elsewhere in Florida the stick nests are small or nonexistent. Woodrats often nest in hollow logs and stumps on the forest floor, and they have a weakness for old cabins.

L. N. BROWN

large eastern woodrat nest on Key Largo, Florida

Life History and Reproduction: Woodrats are nocturnal and very rarely venture forth during the daytime. They are active year-round and do not hibernate. Evidence of woodrat presence often comes from accumulations of their half-inch-long oval droppings that are left in piles not too far from the nest. The droppings and piles of sticks are obvious indicators of their occurrence.

Woodrats are good climbers and probably forage a great deal in trees. I have flushed them from the large stick nests on the coral limestone at Key Largo, and almost invariably, they climb a tree to seek refuge. They are almost entirely vegetarian, eating all types of plant foods including leaves, stems, buds, seeds, fruit, tubers, roots, and nuts of trees and shrubs. They also eat insects including beetles and lepidoptera, as well as mushrooms and other fungi. Food is sometimes hoarded or cached in and around the nest.

The woodrat is not nearly as prolific as most small- to medium-sized rodents. They produce small litters and few litters per year. In Florida, offspring can be born in almost any month of the year. Females usually breed two or three times a year, and give birth to 1-5 offspring (usually two) per litter. Gestation averages 35 days, and the young are naked, helpless, and blind at birth. They attach themselves so firmly to their mother's teats that she can only dissociate herself with difficulty. If she is disturbed or leaves the nest suddenly, the babies are usually dragged along the ground, without apparent harm, still attached firmly to her nipples. When young woodrats are about 15 days old, they are fully furred and the eyes open. Weaning takes place when young woodrats are four weeks old, but they don't reach adult size or start breeding until about eight months of age.

Economic Importance and Remarks: The eastern woodrat rarely has any economic impact on man, but they are sometimes blamed for the extensive damage caused by two introduced species, the black rat and Norway rat. They do occasionally live in cabins and summer cottages built in the deep woods.

Gnawing Mammals

Nuisance individuals are easily trapped and removed with snap traps or live traps.

The nests of woodrats serve as homes for a wide variety of other creatures including several rare insects, spiders, mice, shrews, snakes, frogs, toads, and lizards. The eastern woodrat is preyed upon by many carnivores, including foxes, bobcats, large snakes, hawks, owls, weasels, skunks, raccoons, and cats. Their droppings serve as a rich source of organic fertilizer, providing nutrients for future plant growth, as well as food for a scavenging insects.

The Key Largo race of the eastern woodrat is listed as endangered by both the State of Florida and the U.S. Fish and Wildlife Service, and faces extermination if development gobbles up the remaining mature hammock on the north end of the island. The recent solution has been state and federal purchase of the best remaining hammocks to preserve this and several other organisms found nowhere else in the United States.

Hispid Cotton Rat (Sigmodon hispidus)

Description: Often called the "field rat," this is a medium-sized, robust rodent with a tail a good deal shorter than the head and body combined. The ears are blackish, medium in size, rounded, and buried in the neck fur. The upper pelage has a coarse, grizzled appearance and is a combination of brown, black, and light tan banded hairs. The belly is grayish or buffy. The tail is sparsely haired and weakly bicolored, black above and buff below.

The skull is the size of that of a small rat and identified by cheek teeth that show an S-shaped pattern of enamel folds of the grinding surfaces.

Geographical Range: The hispid cotton rat is one of the most common mammals in Florida and occurs statewide. In the United States, the range occupies the southern half of the country. It also is found in Mexico, Central America, and parts of South America.

Habitat Preference: Cotton rats occur in a wide variety of open and semi-open habitats. They are most abundant in old fields composed of dense grasses, especially broomsedge, and weeds. They are also common in brush and palmettos where some grass is present. During periods of high rat populations, they invade other plant communities such as sand pine scrub, pine-turkey oak and scrubby flatwoods.

Life History and Reproduction: Cotton rats make well-defined runways (about 3 inches wide) through the grass that are good indications of their presence. However, in areas where the grassy vegetation is sparse, they do not always make runways. A small bulbous nest is constructed of dry grass or fibers stripped off the stems of larger plants. It is usually placed underground in a shallow tunnel, but occasionally the nest is built on the surface in dense vegetation. Cotton rats eat the leaves, stems, roots, and seeds of many grasses, sedges, legumes, and other herbaceous plants. They also take some insects, bird eggs, and will even feed on carcasses.

Cotton rats have a 3-5 year population cycle, reaching peak numbers as high as 10-15 per acre in some areas. This is followed by a die-off of much of the population to densities of less than one cotton rat per acre. They then slowly increase in numbers over several years to a peak once again. Cotton rats seldom live more than a year in the field, but in captivity they can live 3-4 years.

Hispid cotton rats are active both day and night. It is common to see them during the daytime, running rapidly along a runway to escape human disturbance of their habitat. It is also not unusual to set a snap trap across one of their runways, then take a few steps, and hear the trap go off because a cotton rat ran across it.

The reproductive rate of cotton rats is very high, with breeding occurring throughout the year. In central Florida, there are breeding peaks in the early spring (March) and early fall (September-October) respectively. The average litter size in Florida is five, but the range is 2-10. Litters average larger in northern populations. The gestation period is 27 days, and females come into estrus and breed again right after giving birth. Adult females produce several litters each year and are normally pregnant and nursing all the time. The eyes open when offspring are two days old. The young grow rapidly, and they are weaned within two weeks. Sexual maturity is attained at the age of 40-50 days, and adult size is reached at five months of age.

Hispid cotton rats are a staple food item for many of Florida's predators, including hawks, owls, snakes, foxes, coyotes, dogs, cats, minks, bobcats, skunks, and weasels. When cotton rats are numerous, many other species of wildlife are under less predation pressure.

Economic Importance and Remarks: Cotton rats are generally destructive to many cultivated crops, including sugarcane, small grains, sweet potatoes, legumes, cotton, and truck garden vegetables. They also impact bobwhite quail directly by eating their eggs, and indirectly by consuming plants that the quail could use for food.

The best control methods involve removing or reducing heavy plant cover adjacent to a cultivated crop. This can usually be accomplished by burning or plowing the heavy cover areas. Less effective methods involve trapping or poisoning with coated grains. The latter can be extremely dangerous to other valuable wildlife such as perching birds, turkeys, and quail. Predators can also be inadvertently poisoned when they consume sick, dead, or dying cotton rats.

Eastern Harvest Mouse *(Reithrodontomys humilis)*

Description: This is Florida's smallest mouse and one of its least known. The upper side is grayish brown sprinkled with black hairs, and the underparts are grayish white or gray. The tail is not long (range 1.7 to 2.5 inches) and is sparsely haired. The leaf-like ears are short, broad, and rounded. The feet are white or light gray.

The skull is identified by its small size and by a pair of lengthwise grooves located on the front surface of the upper incisors. A similar species, the house mouse, lacks grooves on its upper incisors.

U.S.F.W.S.

cotton rat, 7.1-9.4 in. (180-240 mm) overall, tail 2.8-3.9 in. (72-100 mm)

J. F. PARNELL

harvest mouse, 3.5-4.7 in. (90-120 mm) overall, tail 1.7-2.5 in. (42-63 mm)

Geographical Range: This diminutive species is known from portions of the northern two-thirds of Florida. See map on page 203. Its range in the United States occupies the southeastern quadrant of the country, from Maryland southwestward to eastern Texas.

84   Gnawing Mammals

Habitat Preference: The eastern harvest mouse prefers old fields where tall grasses such as broomsedge predominate. It is also found in weedy fields, blackberry brier patches, grassy pastures, and roadside ditches.

Life History and Reproduction: This mouse is not often seen or collected and apparently is wary of entering traps. Their skeletal remains are often found in the cast pellets of owls, but few specimens have been trapped in Florida.

The nest is a small, spherical ball of dried grasses constructed above the ground in a thick clump of grass. Harvest mice are active at night and feed on weed seeds and some green vegetation.

In Florida, breeding occurs throughout the year. The gestation period is 21-22 days, and the litter size averages three (range 2-5). Their eyes open at 7-10 days of age, and the young are weaned at three weeks. They become sexually mature and can breed when around 12 weeks old.

The home range size of these little mice is not large, varying only from one-half to one acre. Males have slightly larger home ranges than females.

Economic Importance and Remarks: The eastern harvest mouse, as a result of its seed-harvesting habits, aids in the dispersal of certain grasses and herbs. In Florida, it has little or no economic significance.

Although harvest mice and cotton rats occupy the same type of habitat, they seldom coexist. When cotton rats are abundant in a field, harvest mice are absent, and vice versa. This strongly suggests there is some degree of mutual exclusion (possibly behavioral) in the two species.

Marsh Rice Rat *(Oryzomys palustris)*

Description: This is a small rat-sized rodent having a slender, scantily haired tail that is about equal to the length of the head and body combined. The upper parts are buffy brown slightly sprinkled with black. The color is darkest down the middle of the back with more brown on the sides. The underparts are grayish white and the feet are white. The tail is bicolored, brownish above and grayish white below. The body fur is coarse and moderately long. The leaf-like ears are medium sized, rounded, and extend beyond the body fur.

The skull is identified by a prominent ridge (supraorbital

FLORIDA DNR

marsh rice rat, 6.5-9.8 in. (165-250 mm) overall, tail 3.5-5.7 in. (90-130 mm)

rice rat nest in marsh

ridge) running anteriorly just above the eye socket on each side. The grinding surfaces of the cheek teeth have small rounded cusps covered with enamel.

Geographical Range: The marsh rice rat has a statewide range, including the Florida Keys. In the United States, the marsh rice rat occurs in the southeastern quadrant of the country, from New Jersey southwestward to eastern Kansas, Oklahoma, and Texas.

Habitat Preference: This species is most abundant in freshwater marshes, saltwater marshes, and wet grassy meadows. It is sometimes also found along wet ditches and the open edges of lakes and streams. It seldom occurs in dry fields or woodlands. The marsh rice rat is a good swimmer and very much at home in the water.

Life History and Reproduction: Rice rats are active to some extent during the day, but most active at night. They eat the seeds of grasses and sedges, tender green plants, as well as berries, fruits, fungi, snails, insects, crustaceans, and bird eggs. Like cotton rats, they make an extensive runway system where the vegetation is thick enough. The nests are grapefruit-sized globular masses made of woven dried grasses. They are built in a shallow burrow on land or suspended in thick vegetation over water. Feeding platforms of matted vegetation are sometimes constructed in marshy environs.

In Florida, the breeding season is year-round. Females are prolific and can produce as many as 6-8 litters per year. The gestation period is 25 days, and females normally become pregnant again the day they give birth. When born, the babies are covered with a sparse coat of hair, but the eyes do not open until the sixth day. The litter size is 2-7 and averages four, but it varies somewhat with the population density, food supply, and weather. Smaller litter sizes and fewer litters are produced when the population density is high, food is scarce, or the weather is severe. Young rice rats become sexually active when about six weeks old and reach adult body size at eight weeks of age. They rarely live more than a year in the wild, but marsh rice rats have survived up to five years in captivity.

Rice rats, like the cotton rat, are an important food staple for many of Florida's predators, including hawks, owls, water snakes, minks, foxes, weasels, raccoons, skunks, and bobcats.

Economic Importance and Remarks: The marsh rice rat can cause serious economic losses to agricultural operations in wetland habitats. The worst damage occurs to rice and sugarcane fields. Population densities as high as seven rats per acre have been reported in Louisiana. The best management practice is to eliminate rice rat cover near the fields. This is usually accomplished by mowing, plowing, burning, or using herbicides.

Two races of the marsh rice rat are on some rare and endangered species lists. One of these is the Sanibel Island rice rat, threatened by development and limited habitat available on Sanibel Island. The other is the Key rice rat which is restricted to the lower Florida Keys. The latter form appears to prefer mangroves, buttonwoods, and brackish salt marshes. The Key (or silver) rice rat was originally described as a separate species *(Oryzomys argentatus)*, but some authorities consider it to be an insular form of the marsh rice rat. Due to its isolated geographical distribution and morphological differences, it should at least be recognized as a subspecies of the marsh rice rat if not a unique species in its own right.

Florida Mouse *(Peromyscus floridanus)*

Description: All members of the genus *Peromyscus* are called deer mice because they are tan or fawn on the back, like a deer. They are also called white-footed mice. This is Florida's largest deer mouse, and is sometimes called the gopher mouse because of its association with gopher tortoise burrows. The upper parts are buffy cinnamon or buffy brown mixed with dusky hairs. There is a bright orange-cinnamon wash down each side at the junction with the all-white underparts. The feet are white and the leaf-like ears are large, rounded, and dusky grey. The tail is 3 to 3½ inches long, dusky brown above, and grayish white below, but not sharply bicolored.

The skull is difficult to separate form the cotton mouse and golden mouse, so specimens should be examined by an expert for identification.

Geographical Range: Except for an apparently isolated population along the Gulf Coast in Franklin County, the Florida mouse is confined to peninsular Florida from St. Johns, Clay, Suwannee, and Taylor counties southward to Dade, Highlands, and Sarasota counties. Populations are often isolated and spotty. See map on page 204. The Dade County populations and most of the Pinellas County populations have been exterminated in recent decades by development. This mouse occurs nowhere else in the United States, and is the only mammal species entirely restricted to Florida.

Florida mouse, 7.3-8.2 in. (185-208 mm) overall, tail 3.1-3.7 in. (80-95 mm)

Habitat Preference: Florida mice occur on high, well-drained, sandy ridges covered by pine-turkey oak or sand pine scrub vegetation. Many of these sites exemplify old beach dunes formed along the edges of the Florida peninsula when sea levels were higher and farther inland.

Life History and Reproduction: The burrow of the Florida mouse is often situated within the large tunnels dug by Florida gopher tortoises. The mouse merely digs a short tunnel and nest chamber at right angles to the large gopher tortoise burrow. Since armadillos are also widely established in many Florida habitats, Florida mice also use their numerous burrows for nesting sites. The nest is usually a simple concave platform composed of leaves and grasses. Florida mice usually have several burrows in an area and rotate their use frequently except when the female has young; then only one nest site is used.

Florida mice are active at night and semifossorial, doing much foraging in the underground tunnel systems of the gopher tortoise. They also forage on the surface when certain seeds are available. Favorite foods include acorns, pine seeds, palmetto berries, mushrooms, insects, and various other arthropods found in the burrow systems.

Florida mice start breeding in August and continue through the fall and early winter. The gestation period is about 23-24 days and the average litter size is 3-4 (range 1-6). Females sometimes produce two litters per year.

Economic Importance and Remarks: The Florida mouse is an interesting rodent, but has little or no economic impact. As a seed eater, it aids in the dispersal of several plants that grow in dry, sandy plant communities.

The habitats of the Florida mouse are rapidly disappearing because of their prime value for citrus and commercial developments of all types. So much sand pine scrub and pine-turkey oak habitat has been lost that the Florida mouse is listed as a "species of special concern" by the Florida Game and Fresh Water Fish Commission. Unless these plant communities can be protected, this mouse

88   Gnawing Mammals

may become very rare and may only be found in a few protected parks and preserves. It has already been eliminated from most of the east coast ridge in Dade, Broward, and Palm Beach counties, and from nearly all of the sand pine scrubs in Pinellas, Manatee, and Sarasota counties, due to urban development.

Known predators of the Florida mouse include rattlesnakes (with whom they share burrow systems), pine snakes, rat snakes, indigo snakes, raccoons, foxes, bobcats, hawks, owls, skunks, and weasels.

The life span of Florida mice in the field seldom exceeds two years. In captivity, however, there is an incidence of one living to an age of just under 7½ years.

A few taxonomists have placed this species in the genus *Podomys* rather than *Peromyscus,* but the characteristics cited are both weak and superficial. Therefore, the long-used genus name, *Peromyscus,* will be retained here.

Beach or Oldfield Mouse *(Peromyscus polionotus)*

Description: The beach mouse or oldfield mouse is Florida's smallest deer mouse. The upper pelage of this species is extremely variable and ranges from white with a narrow buffy stripe to cinnamon or a dull buffy gray. The underparts and feet are white, and the tail is rather short, ranging from 1½ to 2½ inches long. The leaf-like ears are medium sized and rounded. In general, the pelage of oldfield mice living on light-colored sandy soils is light in color, whereas mice from areas of dark soils are much darker.

The skull is somewhat smaller than those of other deer mice, but positive identification requires an expert.

Geographical Range: This species can be found throughout most of Florida except the southwestern portion of the peninsula and the Keys. See map

FLORIDA DNR

oldfield mouse (white beach form), 4.7-5.3 in. (120-135 mm) overall,
tail 1.2-2.0 in. (40-52 mm)

on page 204. The range in the United States is confined to the southeastern states, southward from South Carolina and northeastern Mississippi.

Habitat Preference: As the two common names for this species suggest, these mice prefer sparse sandy beach vegetation and the early weedy-grass stages of oldfield succession. They do not thrive in dense vegetative ground cover, but are ideally suited for disturbed open areas having much bare soil.

Life History and Reproduction: The beach mouse always constructs a very stylized and predictable burrow. It consists of three parts: a downward sloping entrance tunnel that is loosely plugged during the daytime with soil approximately six inches back from the entrance; a spherical nest chamber 6-8 inches in diameter, at a depth of 2-3 feet below the surface; and an escape tunnel that rises steeply from the back side of the nest chamber to within about an inch of the surface. I have excavated hundreds of burrows to collect beach mice, and every burrow system exhibited all three components. Beach mice always enter the escape tunnel when danger threatens, and often they will pop through to the surface and run if pressed. The nest is a cup-shaped pad of dried grasses, plant fibers, and sometimes shredded paper or rags, if available.

It is common to find a paired male and female or a female and her young in a burrow. Beach mice are social, sometimes forming fairly large groups in a single nest during the colder months. This species feeds mainly on the seeds of grasses and herbs such as bluestem, sea oats, dropseed, buttonweed, sheep sorrel, lespedeza, and others. They are active above ground only at night.

Breeding occurs during all months of the year, but is at its peak in the late summer and fall (August-November). The average litter size is three young (range 1-6) in Florida. The gestation period is 21 days. The babies are naked and blind at birth, but they grow rapidly and wean in three weeks. In the laboratory, first breeding can occur when young beach mice are about 30 days old.

Economic Importance and Remarks: The beach mouse has little or no economic impact on agriculture because it lives in fallow fields and abandoned farmland. They sometimes eat grain in mature cornfields that have not been harvested.

This mouse is preyed upon by owls, skunks, foxes, raccoons, weasels, snakes, cats, and many other small carnivores. In disturbed, sparsely vegetated areas, they are often the commonest rodent present and a staple food for small predators.

Four races or subspecies living in beach habitats are currently listed as endangered and one is listed as extinct by the Florida Game and Fresh Water Fish Commission and the U.S. Fish and Wildlife Service. Three of these are the Choctawhatchee beach mouse, St. Andrews beach mouse, and the Perdido Bay beach mouse, which live on the rapidly developing barrier islands of the western Florida Panhandle. The other one is the Anastasia Island beach mouse found on the Atlantic coastal dunes of Flagler and Volusia counties. The pallid beach mouse, formerly found in St. Johns county, has been declared extinct; during the past thirty years, mammalogists have been unsuccessful in trapping it in areas where it was formerly taken. Another lower Florida east coast race, the

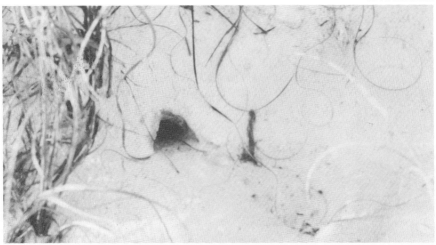

beach mouse burrow in sand

southeastern beach mouse was also recently added to the threatened species list by both the U.S. Fish and Wildlife Service and the Florida Game and Fresh Water Fish Commission. The coastal forms of the oldfield mouse are not faring well in the path of development on barrier beaches and islands.

Cotton Mouse *(Peromyscus gossypinus)*

Description: The cotton mouse is a fairly large deer mouse, but slightly smaller than the Florida mouse. The upper parts can vary from chestnut brown to dark brown or grayish brown. The middle of the back is darker than the sides. The underparts are white and, unlike the Florida mouse, there is no orange wash down the sides where the white meets the dark upper pelage. The tail is equal to or slightly longer than the head and body combined. It is also sparsely haired and distinctly bicolored (upper side dusky brown and underside white). The leaf-like ears are large, rounded, and dusky gray.

The skull is very similar to other deer mice and should be examined by an expert for positive identification.

Geographical Range: Cotton mice occur in every woodland habitat found in Florida, but they are probably most abundant in mature hardwood forests of various types. They are rare or absent only in open grassy treeless situations.

Life History and Reproduction: Cotton mice are probably the most numerous mammals found in Florida. Their closest rival for that distinction might be the cotton rat, which lives in open grassy areas instead of forests. Cotton mice are active at night and often nest in logs, hollow stumps, holes in the ground, and even old cabins. They also climb trees readily and build a spherical nest of leaves and plant fibers in hollow cavities.

cotton mouse, 6.7-7.8 in. (170-198 mm) overall, tail 2.7-3.5 in. (70-90 mm)

Cotton mice eat all kinds of acorns, nuts, and seeds of trees, as well as animals including snails, slugs, spiders, insects, and various other arthropods. They also take several types of mushrooms and other fungi.

In Florida, the cotton mouse breeds throughout the year except possibly early summer (May and June). The peak breeding time is August through December. The gestation period is 23 days and the average litter size in Florida is four young (range 2-7). Females can produce 4-5 litters per year, and often they become pregnant again right after the birth of a litter. The newborn are pink, naked, and blind, but they grow rapidly and are weaned when 20-25 days old. The juvenile pelage is dusky gray dorsally, and the young do not turn brown until the post-juvenile molt. Breeding can occur at 10 weeks of age.

The longevity of cotton mice in the wild is short, seldom exceeding 1½ years. In captivity, however, they have lived as long as 5-6 years. Cotton mice are eaten by every medium- and small-sized predator of the Florida woodlands, including snakes, owls, hawks, foxes, cats, dogs, raccoons, bobcats, skunks, and weasels. In spite of predation, a high reproductive rate ensures that the cotton mouse maintains high population levels. One study in Florida reported that 2-5 cotton mice per acre occurred in suitable forested habitat.

Economic Importance and Remarks: Cotton mice are an important link in the food chain for many carnivores, and they also aid in the dispersal of many tree seeds. They also occasionally forage on the seeds of rowcrops, such as corn, cotton, and soybeans planted adjacent to wooded cover. They sometimes invade corn cribs and granaries to consume stored grain, and they will commonly enter cabins and homes that are located in wooded areas. Snap traps are usually effective for control of cotton mice in buildings and grain storage areas.

Gnawing Mammals

Two races of the cotton mouse in Florida can be considered threatened or endangered because of development and limited ranges. These are: the Key Largo cotton mouse, found only on Key Largo and Lignum Vitae Key (introduced there in 1970) in Monroe County; and the Anastasia Island cotton mouse, which occurs only on Anastasia Island in Florida and Cumberland Island in Georgia. The Chadwick Beach cotton mouse is now considered extinct in Florida, and all beach forms may eventually disappear if sufficient acreages of their natural habitats are not preserved and protected from development.

Golden Mouse *(Ochrotomys nuttalli)*

Description: This medium-sized mouse has a strikingly beautiful coat that is golden cinnamon or burnt orange in color. The belly and feet are white, usually tinged with some cinnamon or gold. The tail is slightly shorter than the body and head combined, scantily furred, and not bicolored. The leaf-like ears are medium large, rounded, and the same color as the body.

The skull looks much like those of the closely related deer mice (Florida mouse, oldfield mouse, and cotton mouse), and should be examined by an expert for positive identification.

Geographical Range: The golden mouse is common throughout the northern two-thirds of Florida. See map on page 204. The southernmost record of the species is west of Lake Okeechobee in Glades County. The range of the golden mouse in the United States occupies the southeastern quadrant, extending from Virginia west to eastern Oklahoma and eastern Texas.

FLORIDA DNR

golden mouse, 5.5-7.3 in. (140-185 mm) overall, tail 2.6-3.5 in. (67-90 mm)

Habitat Preference: This mouse prefers dense woodland with heavy vines, brush, or palmettos in the understory, usually in moist situations. The golden mouse is an arboreal species, nesting and foraging above the ground in thick vegetation, vines, or clumps of Spanish moss.

Life History and Reproduction: Golden mice build a spherical, domed nest 5-8 inches in diameter with a single small entry hole on one side. Each mouse usually builds several nests within its home range. The nests are composed of a finely woven mass of shredded cabbage palm or palmetto fibers, sometimes combined with inner tree bark or leaves. The nest is a neat, compact, woven ball, and is placed inside a clump of Spanish moss, in a tangle of

hanging nest of golden mouse in Spanish moss

greenbrier, or on top of a palmetto frond. The nest may be built from a few inches above ground to over 15 feet in the air. These mice are known to forage even higher, into the treetops. They also construct flat feeding platforms, well above the ground, scattered throughout the home range. Golden mice sleep during the day and forage at night. The diet consists of seeds, berries, fruits, buds, leaves, and some insects. Preferred seeds include those of dogwood, oak, magnolia, wild cherry, and palmettos.

The breeding season in Florida extends throughout the year, but peaks in the spring and fall. The gestation period is 25-30 days, and the litter size averages 2-3 young (range 1-4). Litters born in fall are larger than spring ones, and several litters may be produced each year. Newborn babies are pink, blind, and helpless. The first hair appears on the fifth day, and the eyes open on the thirteenth day. Weaning occurs at 3-4 weeks of age. Females frequently come into estrus immediately after birth of a litter and are impregnated again. Adult females can produce as many as 5-6 litters per year in Florida. Young golden mice become sexually active when about two months of age.

Economic Importance and Remarks: This beautiful mouse has little or no economic impact. It is valuable as a disperser of tree seeds and as a consumer of certain harmful forest insects.

Golden mice can readily be captured by hand from their globular nests.

Interestingly, nests are invariably made of reddish-brown plant fibers that closely match the color of the golden mouse. This is a rather docile rodent and does not bite when handled. They are excellent climbers and are able to cling tenaciously to vertical objects. They make attractive and interesting pets.

In the wild, longevity rarely exceeds 2½ years, but in captivity I have had several that lived more than five years. The longest life span ever recorded for a golden mouse in captivity was just under 8½ years, the record longevity for any small rodent in North America.

Pine Vole *(Microtus pinetorum)*

Description: Also known as the woodland vole, this small blocky vole has a short tail (only slightly longer than the hind foot), and a chestnut-brown upper coat. The underparts are grayish, washed with buff and chestnut. The flanks are paler than the back and the tail is not sharply bicolored. The leaf-like ears are small, rounded, and nearly concealed in the fur. The eyes are small and beady. The Florida form of the pine vole is only about half the size of northern races of this vole and it may be a separate species.

The grinding surfaces of the upper cheek teeth have a pattern of angular enamel folds, surrounding dentine, that are triangular and prism shaped. The second upper molar has four islands of dentine surrounded by enamel, compared to the meadow vole which has five.

Geographical Range: The pine vole is known only from the northern third of Florida, having been recorded as far south as Lynne in Marion County. See map on page 204. The range of the pine vole in the United States occupies roughly the eastern half of the country.

Habitat Preference: This species was first taken in the pinelands of Georgia and given the name pine vole for that reason. This is something of a misnomer, because this vole prefers to live in the heavy leaves, humus, and soil of hardwood forests. They also live in fruit orchards and in fallow fields along the edge of a hardwood stand, but only occasionally in pinelands. Pine voles are fossorial, spending most of their time in extensive underground tunnel systems, which they excavate just beneath the surface of the ground. They often take over the old tunnels of moles as well. Their burrow systems normally have multiple entrances that are left open and not plugged.

Life History and Reproduction: Pine voles forage both day and night in their underground burrow systems. They mainly eat tubers, roots, bulbs, sprouts, tender bark, and occasionally insects encountered underground. Food is cached in subterranean storage chambers as a hedge against periods of scarcity. The home range size of a pine vole is small, only 1/3 to 1/2 acre. A globular nest (4-6 inches in diameter) of dead leaves and shredded grasses is constructed just beneath the ground surface, often at the base of a tree stump, or under a rotting log. There are usually 3-4 nest openings that lead to various interconnecting tunnels. Pine voles are surprisingly social; small groups of adults or several females with litters have been recorded in a single nest.

Gnawing Mammals

pine vole, 3.8-4.3 in. (98-110 mm) overall, tail 1.0-1.3 in. (25-32 mm)

The breeding season occurs year-round in Florida, but activity is somewhat reduced during the hot summer months. The gestation period averages 21 days (range 20-24), and the average litter size is three young (range 1-8). Each adult female can produce 5-6 litters per year, and she often comes into estrus and is impregnated again on the day a litter is born. The offspring are blind, naked, helpless, and pink at birth. When they are 5-6 days old, hair appears, and the eyes open around the tenth day. Young voles are weaned when about 20 days of age, just before the birth of another litter. They breed for the first time at 2½ to 3 months of age.

In the wild, few pine voles survive beyond two years of age and most die much sooner. Owls, hawks, snakes, weasels, opossums, skunks, foxes, cats, dogs, raccoons, and bobcats all eat pine voles, but their largely underground lifestyle limits predation. Most voles are probably taken at the burrow entrances or on short excursions above ground to feed on green vegetation.

Economic Importance and Remarks: Pine voles often cause damage to the root systems of trees and shrubs, including peaches, apples, and blueberries. Tunneling severs small roots, and foraging results in girdling of larger roots. They also can damage row crops and gardens located near wooded areas (such as corn, soybeans, sweet potatoes, Irish potatoes, and peanuts). On the plus side, tunneling by voles aerates the soil and mixes organic matter to depths where plant roots can benefit.

Pine voles are best captured by placing snap traps set at right angles across their underground burrows. The tunnels, usually less than one inch below the surface, can be easily exposed by probing with the fingers. I have trapped many

Gnawing Mammals

pine voles using this method in fallow agricultural fields located near forests throughout much of northern Florida.

Meadow Vole *(Microtus pennsylvanicus)*

Description: In Florida, a recently discovered relict population of this vole has been called the saltmarsh vole because of its habitat affiliation. However, other races of the meadow vole also inhabit salt marshes along the east coast of the United States, so the use of that common name may be misleading. The meadow vole is a medium-sized vole, having a dark brown upper coat, and a tail that is about twice the length of the hind foot. The underparts are silvery gray and the leaf-like ears are small, rounded, and partly hidden in the fur.

Meadow vole skulls are identified by the number of angular enamel loops surrounding dentine islands in the grinding surfaces of the cheek teeth. The meadow vole has five (or rarely six) dentine islands on the second upper molar, instead of four as in the pine vole.

Geographical Range: The meadow vole in Florida is recorded only from the general area of Waccasassa Bay, just northeast of Cedar Key in Levy County. See map on page 205. However, suitable habitat extends along the west coast of Florida almost continuously from Taylor County southward to Citrus County, so other undiscovered populations of the saltmarsh form of the meadow vole undoubtedly will be found. In the United States, the meadow vole ranges over most of the northern two-thirds of the country. In the East, the range extends as far south as South Carolina and northcentral Georgia, plus the relict population present on the west coast of Florida. There are similar isolated relict populations of the meadow vole found in New Mexico and northern Mexico.

J. F. PARNELL

meadow vole, 5.7-7.7 in. (145-196 mm) overall, tail 1.3-2.2 in. (32-56 mm)

Habitat Preference: In Florida, the meadow vole is known to occur only in tidal salt marshes. They have been trapped most frequently in strands of seashore saltgrass. Other dominant plants in the marshes include cord grass, black rush, glasswort, and saltwort. Elsewhere in its range, the meadow vole occurs in many types of wet meadows and marshlands.

Life History and Reproduction: Almost nothing is known about the life history of the Florida population of the meadow vole. It was discovered quite by accident in 1979 when a vole skull was found among skeletal remains discarded by marsh hawks in the salt marshes along State Highway 24 in Levy County, Florida. Trapping throughout the salt marshes revealed that meadow voles live in a zone subject to daily tidal flooding. It is somewhat of a mystery how the voles survive in such a harsh environment, but apparently they swim very well and hide in the thick vegetation mats during high tides. Very few meadow voles have been taken in thousands of nights of trapping, so they apparently either occur in low numbers or are reluctant to enter standard live traps. Two species of rats that also occur in salt marshes are the marsh rice rat and hispid cotton rat. It is possible these two prolific species help suppress meadow vole numbers by their abundance and aggressiveness.

The meadow vole is highly herbivorous in the northern states, with vegetable matter comprising more than 90% of its diet. In Florida salt marshes, researchers have evidence that meadow voles might eat more animal food (invertebrates particularly) than their northern cousins. Nests are presumably globular affairs built in the marsh vegetation.

The breeding cycle is completely unknown in Florida, but the species has higher fecundity than most mammals in other areas. In New York, the gestation period of the meadow vole is 21 days and the average litter size is five (range 2-11). The average litter size is probably lower than this in Florida, based on evidence from other species of mice having large north-south geographical ranges. A sequence of post-partum pregnancies is the norm, a new litter born every 21 days. Young meadow voles mature rapidly, weaning at 12-14 days of age and breeding when 1 to 1½ months old. Very few meadow voles survive beyond one year of age in the field; in the laboratory, they have lived as long as five years.

Economic Importance and Remarks: The meadow vole, because of its habitat restrictions in Florida, has no economic importance. It is listed as a "endangered" by the U.S. Fish and Wildlife Service and the Florida Game and Fresh Water Fish Commission because of its apparent rarity and small range. A much more intensive study of its natural history is required before its real status can be correctly determined.

In some northern areas, meadow voles show cyclic population fluctuations, reaching peak numbers every 3-4 years. They then die off to very low numbers in a short time, and over the next 2-3 years, gradually increase to high population densities again. It is not known whether this cycle also occurs in the Florida meadow vole.

Gnawing Mammals

In addition to marsh hawks, Florida meadow voles are almost certainly preyed upon by owls, snakes, alligators, raccoons, bobcats, minks, and various carnivorous fishes.

Round-tailed Muskrat *(Neofiber alleni)*

Description: This aquatic vole is also called the Florida muskrat or Florida water rat. The body size is less than half that of the common muskrat (found north of Florida) and the sparsely-haired tail is round rather than laterally compressed. The upper fur is shiny blackish brown or deep chocolate brown, and the underside is grayish white with a buffy wash. The leaf-like ears are small, rounded, and hidden in the fur. The tail is blackish brown and covered with bristle-like hairs.

The skull is very large compared to those of meadow voles and pine voles. The first lower molar has five dentine triangles (rather than six in the common muskrat) on the grinding surface, surrounded by enamel loops. The postorbital processes are prominent and extend forward into the orbital area.

Geographical Range: The round-tailed muskrat occurs throughout the peninsula and eastern half of the panhandle in Florida. See map on page 205. An isolated population has also been reported on the northeast shore of Choctawhatchee Bay in Walton County. It is absent in the Florida Keys. The range of this species is limited to Florida and southeastern Georgia.

Habitat Preference: The round-tailed muskrat occurs widely in grassy freshwater marshes and certain brackish coastal marshes. In freshwater situations they show a particular affinity for stands of maidencane, an emergent aquatic grass. They are most abundant in areas of the marsh that are choked with vegetation.

Life History and Reproduction: This muskrat constructs a small dome-shaped nest of grasses and stems of water plants, slightly above the water level. The nest is anchored to emergent vegetation such as maidencane, willows, small cypress trees, buttonbush, or cattails, and is 10-24 inches in diameter and 10-15 inches high. All nests have two escape or "plunge" holes leading downward into the water from the bottom of the nest. The muskrats can enter or leave the nest quickly via these paired entrances that are about 3 inches in diameter. Round-tailed muskrats build and maintain more than one house, usually two (range 1-4) per animal.

Two versions of muskrat houses are built, one for protection and care of the young, and another for ordinary daily use by one individual. The non-breeding nest has thinner walls (2-3 inches thick) and is smaller. Before the birth of a litter, females enlarge the nest, reinforce the walls (up to a thickness of 6 inches), and line the inner nest chamber, which is about 4 inches in diameter, with dry fine-textured grasses.

round-tailed muskrat, 11-14.9 in. (28-38 cm) overall, tail 4.3-6.7 in. (11-17 cm)

Breeding occurs throughout the year if food is abundant and water conditions are favorable. Peaks in the number of pregnant females occur in April, August, and November in northcentral Florida. The gestation period is 26-29 days and the average litter size is 2-3 young (range 1-4). The babies are naked, helpless, blind, and pink at birth. They become fully furred by one week of age, and the eyes open at about two weeks. Young muskrats attach tightly to the mother's teats and are often carried with her into the water when she is frightened from the nest. The ability of the young muskrats to hold their breath while being dragged through the water is phenomenal. Weaning takes place at about one month of age. Each adult female may produce 4-5 litters per year. Young animals attain sexual maturity when 90-100 days old.

Round-tailed muskrats are primarily herbivores, eating the stems, roots, leaves, and seeds of aquatic vegetation, particularly maidencane, arrowhead, rice cutgrass, water shield, green arum, caladium, and lemon bacopa. They also may eat an occasional crayfish or insect. Feeding platforms are routinely constructed of matted vegetation throughout the marsh. Plant cuttings and fresh droppings are readily visible on active feeding platforms.

When the marsh dries up, round-tailed muskrats live underground and make runways through the marsh vegetation much like other voles. They presumably suffer much greater mortality and stress during such periods of drought. The list of predators that take muskrats includes marsh hawks, barn owls, barred owls, great horned owls, bobcats, raccoons, minks, foxes, cottonmouth water moccasins, rat snakes, indigo snakes, and alligators.

Gnawing Mammals

Economic Importance and Remarks: This aquatic vole periodically causes damage to sugarcane and rice farming interests in southern Florida. They also sometimes compete to a minor degree with cattle for herbaceous forage in some wet prairie habitats. The best agricultural practices involve habitat manipulation and elimination of cover for water rats in croplands. They also can be controlled by trapping or poisoning, but the latter is very dangerous to other resident animals.

It is possible that the round-tailed muskrat has a regular population cycle every 3-4 years like the common muskrat. They are sometimes abundant in a given habitat, but later become uncommon. Long-term field research is needed to explore this possibility.

The potential longevity is not known for this species, but in the wild they probably seldom live more than two years. They have not been maintained in captivity for long periods.

The houses built by round-tailed muskrats are also used by a variety of other marsh residents including marsh rice rats, cotton rats, snakes, lizards, frogs, wrens, rails, bitterns, ants, spiders, and other arthropods.

House Mouse *(Mus musculus)*

Description: The house mouse is small with a long scaly tail that is only slightly shorter than the head and body combined. The upper pelage is grayish brown or olive brown and the underparts are ashy gray, buffy gray, or whitish. The leaf-like ears are large and naked. The nose is rather pointed; the eyes are small.

The skull is identified by small size and by the presence of a notch in the cutting surface of the upper incisors, readily visible from the side. There is no lengthwise groove on the front border of the upper incisors as in the eastern harvest mouse.

J. F. PARNELL

house mouse, 5.8-7.9 in. (148-200 mm) overall, tail 2.7-3.3 in. (69-85 mm)

Geographical Range: The house mouse is an introduced species that is found in all areas of the state of Florida. It occurs throughout the United States, as well as the rest of North America, Central America, and South America. In early historic times it was restricted to Europe and Asia.

Habitat Preference: This is a cosmopolitan species that occurs in most habitats in association with humans. In addition to dwellings, house mice live in granaries, warehouses, factories, restaurants, office buildings, supermarkets, farm buildings, garbage dumps, etc. House mice also can live in natural habitats such as abandoned fields, fence rows, grain fields, beach dunes, weedy roadsides, and pastures.

Life History and Reproduction: House mice are social and form colonies both in buildings and in the wild. They consume almost anything edible, but prefer grain and vegetable products. They also eat a wide variety of animal foods, when available.

House mice are extremely prolific and breed year-round. The gestation period is only 19-21 days and the litter size varies from 2-12, averaging around six. There is a post-birth estrus in adult females, and they can produce 14 litters per year, but 4-10 is normal. If all the young survived and bred, we would, of course, be hip-deep in house mice in a few months. Fortunately, most do not reach maturity. At birth, the babies are pink, blind, naked, and helpless. They are fully furred when 10 days old, and their eyes open at about 14 days of age. House mice wean at 20 days of age and can become sexually mature as early as 4-6 weeks old.

Economic Importance and Remarks: House mice are obnoxious and destructive pests in homes, where they gnaw holes in walls and woodwork, consume and contaminate food, and chew up clothing and books for nest material. On farms and in agricultural feed stores, they are particularly destructive to stored grain, seeds, fruits, and vegetables. Control is achieved either by trapping or poisoned baits. The latter is always a potential danger to children, pets, livestock, and predators.

The highly inbred albino form of the house mouse is the world's basic laboratory animal for most medical and scientific research. White mice and other color phases of house mice are commonly sold as pets or as food for pet snakes, lizards, hawks, and owls. House mice have strong scent glands located near the anus. If their cages and nest materials are not kept clean, they develop a characteristic pungent odor from the scent glands and from accumulated droppings and urine.

Longevity of house mice in feral populations is rarely more than one year, but in the laboratory they may live four years or slightly longer. In the wild, house mice are preyed upon by every kind of avian, reptilian, and mammalian carnivore that consumes rodents.

Black Rat, Roof Rat *(Rattus rattus)*

Description: Contrary to its common name, this introduced rat is usually not black, but grayish brown on the upper side. It also has a long, bare, scaly tail that is longer than the head and body combined. The underparts are variable in color, but are usually slate gray, creamy, or white. There is also an all-black color phase of this species (fairly rare in Florida) that is the source of the common name. The leaf-like ears are large and rounded; the nose is long and pointed.

The skull is difficult to distinguish from the Norway rat and eastern woodrat, and should be examined by an expert for positive identification.

Geographical Range: The black or roof rat has become established throughout the state of Florida since it was brought here accidentally on the ships of early European explorers and settlers. In the United States, this species thrives primarily in coastal areas and throughout the southern states; however, it can turn up almost anywhere in association with man.

Habitat Preference: The roof rat is widely associated with buildings, garbage dumps, granaries, warehouses, wharves, factories, etc. They are agile climbers, quite at home in roofs, attics, and rafters of most houses and buildings. The common name, roof rat, originated from their tendency to nest in the attics of buildings. Despite its common association with humans, a large segment of the Florida black rat population lives in feral conditions, completely separate from man. These black rats build arboreal leaf nests in all types of dense forest habitats, including floodplain forests, oak hammocks, tropical hardwood hammocks, mangrove swamps, oak scrub, and thick coastal strand vegetation. They are agile climbers and forage throughout the canopy as well as on the ground. This species is also the "orange grove rat" commonly found foraging on ripe or fallen fruit in our citrus groves.

Life History and Reproduction: Roof rats, with their longer tails and smaller body size, are much better climbers than Norway rats. Sometimes both species will coexist in the same building. The bigger, more aggressive Norway rats will live on the ground floor and the slim, agile black rats occupy the rafters, attics, and upper floors. The species are behaviorally incompatible, and they never interbreed.

Black rats will eat virtually anything that is consumable. They prefer vegetative food, but consume a wide range of animal matter as well. In poultry houses, they have been known to eat eggs and kill chicks.

Black rats are quite prolific and breed year-round. The gestation period is 21 days and the average litter size is six young (range 2-12). Baby rats are pink, blind, naked, and helpless. They grow rapidly, the eyes open when about 14 days old, and they are weaned at three weeks. Adult females have a post-birth estrus and immediately become pregnant again. Young rats become sexually active when 3-4 months old. Females can produce as many as 14 litters per year, but most average 6-8 litters, depending on the food supply.

Economic Importance and Remarks: Black rats are destructive to most of man's agricultural activities and cause much damage to homes and businesses. Their habit of gnawing off the insulation around electrical wiring in attics and walls of older buildings produces a fire hazard. Black rats also carry fleas that can spread diseases such as typhus, bubonic plague, spotted fever, leptospirosis, and rat-bite fever.

black rat, 12.6-16.9 in. (32-43 cm) overall, tail 6.3-10.2 in. (16-26 cm)

The best way to control rats is to exclude them from the premises with good barriers, and eliminate or protect all potential food sources. If that is not successful, trapping and the use of poison baits are the main recourses. Poisons, however, carry a risk to children, pets, and livestock. Also, dying rats often crawl into some inaccessible location to die, and the decomposition of their bodies can create strong odors.

Norway Rat *(Rattus norvegicus)*

Description: The Norway rat or wharf rat is an introduced species. It has a large robust body and a long, bare, scaly tail, the length of which is slightly shorter than the head and body combined. The upper side is grizzled grayish brown, and the underparts vary from pale gray to grayish brown. The leaf-like ears are large and rounded; the nose is quite long and pointed.

Norway rat skulls are difficult to distinguish from those of the black rat and eastern woodrat, and should be examined by an expert for positive identification.

Geographical Range: The Norway rat has been recorded throughout Florida, especially in port cities and urban slums. It was first introduced to the United States from Europe in the late 1700s and there are records from every state in the Union.

Habitat Preference: In Florida, the Norway rat is not as widespread or abundant as its smaller cousin, the black rat. Most populations are found in the inner city slums, near shipping wharves, warehouses, grain elevators, and other urban facilities. Farm populations of the Norway rat are much less common in Florida than in northern states.

Life History and Reproduction: Norway rats are sedentary animals that remain near a food source and rarely have home ranges greater than 200 feet in diameter. However, they will disperse to a new location if food or cover is not available.

Norway rats dig tunnels in the ground where conditions are suitable. The burrow systems usually have several entrances and a labyrinth of interconnecting tunnels, and contain one or more nest chambers. They commonly live in colonies of 10-20 individuals. A dominance hierarchy is maintained within the

(ASM)—E. J. TAYLOR

Norway rat, 12.6-18.9 in. (32-48 cm) overall, tail 5.9-8.7 in. (15-22 cm)

L. N. BROWN

nutria, 32.6-39.8 in. (83-101 cm) overall, tail 11.8-13.4 in. (30-34 cm)

Gnawing Mammals

colony, with the largest, most aggressive male at the top of the peck order.

Norway rats are among the most omnivorous of all mammals, feeding on any vegetable or animal food source. They eat all types of plant matter including vegetables, grain, roots, tubers, fruit, berries, and garbage. Animal foods include baby chickens, eggs, fish, cheese, milk, meat, carrion, leather, baby rabbits, ducklings, lizards, insects, snakes, and others.

Norway rats breed year-round in Florida. The gestation period is 22 days, but a slightly longer duration may occur when the female is nursing one litter while pregnant with the next. The litter size averages nine young and ranges from 2-16. Baby rats are pink, blind, naked, and helpless at birth. The eyes open at 14 days and the young are weaned around 21 days of age, before the birth of the next offspring. An adult female could potentially produce 14 litters per year, but most average 6-8. Norway rats can breed as young as three months of age, and the species probably has the highest fecundity of any mammal on earth. If all their offspring survived, the entire world would be covered with Norway rats in just a few years. Fortunately, most do not survive to breed.

Economic Importance and Remarks: Norway rats, because of their large size and aggressive nature, are even more destructive to business and agricultural activities than the ubiquitous black rat. However, they are fortunately not as common in Florida as in northern locations. They do cause problems for residents of urban slums, to some ship docks and wharf storage areas, to food warehouses, and to animal feed-mixing operations. They are best controlled by excluding them from those areas having food and cover. Poison baits are also used extensively in most areas. Norway rats have been found to carry and occasionally transmit a variety of diseases, including rat-bite fever, spotted fever, scarlet fever, typhus, diphtheria, tularemia, bubonic plague, and trichinosis.

This species is the source of the "lab rat or white rat," widely used in medical and biological research. These rats are highly inbred strains of the Norway rat (most are true albinos) that have been maintained and propagated in captivity for decades. White rats are extremely docile and easy to handle compared to normal wild Norway rats, which are noticeably aggressive and high-strung. In its laboratory form, the Norway rat is extremely beneficial to mankind as an all-purpose experimental animal.

Nutria *(Myocastor coypus)*

Description: The nutria or coypu is an introduced, giant, aquatic rat that has a long, round, scaly tail and large orange-edged front teeth. It is almost as large as a beaver, and the upper parts are glossy dark amber or blackish brown. The belly is a slightly paler gray brown, and the ears are short, rounded, and almost completely buried in the fur.

The skull is very large and identified by an immense opening (infraorbital foramen) located at the anterior junction of the cheek bone (zygomatic arch) with the snout. The opening is large enough to admit the end of your little finger. In this way, it can easily be distinguished from the skull of the beaver, which lacks this large canal or foramen.

Geographical Range: The nutria has been released and become established in several locations scattered throughout the state of Florida. In the United States, there are feral populations established along the Atlantic coast and throughout the southern states as far west as Texas. There are also scattered populations in some Pacific coast and mountain states. The nutria is native to the southern third of South America.

Habitat Preference: Nutria prefer freshwater marshes, ponds, and canals. They are adaptable to many aquatic situations that have emergent, floating, or submergent vegetation. They also occasionally are found living in brackish coastal marshes.

Life History and Reproduction: Nutria feed on a wide variety of aquatic plants, including some that are introduced and choking Florida waterways, like water hyacinth, milfoil, hydrilla, and elodea. Unfortunately, most of these aquatic plants grow faster than nutria can consume them. Nutria are active both day and night, but they forage primarily during the nocturnal hours. They do not take any animal food, but are strict vegetarians. Nutria sometimes construct feeding and resting platforms composed of matted or interwoven vegetation. They live in sizeable tunnels dug into vegetated banks or levees containing crude nests made of plant cuttings. Often there are two or more entrances to each burrow system, one frequently below water level and one or more above.

Breeding occurs throughout the year in Florida. The gestation period is about 130 days and the litter size averages 6 offspring (range 1-12). Baby nutria are precocial and are born completely furred and with open eyes. Following the birth of a litter, the female usually comes into estrus and breeds again. Young nutria can swim shortly after birth, and they can nurse when in the water, because the mother's teats are located along each side. Nutria wean when 6-8 weeks old. Sexual maturity can occur before nutria reach their adult body size. This is called juvenile breeding and can occur at four months of age. However, most nutria do not breed until they are eight months old.

Alligators are the nutria's chief predator, and they take a heavy toll. Young nutria are also taken by hawks, owls, gars, snakes, foxes, and bobcats, but the adults are too large to be vulnerable to these predators.

Economic Importance and Remarks: Nutria are sometimes extolled as a valuable fur animal, but actually the pelt is not of great quality and only the belly fur is usable. Unscrupulous operators often sell breeding stock to would-be nutria farmers for high prices. When such breeding operations fail, the nutria are often released into the wild. Many introductions in new areas of the United States have resulted from failed attempts at nutria farming.

Nutria eat aquatic weeds that clog our waterways, but they never consume enough to control the vegetation. Their tunnel systems do considerable damage to dikes and levees.

A few years ago, I studied a population of nutria living on a large dairy farm in westcentral Florida. They often fed on commercial dairy feed intended for cows. The nutria were also able to thrive and breed in ponds and canals of the dairy that contained water highly polluted with fecal material from the cattle feed lots and milking areas. Nutria occasionally do damage to cultivated crops including sugarcane, rice, and soybeans. Except for trapping or shooting, few methods are effective in controlling problem nutria.

ORDER CARNIVORA
Flesh-eating Mammals

The flesh-eating mammals or carnivores are mainly specialized for killing other animals and feeding on their flesh. Their adaptations include the large conical canine teeth located near the front corners of the mouth that are excellent for penetrating and holding the prey. Many carnivores also have specialized flesh-cutting and bone-shearing teeth (the carnassials) located toward the back of the jaw. They are blade-like, functioning much like scissors, just sliding past each other, and have great shearing power. The carnassial teeth are the last upper premolar and the first lower molar. The jaw muscles are powerful and jaw movement is in the vertical plane. All male carnivores have a well developed penis bone, called the os baculum. These mammals also have keen senses of smell and sight that enhance their ability to locate and catch prey.

Carnivores have a highly developed brain, and the group exhibits a high order of intelligence. The dogs and cats are specialized to walk up on their toes (called digitigrade), while most other carnivores walk on the soles of their feet (called plantigrade). Carnivores travel with a running gait which is called cursorial locomotion. Some carnivores are not exclusive flesh eaters but consume much vegetable matter as well (bears and raccoons for example). A few live on insects (the aardwolves of Africa) and others are scavengers (the hyenas of Africa).

Carnivores have a worldwide distribution except for some oceanic islands. There are 12 species of flesh-eating mammals living in the wild in Florida.

Black Bear *(Ursus americanus)*
Description: The black bear is the largest carnivore living in Florida. It is a heavily built, bulky carnivore with long, dense, glossy, black hair above and below. The tail is very short and inconspicuous, but well haired. The face is rather blunt and broad, the eyes are small, and the nosepad is broad. The muzzle is yellowish brown and white spotting often occurs on the throat and chest. Each foot has five toes with short, heavy, downward-curved claws. In the western states and Canada there are brown, cinnamon, blue-gray, and creamy-white color phases of the black bear, but none of these are found in the Florida populations.

black bear, 50-78.8 in. (127-200 cm) overall, tail 3.9-11 in. (10-28 cm)

The skull is identified by its large size, broad profile, large pointed canines, and flat-topped molars (bunodont molars).

Geographical Range: The black bear, at least historically, occurred throughout the state of Florida. Many areas are now too developed or ecologically modified to support a bear population. Black bears are still found in the more remote areas of the state. The range in the United States extends from coast to coast, except a few of the plains states.

Habitat Preference: Bears are found in all types of heavily wooded terrain. In Florida, they are most often found in large tracts of swamp forest and undisturbed upland forest.

Life History and Reproduction: Bears make dens in a variety of situations, including large hollow logs and stumps, tree cavities, caves, under banks, and even in culverts. Black bears are good climbers and frequently make their dens in cavities well above ground level. One bear in Louisiana nested in a hollow cypress tree with the entrance hole almost 100 feet above the ground.

Most Florida black bears probably do not hibernate for extended periods, but they can be found in torpor in northern Florida during cold snaps in the winter months. Each black bear usually dens alone, but a female may be accompanied by her cubs.

Bears forage and move about primarily from dusk to dawn. Occasionally, they also are active during daylight, when a berry crop is ripe, for example. Black bears walk with an ambling, flat-footed gait (plantigrade locomotion), but can run as fast as 30 miles per hour in short charges or sprints. They often rear up on their back legs to get a better view of their surroundings.

Flesh-eating Mammals   109

Black bears eat much vegetable matter and are truly omnivorous, much like humans. They eat berries, fruits, grass, honey, seeds, nuts, buds, roots, tubers, the inner bark of twigs, insects of all types, grubs, lizards, snakes, frogs, fish, rodents, armadillos, bird eggs, young deer, and carrion of all kinds. When searching for food, they often do a lot of digging, turning over logs, and clawing open rotten stumps. They sometimes make long scratches in the bark of trees when sharpening their claws. In some areas of the country, bears become obnoxious feeders at garbage dumps and sometimes are dangerous in camp-grounds when they steal food and tear up equipment. However, they are not a problem to campers anywhere in Florida.

Adult females breed only in alternate years during June or July, after which the sexes separate and return to solitary living. The female releases 1-4 (usually 2) ova and these are fertilized by the sperm immediately after mating. The tiny embryos then undergo arrested development (called delayed implantation) for the next 5-6 months. During midwinter, the embryos finally implant in the uterus and complete development. The period of gestation can range from 200-240 days, depending on the duration and degree of hibernation. Most young are born in January or February and cubs are tiny (weighing only 6-8 ounces), naked, and blind at birth. They grow slowly; their eyes open and first teeth appear when they are about 40 days old. At this time they are also well furred and weigh about two pounds. When they are about two months old, the cubs leave the den with their mother for the first time. They remain with her and continue to nurse throughout the summer and part of the fall. They normally do not leave their mother until the spring of their second year, when they weigh about 100 pounds. After that, the cubs usually stay together through their second summer. Adult males take no part in rearing the young.

Females can give birth at three years of age, but most are 5-7 years old before bearing young. Black bears do not reach their full growth until about six years old, and they have a life expectancy of 15-20 years in the wild. In zoos, they can live 25-30 years.

The most famous black bear was *Smokey the Bear,* the mascot of the U.S. Forest Service and its "prevent forest fires" campaign. He was found as a burned cub after a forest fire in New Mexico in 1950, and lived 27 years.

In bears, age is determined by tooth wear or by counting the number of growth rings (annuli) in the roots of canines or first premolars. The latter method requires the removal of a tooth, but is more accurate than estimating age by tooth wear.

Bears have large home ranges, with adult males covering much larger areas than females. One study in Louisiana found that the minimum home range for males averaged more than 27,000 acres and was just under 5,000 acres for females. Studies in Florida report that individual bears range over 25 to 100 square miles. Radio tracking of black bears wearing transmitters reveals that they move as much as 20 miles in a single 24-hour period. On occasion, transplanted bears have wandered as far as 300 miles from their release site in a few days.

Bears gain weight rapidly when food is abundant. One adult gained 60

Flesh-eating Mammals

pounds during one fall month as a result of feeding on the heavy mast (nut and acorn) crop. This represents a gain of roughly two pounds per day.

Economic Importance and Remarks: Bears are hunted as game animals primarily to secure a "trophy," but the meat also can be eaten, especially that of younger animals. The tanned pelt is often used as a floor rug or wall decoration.

Occasionally, black bears develop a taste for livestock, pigs, sheep, goats, or poultry, and they sometimes damage corn crops and vegetable gardens in remote forested regions. Bears like honey and honey bees, and in Florida often do considerable damage to hives. Electric fences or elevated, bear-proof platforms for the hives are recommended where bears are numerous.

On very rare occasions humans have been attacked, clawed, bitten, or even killed by black bears. I was once clawed by a large female black bear in the Rocky Mountains when I approached her twin cubs too closely in an attempt to photograph them. She swatted me out of the way with one blow to the head, and then quickly retreated, herding her babies before her. I then went for stitches in my temple at a nearby aid station.

Black bears have gradually declined in numbers in Florida, primarily because of habitat loss and exploitation. The Florida Game and Fresh Water Fish Commission currently lists them officially as "threatened" in all areas except Baker County, Columbia County, the Osceola National Forest, and the Apalachicola National Forest. Currently, those areas still have a hunting season because their bear populations have remained stable and can support a regulated harvest. There is a strong bear-hunting, sportsman lobby present in the state. If the downward trend in bear populations continues, and habitat destruction keeps pace as people move to Florida, then the black bear may no longer be a viable big game animal anywhere in Florida.

Raccoon *(Procyon lotor)*

Description: The raccoon is about the size of an average dog, has a black mask across its eyes, and a long bushy tail encircled by 5-7 black rings. The upper coat is grizzled gray, brown, and black, washed with yellow; the underparts are pale brown, mixed with grayish yellow. The face is whitish except the prominent black mask, and the ears are grayish with black on their back sides. There is a great deal of color variation in raccoons, ranging from a pale yellow-brown coat to others that are almost totally black.

The skull is broad and robust, and the hard palate extends well posterior to the bunodont (flat-topped) molars.

Geographical Range: The raccoon is common to abundant in every corner of the state, including the Keys. In the United States, they are found in virtually every state. Raccoons also range through southern Canada, Mexico, and Central America.

Habitat Preference: This species occurs in every plant community having trees. Raccoons are most numerous in mature forests containing many hollow

raccoon, 29.5-35.4 in. (75-90 cm) overall, tail 9.4-11.8 in. (24-30 cm)

trees. They are also very abundant in tropical hammocks and the mangrove zone in southern Florida.

Life History and Reproduction: The raccoon, like its relative the black bear, is omnivorous, taking both plant and animal matter readily. Raccoons are also opportunistic, eating whatever is available. Their animal foods include crayfish, snails, clams, frogs, turtles, lizards, snakes, insects, fish, rodents, birds, eggs, rabbits, and grubs. Their plant foods are mainly fruits, seeds, berries, nuts, vegetables, tubers, and buds. They often forage at dumps, garbage cans, and campgrounds.

Raccoons usually sleep during the daytime in a tree den or on a platform of sticks in a tree, but they become active in the late afternoon and continue through the night. If hungry, they will also forage during the day. A popular misconception is that raccoons always wash their food before eating. Most of the time they are not near water when food is found and even when water is available, they do not wash food before eating.

Male raccoons usually occupy a home range about one mile in diameter, but they will sometimes travel much greater distances, especially during the mating season. Females have smaller home ranges that are about three-fourths of a mile in diameter. Within each home range there are several den sites which are used on a rotating basis as the raccoon moves from place to place. One study found the average distance between den sites is about 1,400 feet. Raccoons do not hibernate, but I have seen them sleep so deeply that they were difficult to arouse when shaken vigorously. Raccoons usually den in trees, and they are agile climbers. When descending trees they can go either headfirst or tail first and they frequently jump the last few feet. They are good fighters and when cornered by a dog usually give a good account of themselves.

Raccoons normally produce one litter a year, and mating in Florida usually occurs in December and January, but sometimes later. The gestation period is 63 days and the average litter size is 3-4 offspring (range 1-7). Males are promiscuous and only the female provides care for the offspring, called pups, kits, or cubs. Newborn raccoons are fully furred, but their eyes are closed. Eyes open when they are about two weeks of age, and pups first leave the den when 8-10 weeks old to forage with the mother. They are not completely weaned until 12-14 weeks. Some young females can breed near the end of their first year, but most males and about 60 percent of females do not mature sexually until their second year.

Most raccoons in the wild live a maximum of 6-8 years, but the record longevity reported in a free-ranging population is 16 years (based on dental annuli). In captivity they have lived to 18 years of age. Age is most accurately determined by examining the concentric growth rings or annuli found in the roots of incisor or canine teeth. The rate of tooth wear is also used for determining age. Also, males can be aged by the increasing size and weight of the elaborately curved os baculum.

Economic Importance and Remarks: Raccoons are hunted extensively for sport, food, and fur. "Coon" hunting is a time-honored sport in the rural South. Hounds are specially bred and trained for the sport and are adept at trailing and "treeing" the raccoon. The hunter then uses a rifle or shotgun to shoot the raccoon out of the treetops. Some purists let the 'coon go to be hunted another night. In some locations raccoon pelts are sold to supplement farm incomes. The fur is of moderately good quality and is used to trim coats.

K. MASLOWSKI

mink, 20-24.4 in. (53-62 cm) overall, tail 7.1-8.3 in. (18-21 cm)

Flesh-eating Mammals

Raccoons can damage crops such as corn, grapes, watermelons, cantaloupes, and tomatoes. Occasionally they will kill chicks, ducklings, or other poultry. Problem raccoons are usually shot, trapped, treed by dogs, or poisoned.

Regarding disease transmission, most rabies outbreaks in Florida have been associated with raccoons. The disease has a long incubation period, and for this reason, adopting pet raccoons (even as babies) carries some risk that the disease may manifest itself later. For this reason, raccoons should not be kept as household pets (unless bred and reared in captivity). In addition to rabies, raccoons can carry distemper, tuberculosis, and fungal skin diseases.

Raccoons have few predators besides man and his dogs. However, young ones are sometimes taken by bobcats, great horned owls, and panthers. Before its decline in the eastern United States, the red wolf was probably a significant predator of the raccoon.

Mink *(Mustela vison)*

Description: The mink is a medium-sized, slender carnivore similar to but larger than the weasel. Both the upper and lower pelage are a glossy chocolate-brown color. The tail is long, bushy and dark chocolate brown on the basal half, but becomes progressively blacker toward the tip. The chin is white, and there are irregular white splashes on the throat and sometimes on the belly and chest. The ears are short and round, and the head is flattened. Males average about one-third larger in body size than females.

The skull has 34 teeth, the last upper molar is dumbbell shaped, and the palate extends well beyond the last molar. It closely resembles the skull of the long-tailed weasel but is larger, and the auditory bullae protecting the inner ear are much smaller than in the weasel.

Geographical Range: The mink occurs in two distinctly different parts of Florida. One form, the Everglades mink, occurs from Lake Okeechobee southward and westward in the Everglades and Big Cypress Swamp areas. The other form occurs only in certain coastal habitats along the Gulf Coast as far south as Hernando County, and along the Atlantic Coast as far south as Matanzas Inlet. See map on page 205. The United States range of the mink covers the entire country except the southwestern desert areas.

Habitat Preference: Minks in Florida are found either in coastal salt marshes or in freshwater habitats including streams, ponds, lakes, marshes, and swamps.

Life History and Reproduction: Minks are always semiaquatic in their habits. They are active mainly at night and occasionally during the day. They forage for food both in the water and along banks and wetland borders. Minks den in a variety of places including hollow stumps, bank cavities, under logs, and even in rodent nests. Males may have a large home range, up to five miles in diameter. Females are more sedentary and have a home range that averages only one-fifth that size. Minks living along streams have much more linear home ranges than those living in marshes.

Flesh-eating Mammals

Their diet is strictly animal matter, both aquatic and terrestrial animals, including frogs, snails, crayfish, fish, Florida muskrats, rice rats, cotton rats, clams, insects, mice, rabbits, birds, and reptiles. The mink is an opportunistic carnivore and will catch whatever animal is most available.

The breeding season begins in the late winter and extends into spring. Only one litter is produced annually, and the gestation period ranges from 40-75 days (average 51 days) because of suspended development of the tiny embryos in the mother's uterus. After implantation finally occurs, development of the embryos to term requires only 30 days. The average litter size is 3-4 offspring (range 1-12). The kits weigh around one-half ounce at birth, are blind, and are covered with a fine silvery-white fur. By two weeks of age the fur color has changed to a pale reddish gray. The eyes finally open when they are about five weeks old, and weaning occurs shortly thereafter. An adult male usually mates with several females each season, but he sometimes remains with the last mate and assists in the care of the young. Juvenile minks usually catch their own food by eight weeks of age, but they typically remain with their mother as a family group until late summer. They reach full adult size when five months old. Both sexes become reproductively active when about 10 months of age.

A few minks live as long as 6-8 years in the wild, but in captivity ranch mink have lived for 12 years. In Florida, minks are preyed upon by alligators, bobcats, great horned owls, and probably by large cottonmouth water moccasins and eastern diamondback rattlesnakes.

Economic Importance and Remarks: Minks have fur that is the highest quality of any Florida mammal. However, the species is seldom trapped here because of its secretive nature and rarity. Some of the vast salt marshes located along the upper west coast of Florida are believed to support good mink populations.

The Everglades mink is currently listed as "threatened" by the Florida Game and Fresh Water Fish Commission. Fortunately, most of its habitat in the Big Cypress Swamp and Everglades is now federal- and state-owned, so it should survive even with continued development in southern Florida.

Long-tailed Weasel *(Mustela frenata)*

Description: The long-tailed weasel is a small, slender carnivore with short legs and a long tail. The upper pelage is chestnut brown and the hair is short and uniform in color. The underparts are yellowish white or creamy white. Ears are short, rounded, and inconspicuous. The tail is about the same length as the head and body combined, brown dorsally, and tipped in black. The eyes are small and beady, and the nose is pointed.

The skull is identified by its small size for a carnivore (Florida's smallest) and inflated, elongated auditory bullae surrounding the inner ears.

Geographical Range: The long-tailed weasel occurs throughout Florida except the Keys. It is less common in the southern third of the peninsula and may be absent in the southeastern corner of the state. I have taken this weasel as far south as Collier County on the west coast of Florida, presently the southernmost record for the animal. The species occurs throughout the United States, as well as Mexico and Central America.

Habitat Preference: The long-tailed weasel appears to have no real habitat preference. It has been taken in most types of terrestrial plant communities in Florida, including both forested and open areas.

Life History and Reproduction: The long-tailed weasel is an aggressive little carnivore, and does not hesitate to attack and kill prey larger than itself. It is extremely fast, agile, and usually leaps on the back of the prey and sinks its sharp teeth into the brain or severs the jugular veins in the neck. They are strict meat eaters and prey largely on rodents, birds, reptiles, and rabbits. They sometimes invade the farmyard to take rats as well as poultry.

The weasel's home is a shallow burrow in the ground, in a log, or in a stump, often taken from one of its prey species. The long, slender weasel can easily forage in the burrows of most medium- to small-sized rodents. The presence of a weasel is often indicated by a cache of food or a pile of discarded bones found within a burrow entrance. They hunt both day and night, but generally are more active nocturnally. They are very inquisitive and will explore every nook and cranny of a structure or habitat looking for prey.

Males have larger home ranges than females, averaging about 400 acres in size. It usually requires several days for a weasel to cover the entire home range. Females are more sedentary and have an average home range of about 150 acres.

Almost nothing is known about the breeding cycle of Florida weasels, because they are rare and difficult to study. Elsewhere, the species breeds in July or August and produces a single annual litter, usually born in April or May. Because of the warm climate, litters are probably born earlier in the spring in Florida. The gestation period is extremely variable in length because weasels have delayed implantation of the fertilized eggs of up to 6-7 months. Once the embryos

FLORIDA DNR

long-tailed weasel, 14.5-17.7 in. (37-45 cm) overall, tail 5.8-7.1 in. (13-18 cm)

Flesh-eating Mammals

implant in the uterus, the development to full term requires only about 25 days. Thus, the gestation period can be as long a 8-9 months. The annual litter contains 1-12 young, but averages six. At birth the babies are pink, blind, nearly hairless, and helpless. They are well furred by three weeks of age, but the eyes do not open until the young weasels are about five weeks old. Adult males sometimes assist in caring for the young. Weaning takes place shortly after the eyes open, after which the young begin foraging with their mother until they are nearly full grown. Young females reach sexual maturity when 3-4 months old, but males do not become sexually active until they are a year old.

The size and weight of the os baculum is sometimes used to determine the age of male weasels. In the wild, weasels seldom live beyond 3-4 years, but in captivity they have survived as long as seven years.

Economic Importance and Remarks: Weasels, while rare in Florida except the northern part of the state, are very beneficial in consuming harmful cotton rats, rice rats, black rats, and many species of mice. On infrequent occasions, they attack poultry and may kill more than they can eat, although such behavior is not well documented. Problem weasels are usually controlled with traps, shooting, or dogs.

In the northern parts of its range, long-tailed weasels molt to an all-white winter pelt with the tail still tipped in black. This protective coloration makes them almost invisible on snow. In the southern half of the United States, including Florida, weasels remain brown year-round. When weasels are in the white winter coat, fur dealers call them "ermine." There is no fur market for weasel pelts in Florida, but in the north they are an economically important furbearer.

I can personally attest to the fearless nature of the long-tailed weasel. I once kept a large male in a cage to observe its habits. One day it somehow unlatched the cage door and got out. I proceeded to chase it around the room several times, while wearing heavy leather gloves to protect my hands. It suddenly turned the tables as I cornered it under a bench. The weasel jumped almost three feet into the air, on the attack, and in the general direction of my head and throat. I deflected him to the side with my gloves and ultimately subdued him, but not without gaining a healthy and permanent respect for the aggressive, fearless nature of Florida's smallest carnivore.

Striped Skunk (Mephitis mephitis)

Description: The striped skunk is about the size of a house cat, stout bodied, and entirely black except for two white stripes that run down the back. Occasionally, the white stripes on the back are very narrow or reduced to a single stripe. They have a small head, short, stocky legs, and a large plume-like black tail that is sometimes marked with white. Each foot has five toes with long, slightly curved claws. Males are slightly larger than females.

The skull is about the same size as the mink's, but the auditory bullae protecting the inner ears are small. Also, the region above the eye sockets is well rounded or arched upward in the skunk.

Flesh-eating Mammals

Geographical Range: Striped skunks are found throughout the state of Florida, except the Keys. The range in the United States extends from coast to coast, plus parts of Mexico and most of Canada.

Habitat Preference: This species occurs in virtually every terrestrial community in the state. Striped skunks are probably most abundant in forest edge habitats, brushy fields, and areas with heavily overgrown fence rows. They sometimes live in suburban and residential areas.

Life History and Reproduction: Striped skunks can be active at any time of the day or night, but they usually venture out in the late afternoon and remain active during the night. They have keen senses of hearing and smell but weak vision. Skunks often dig their own den, but they also remodel those of armadillos, gopher tortoises, or foxes, to suit their needs.

The striped skunk is infamous for its potent scent glands, located on either side of the anus, that spray droplets of acrid, pungent musk on offenders up to 15 feet away. The smell itself can be detected for much greater distances, up to 1½ miles downwind. Skunks cannot squirt the musk if the tail is depressed toward the ground, but they spray it with considerable accuracy when the tail is up.

Striped skunks are omnivorous, eating plant and animal foods in about equal amounts. Their diet includes insects, grubs, mice, rats, reptiles, amphibians, small birds, eggs, young rabbits, crayfish, plant buds, roots, tubers, nuts, seeds, mushrooms, and even grass. They are not good climbers but dig very effectively and locate food in that manner.

The breeding season begins in February or March and continues into the spring. Gestation is variable, ranging from 59-77 days, but averages 65 days. The tiny embryos often undergo a period of arrested development before implantation in the mother's uterus, which extends the length of gestation. One litter of 2-10 young, but averaging five, is produced annually. Young females generally have smaller litters than older females. At birth, the kits weigh about one-half ounce, the eyes are closed, and they are almost naked but show delicate black and white color markings. At the end of two weeks they are well furred. Eyes open by about 18 days of age and the young skunks will assume a characteristic defensive pose at this time. They leave the nest and accompany their mother on foraging trips for the first time when 6-7 weeks old. Weaning occurs at 8-10 weeks of age. Young striped skunks are not able to throw scent until they are about one month old. After weaning, the mother and young usually stay together as a family group until late summer.

In the wild, striped skunks usually live a maximum of 5-6 years. However, in captivity, where they are often kept as pets, some have lived for 10 years. Skunks do not hibernate, but they become obese in the fall, and sleep for extended periods during the cool snaps of winter, living off their stored fat.

Economic Importance and Remarks: Striped skunks are trapped and sold for their fur in many northern areas, where the pelts are frequently used to trim garments. Striped skunks occasionally cause problems by killing young chickens and other poultry, but this is uncommon.

Flesh-eating Mammals

The odor of skunk musk is very difficult to completely eradicate. If a person is accidentally sprayed by a skunk, clothes are usually burned, but various solvents and deodorants may be tried to salvage them. Those often recommended are laundry bleaches, ammonia, turpentine, tomato juice, and vinegar. I have found none to be totally effective, however.

Since skunks often carry and transmit rabies and leptospirosis, there is some danger in handling skunks from wild populations. Also, there is a risk in buying skunks as pets because the incubation period for rabies is long, and the history of the skunk may be unknown. Almost 50 percent of the animal rabies cases reported in the United States each year occur in skunks, so the risk is real.

Striped skunks have very few predators because of their potent defense system. Great horned owls, however, are not deterred by the scent, and they frequently eat skunks. A few young skunks are also taken by hungry bobcats, foxes, and stray dogs. Dogs commonly attack and kill adult skunks, but seldom a second time.

Eastern Spotted Skunk *(Spilogale putorius)*

Description: The eastern spotted skunk or "civet cat" is a small carnivore the size of a squirrel, having a black coat with numerous conspicuous white stripes and spots scattered over the upper parts. There is always a large white spot on the forehead and one located in front of each ear. The tail is long, bushy, and usually all black, but it may have a prominent white tip. The legs are short and stocky, the ears and eyes are small, and the toes have long claws.

The skull is much smaller than that of the striped skunk and the region above the eye sockets is flat, lacking an arch. The auditory bullae over the internal ears are slightly inflated.

Geographical Range: Spotted skunks occur throughout the state of Florida, except the Keys. The range in the United States is nearly nationwide except the Great Lakes area and northeastern states. Spotted skunks also range throughout Mexico and most of Central America.

Habitat Preference: Habitats clearly preferred by the spotted skunk are old fallow fields, weedy pastures, blackberries and brush, dry prairies, field fence rows and open disturbed areas. They are uncommon to absent in mature forests and dense timber of any type. Spotted skunks are strictly terrestrial and do not occur in wet, swampy, or marshy habitats.

Life History and Reproduction: Spotted skunks sleep during the day in underground dens and are active at night. They sometimes dig their own burrow, but often modify the tunnel of another burrowing animal to suit their own needs. They like to dig their dens under barns, sheds, old foundations, woodpiles, rock piles, logs, brush heaps, and even houses (where they are seldom appreciated).

The spotted skunk has potent anal musk glands like those of the striped skunk. The vile-smelling scent is often described as a more sickening, sweeter smell than that of the striped skunk. The droplets are sprayed for a distance of 12-15 feet, but the odor travels for long distances downwind. The defensive posture of the

Flesh-eating Mammals

striped skunk, 23.2-28 in. (59-71 cm) overall, tail 8.3-13.8 in. (21-35 cm)

spotted skunk, 16.5-20.5 in. (42-52 cm) overall, tail 6.3-8.3 in. (16-21 cm)

Flesh-eating Mammals

spotted skunk is stereotyped. Before spraying scent, they do a series of rapid handstands with the rear end of the body and tail held high in the air. When approached too closely, they drop back to all fours, assume an U-shaped stance, with the tail lifted and the anus and head directed toward the intruder, and let the spray fly.

Spotted skunks are omnivorous and consume a wide variety of plants and animals. Insects make up a large part of the diet, but they also eat mice, rats, amphibians, reptiles, small birds, eggs, fruits, nuts, mushrooms, and plant tubers. They are very good climbers and can scurry up and down trees like squirrels.

The breeding season begins in the late winter and young are born in the spring. The gestation period varies from 50-65 days but averages about 58 days. There can be a delay of a week or more before the tiny embryos implant in the mother's uterus. The litter size varies from 2-9 and averages 4-5 offspring. The kits are blind and naked at birth, but their black and white color pattern is clearly visible. By three weeks of age, dense fur covers the entire body, but the eyes do not open until they are about 32 days old. Young spotted skunks can first spray musk when 46 days of age, and they wean when about 54 days old. Adult size is reached at 3-4 months and breeding occurs when they are 10-12 months of age. Some adult females appear to mate a second time in late summer and produce a fall litter in Florida.

Spotted skunks in the wild live a maximum of 5-6 years, but in captivity they have survived to 10 years of age. Spotted skunks are preyed upon by great horned owls and barred owls and occasionally by bobcats, foxes, dogs, and coyotes. Humans also often kill them for no good reason.

Economic Importance and Remarks: The pelts of spotted skunks are sold in most northern areas for use as trim on coats and other garments. This species rarely kills poultry, but individuals often develop a fondness for chicken eggs. Usually the skunk bites off the end of an egg and laps the contents out. However, sometimes a skunk will straddle an egg and give it a quick kick backward with the hind feet, propelling the egg with considerable force against a wall or other suitable object. The swift kick may be repeated several times until the egg breaks.

Spotted skunks are not kept as pets as frequently as striped skunks, but in many ways they are cuter and more cuddly (when descented) than their big lumbering cousins. This species also can carry rabies and leptospirosis, so wild-caught stock should never be kept as pets.

River Otter *(Lutra canadensis)*

Description: The river otter is a large, elongated, torpedo-shaped carnivore with a small flattened head and broad muzzle. The tail is long, muscular, and tapers gradually from the broad base to a point at the end. The legs are short and stout, and the feet have webbed toes. The upper fur is glossy brown, and the underparts are paler brown or grayish tan. The ears are small, rounded, and conspicuous.

The skull is large, broad, and has a very short rostrum in front of the eye sockets. There is also a narrow constriction of the upper surface of the skull between the eye sockets.

Geographical Range: The river otter is found throughout the state of Florida, except the Keys. The range in the United States is nationwide, excluding only the southwestern desert region. However, it has been exterminated by man and his pollution in several states where it once occurred widely. They also range through Canada and Alaska.

Habitat Preference: River otters can be found in almost every aquatic habitat in Florida. They do very well in rivers, creeks, lakes, ponds, swamps, marshes, and bayous. They are less often found in brackish and salt water, except in the tidal zones of some large rivers. They are never found far from water, except when dispersing in search of a new home.

Life History and Reproduction: Otters live in bank burrows, usually located under the roots of a tree, a stump, or in thick vegetation. They may excavate their own tunnel, but frequently take over and remodel the den of another animal, such as the beaver or nutria. Otters feed almost entirely on animal foods, with crayfish and fish as their favorite items in Florida. They also occasionally eat frogs, snails, salamanders, snakes, turtles, clams, rodents, birds, and aquatic insect larvae.

River otters are among the most playful of mammals and take particular delight in sliding down mud banks into the water. They are sociable animals that appear to enjoy group interactions.

River otters have large home ranges that may cover 3-10 linear miles along a stream, lake shore, or marsh. Otters are mainly nocturnal, but I have occasionally seen them foraging during the daytime in protected areas where cover is ample. Otters, like all members of the weasel family, have strong musk glands in the anal area. They make scent posts throughout their home range, marking clumps of leaves or sticks with their musk. Such scent markings are important to the social and reproductive interactions of otters.

In Florida, the mating season occurs in the late summer or fall. This is the only time males are not sociable, and they engage in fighting and combat in an attempt to breed with the females. There is a period of dormancy in the tiny embryos that lasts several months, but after implantation, development to term requires only nine weeks. The total length of the gestation period averages 11 months, and varies from 10-12 months. The litter size averages three kits (range 1-6). The mother mates again for the next year's litter immediately after birth. The babies are born blind, helpless, and dark brown in color. The eyes open around 35 days of age, and young otters do not leave the den until they are 10-12 weeks old. The mother will not tolerate adult males near her young until they are about six months old, but weaning occurs around four months of age. The young otters accompany their mother until they are about one year old and fully grown. A few breed at one year of age, but most do not become sexually active until they are two years old.

River otters are fairly long-lived, and some reach 12-15 years of age in the wild. In zoos, they have lived as long as 20 years. Males can be aged by the increasing size and configuration of their os baculum. The relative amount of tooth wear also can be used to age both sexes, but the most accurate method is to count the annuli in tooth enamel. Adult otters can be placed in yearly age classes by counting these tooth rings.

Otters are preyed upon occasionally by alligators, but they have almost no other enemies except humans. The nets of commercial fishermen sometimes drown river otters. Also, I have found a sizeable number of dead otters as road-kills throughout Florida. Automobiles take a heavy toll as otters amble across highways in search of food sources or new habitats.

Economic Importance and Remarks: The fur of the river otter is among the most valuable and durable of all carnivore fur. It is harvested by trappers and the pelts sold for substantial prices in Florida and northern locales. The trapping season is limited to the winter months when the fur is thickest.

River otters make entertaining and playful pets if raised from a young age. Unfortunately, they often cache a portion of the food they are given, which can become very smelly in confined quarters. They also require a large aquarium or pool to frolic in, which can be a problem.

Some fishermen claim that river otters damage fishing, but studies show they take mainly the "trash fish," or nongame species. Their direct effects on bass, bluegills, and other freshwater game fishes are negligible.

Habitat loss in Florida is by far the greatest threat to the health and survival of the state's otter populations. Burgeoning development is gobbling up suitable habitat in many areas that once supported good numbers of river otters. I personally know of several areas in the Tampa Bay region that contained numerous otters a few years ago, but now contain only subdivisions, streets, sewers, and sidewalks.

Gray Fox *(Urocyon cinereoargenteus)*

Description: The gray fox is a medium-sized carnivore that has grizzled salt-and-pepper-gray upper parts and a long bushy tail with a distinct black stripe on its upper side. The underparts are white along the center of the belly and tawny orange along the sides. The muzzle is pointed with a blackish patch above and on the chin. There is tawny orange on the sides of the neck, back of the ears, and sides of the legs. The orange flank and leg markings often lead to the incorrect identification of this species as the red fox, which is orangy red on both sides and back.

Young gray foxes have a juvenile fur that is distinct from the colorful adult pelage. It is a woolly gray-brown color that is replaced, at about 6 weeks of age, by fur that is similar to that of adults.

The skull is easily identified by the presence of a prominent pair of elevated lyre-shaped ridges running lengthwise in the top of the cranium (on the frontal and parietal bones). Also, the upper incisors are evenly rounded on each side, but are lobed in the red fox.

river otter, 35.4-43.3 in. (90-110 cm) overall, tail 11.8-15.7 in. (30-40 cm)

J. WATERS

gray fox, 31.5-44.1 in. (80-112 cm) overall, tail 10.6-15.7 in. (27-40 cm)

Geographical Range: This is the only native fox found in most of Florida and it has a statewide distribution except the Keys. In the United States, the gray fox is found everywhere except the northern Rocky Mountains and portions of the High Plains. They also range throughout Mexico, Central America, and into northern South America.

Flesh-eating Mammals

Habitat Preference: The gray fox occurs at least sparingly in most terrestrial Florida habitats, and they are common in several of them. These include upland hardwood forests, wooded floodplains, and pine-oak woodlands bordering fallow fields and weedy pastures. This species is adaptable and tolerant of man's intrusions in its habitat. I have found them to be abundant in the rapidly developing suburban areas around Tampa, for example.

Life History and Reproduction: Gray foxes are seldom seen because they are active primarily at dawn and dusk and during the night. They spend the day in an underground den or hollow log. The gray fox is the only member of the dog family that regularly climbs trees in pursuit of prey or to escape hounds.

They prey heavily on cottontail and marsh rabbits that often make up nearly half of the total food consumed. Also important food items are cotton rats, rice rats, deer mice, perching birds, insects, acorns, and fruits (persimmons, pawpaws, etc.).

Gray foxes mate during the winter in Florida. The gestation period averages 53 days (range 51-63) and one yearly litter is produced in the early spring. The litter size averages 4 young (range 1-7). The offspring (called pups or kits) are blind, blackish in color, scantily furred, and weigh about 3 ounces. The eyes open at 9-12 days after birth, and the foxes first leave the den for short periods when about 3 weeks old. For the first 5-6 weeks, only the female cares for the young; after that, the male also brings food to the family. When about three months old, young foxes begin to forage for food with the parents, and the family breaks up by late summer. Gray foxes do not breed until the year following their birth.

This species has few enemies other than man and his dogs, but bobcats and great horned owls probably take a few pups. They are rarely hit by automobiles, presumably because of their speed, agility, and cunning nature. Gray foxes normally live a maximum of 8-10 years in the wild, but there are records of them living up to 15 years in captivity.

(ASM)—J. MURIE

red fox, 33.5-43.3 in. (85-110 cm) overall, tail 11-15.7 in. (28-40 cm)

Economic Importance and Remarks: The pelt of the gray fox is of fairly high quality, particularly in the colder states. Foxes are widely trapped and sold for use in a making coats. Gray foxes sometimes take chickens, ducks, geese, turkeys, and other poultry from the farmyard. Such problem foxes are usually trapped, poisoned, or shot.

I have observed that gray foxes in Florida often show little fear of humans shining bright lights on them at night. They are much more wary in other situations. This tameness in response to light has probably led to their demise on many occasions.

Foxes sometimes carry rabies, canine distemper, mange, scabies, or leptospirosis. These diseases are rare in most populations, however.

Red Fox *(Vulpes vulpes)*

Description: The red fox is a medium-sized carnivore that has a reddish-yellow or tawny-red upper coat. The terminal portion of the long, tawny, bushy tail is black tipped with white. The cheeks, throat, and belly are white, but the legs and feet are black. The muzzle and ears are pointed, and the ears are black on the back side.

The skull is distinguished from that of the gray fox by the shallow (rather than deep) depression above and between the postorbital processors. Also, the parietal and frontal ridges on top of the skull are not pronounced or elevated. The upper incisors are distinctly lobed on each side, but they are evenly rounded in the gray fox.

Geographical Range: The red fox is not native to Florida, with the possible exception of the extreme northern border of the panhandle. It has been widely introduced in Florida by fox hunting clubs, and is now well established in many areas throughout the state. In the United States, the range of the red fox extends from coast to coast. It also occurs throughout Canada and Alaska.

Habitat Preference: The red fox prefers mixed pine-oak uplands interspersed with fallow fields and weedy pastures. Unlike the gray fox, it avoids heavy timber and forested floodplains. Red foxes are also rather common in poorly tended or abandoned citrus groves.

Life History and Reproduction: Although primarily nocturnal, red foxes occasionally forage in the daytime and still more often at dawn and dusk. They normally excavate an underground burrow, or sometimes take over and enlarge the burrow of an armadillo or gopher tortoise. Their dens almost always have more than one entrance, and are usually 20-40 feet long and 3-4 feet deep.

Breeding takes place in late fall or early winter. The gestation period is around 53 days (range 50-56), and one litter, averaging 5 young (range 1-10), is produced per year. Red foxes are monogamous and apparently remain mated for life. The number of young per litter increases with the female's age up to 5-7 years, then declines. At birth the pups (or kits) are blind, helpless, and dark grayish brown in color. The eyes open when 7-9 days old, and pups first leave the den to play when they are about three weeks of age. They lose their woolly juvenile fur when about six weeks old, and the subsequent pelage is much like

126   Flesh-eating Mammals

that of the parents. Weaning takes place at about two months of age, and they leave the parents when six months old. Young foxes sometimes disperse long distances before establishing their own homesites.

Red foxes mainly eat small mammals, including rabbits, rats, and mice. They also take wild birds, amphibians, and reptiles when available. If food is plentiful, they may kill more than they can eat and cache the excess in the ground or cover it with grass and leaves.

In the wild, red foxes may live 8-10 years, but in captivity some have survived 15 years. They have few enemies except man, his dogs, bobcats, and possibly coyotes. Great horned owls also may take a few pups at the mouth of the den.

Economic Importance and Remarks: Red foxes are trapped and sold for fur in many parts of the country. The pelts are used extensively for trimming coats and jackets. Foxes feed heavily on rats, mice, and other small mammals and thus are beneficial in rodent control. They occasionally also seriously damage poultry populations. Problem foxes are usually eliminated by hunting, trapping, or poisoning.

The red fox is much admired by sportsmen who love the chase. It has greater speed, endurance, and stamina than the gray fox and is considered to give the hounds a better test of their abilities. Fox-hunting clubs are largely responsible for the introduction and widespread occurrence of the red fox in Florida.

Red foxes occasionally carry and transmit rabies, mange, scabies, canine distemper or leptospirosis. These diseases are fairly rare in Florida populations, however.

Coyote *(Canis latrans)*

Description: This is a large, dog-like carnivore that somewhat resembles a German shepherd. The upper pelage is light gray to yellowish buff, with the outer hairs tipped with black. The underparts are whitish, cream or pale gray. The backs of the ears are rust colored and the muzzle is yellowish or rusty. The tail is bushy and colored like the back, but the tip is black. The front legs are whitish and the outer sides of the hind legs are rust colored. Considerable variation in the pelage occurs, and there are nearly all-black and nearly all-white color phases.

The dog-like skull is much larger than that of the foxes. Compared with dogs, coyotes have longer canine teeth and a lower brow ridge (the bump on top of the skull between the eyes).

Geographical Range: The coyote is not native to Florida but began to expand its range into the state naturally during the 1970s. It has also been illegally released in scattered locations by fox-hunting clubs. Now there are well-established populations throughout much of the state, except possibly for the Everglades and Big Cypress Swamp. The range of the coyote in the United States is nationwide. It also occurs in Canada, Alaska, Mexico, and part of Central America.

Habitat Preference: Coyotes are adaptable but prefer open rangeland, fallow fields, and brushy pastures. They also appear to do well in the vast open

coyote, 41.3-52 in. (105-250 cm) overall, tail 11.8-15.4 in. (30-29 cm)

areas of old phosphate mines that are slowly recovering ecologically or have been reclaimed into grazing land.

Life History and Reproduction: Coyotes are noted for their vocalizations, which include howls, barks, yips, whimpers, and growls. Howling is most prevalent during the mating season and usually occurs at night. Other coyotes in an area respond to a howl with answering calls.

Coyotes dig large dens, often located in a bank or under some protective obstacle. Sometimes they enlarge a fox, armadillo, or gopher tortoise burrow. There are usually at least two openings that measure approximately 10 inches wide by 20 inches high. The tunnel may be 10-20 feet long with an enlarged nest chamber at the end.

Coyotes often travel over an area 20-30 miles in diameter, with males having larger home ranges than females. They deposit urine, feces, and scent at locations that mark their territorial boundaries for the benefit of other coyotes. Coyotes kill a variety of animals and are opportunistic feeders, but rabbits and rodents make up about two-thirds of their diet. They also eat some fruits, seeds, and berries such as persimmons, grapes, melons, blackberries, and pawpaw. In addition, they eat carrion, birds, reptiles, amphibians, and even man's garbage.

The breeding season occurs in the late winter and early spring. Gestation ranges from 58-65 days (average 63 days) and females produce only one litter per year, averaging 5 young (range 2-12). Larger litters are born in years of good food supply (high rodent or rabbit populations). Some coyotes mate for life and

Flesh-eating Mammals

others pair for only one reproductive season. Both parents tend the young, which are blind and helpless at birth and covered by a grayish-brown woolly fur. The eyes open when the pups are 10-14 days old. Coyote pups can be distinguished from fox pups by the shape of the pupils of the eye; coyote pupils are round, whereas those of both red and gray foxes are vertical slits. Young coyotes first leave the den when about three weeks old. The adult male often brings food to the female, which she tears into bits for the offspring. Juvenile coyotes are weaned at about eight weeks of age, when both parents bring food to the den in their stomachs and disgorge it at the entrance for the offspring to eat. The pups are taught to hunt by the parents when they are 8-12 weeks of age. The coyote family then leaves the den but remains together until late summer or early fall, when juvenile coyotes disperse. Young coyotes have been known to travel as far as 150 miles before setting up their own home ranges. A few young coyotes breed when one year old, but most do not become sexually active until two years old.

Coyotes have been known to survive for a maximum of 12 years in the wild and up to 20 years in captivity. The degree of tooth wear on the canines and incisors is often used as an aging criterion in coyotes, but counting the annuli in the enamel or cementum layer of the teeth is a more accurate method of aging in most carnivores.

Economic Importance and Remarks: Coyotes consume large quantities of harmful rodents and rabbits. They also occasionally take young calves, sheep, goats, and poultry. Often, however, coyotes are blamed for the depredations of free-running packs of dogs. With some effort, problem coyotes can be trapped, hunted, or poisoned. Coyotes have no serious predators except man and his dogs. They can transmit the same diseases as foxes and dogs.

Coyotes readily breed with domestic dogs and produce hybrid offspring called "coy-dogs." The coy-dog cross can look like either parent or, more commonly, an intermediate between the two parents. Young resulting from crosses with German shepherds usually look so much like coyotes that it is difficult to determine that they are hybrids. Coyote-dog hybrids are generally fertile and can breed with either parental line or among themselves.

Bobcat *(Lynx rufus)*

Description: The bobcat, or "wildcat," is a carnivore about halfway in size between a panther and a domestic cat. It has a short tail (4-6 inches long), long legs, and pointed ears that sometimes have small tufts of hair (about one inch long) at the tips. Bobcats have a short, broad face, and ruffs of fur extending out from each cheek like sideburns. The upper parts are tawny brown to olive brown, with scattered black spots or streaks giving the coat a splattered-paint spot appearance. The underparts are whitish with black spots, and there are a few black bars on the inner sides of the front legs. The tail is tawny brown with several transverse black bars, the last of which is broad, followed by a small white tip. The toes are all equipped with large, curved, retractable claws. The backs of the ears and tufts (when present) are black.

bobcat, 31.5-43.3 in. (80-110 cm) overall, tail 3.5-5.9 in. (9-15 cm)

The skull is broad, rounded, and has a short facial region. It is identified by having one less upper premolar on each side (two) than the panther and domestic cat (three).

Geographical Range: Bobcats occur throughout Florida including the Keys. There is virtually no region of the state where bobcats cannot be found at least sparingly, and usually they are common. The range of the bobcat in the United States is nationwide, and it is also present in most of Mexico.

Habitat Preference: Bobcats occur in a wide variety of terrestrial habitats ranging from dense forest to open grassy areas. They are absent only from extensive aquatic environments. It is not unusual for bobcats to live on the fringes of semideveloped residential areas and open suburban habitats.

Life History and Reproduction: Bobcats occasionally are seen foraging during the daylight hours, but they are most active during the night and at sunrise and sunset. They are excellent climbers and often forage or rest in trees. One time, when I was searching for fox squirrels in the Big Cypress Swamp, I encountered a large bobcat sleeping in the fork of a large cypress, about 40 feet above the ground. When I rapped on the trunk of the tree with a stick, he awoke, but showed little alarm, apparently because of his safe, lofty perch.

Bobcats are solitary carnivores having sizeable home ranges 15-25 square miles in diameter. Male home ranges are much larger than those of females, and

Flesh-eating Mammals

they defend their territories against other males. The boundaries of the territories are marked with scent posts, which often consists of feces, urine, and scratchings in the dirt. When marking the boundaries, bobcats typically back up to an object and spray copious amounts of urine. In contrast with male bobcats, females are not territorial and have home ranges that overlap broadly.

Bobcats are strict carnivores but opportunistic in their foraging, taking whatever animal is most available. Rabbits usually comprise the largest part of the diet, but also included are rats, mice, squirrels, opossums, quail, wild turkeys, perching birds, snakes, lizards, and an occasional fawn.

Breeding can occur year-round, but it usually peaks during mid- or late winter. Most births occur from March through September, with the peak parturitions in April-May and in July. Adult females normally produce one, but occasionally a second, litter each year. The gestation period is about 62 days, followed by the birth of 1-6 kittens (average 2-3). At birth, the kittens are covered with soft, spotted fur, have sharp claws, and are blind. The eyes open in about 10 days and the kittens leave the den to play for the first time. The mother starts bringing food to the den for the young when they are 7-8 weeks old. Weaning takes place when the young bobcats are 3-4 months old, but they stay with their mother until the following winter. Some females mate as young as one year of age, but most females and all the males wait to breed until they are two years old.

In the wild, bobcats live a maximum of 10-12 years, but in captivity they have reached 25 years of age. The most accurate method of determining age is to examine the growth rings in the cementum layer of the canine teeth. Man and his dogs are the major enemies of bobcats. Kittens may also be taken by great horned owls, foxes, panthers, or coyotes, but these are probably not major sources of mortality. Roadkills by automobiles are common, however.

Economic Importance and Remarks: Bobcats are often hunted or trapped to be mounted as trophy specimens by sportsmen. The fur is also valuable as a trim for coats and other garments. The ban on importation of the fur of most species of spotted cats into the United States from other parts of the world has increased the demand for pelts of Florida's native bobcat.

Bobcats are valuable predators of many problem rodents such as cotton rats, rice rats, and black rats, and they greatly help control Florida's marsh rabbit and eastern cottontail populations. On the negative side, bobcats, like many carnivores, can transmit rabies and feline distemper.

Panther, Cougar (Felis concolor)

Description: The Florida panther is also called the cougar, puma, or mountain lion in the various parts of its range. It is a large, powerfully built cat with a long, heavy, cylindrical tail. The upper parts are grizzled dark brown to tawny, and the underparts are dull white overlaid with buff in some areas. The head is relatively broad; the ears are small, rounded, and blackish on the back side, and never tufted. The sides of the muzzle are black, as is the top side of the furry tail.

The panther skull is almost twice the size as that of a bobcat and contains one more premolar (three) on each side in the upper jaw than the bobcat (two).

Recently, genetic tests have revealed that nearly all the surviving Florida panthers are crossbred with South American pumas released in the Everglades in the 20th century. This calls to question whether their official "listed" status as a distinct endangered subspecies is justified.

Geographical Range: The panther once had a statewide distribution in Florida with the possible exception of the Keys. It is now missing as a viable species over most of the state. A small remnant population still occurs in southwestern Florida in the Big Cypress Swamp and adjacent vast Everglades region. A few panthers also may be scattered throughout the national forests of the north-central and northern portions of the state. In the United States, this big cat once ranged from coast to coast but is now mainly located in the Rocky Mountain states and a few scattered wilderness habitats in the South. Panthers also occur in western Canada, Mexico, Central America, and across South America to the southern tip.

Habitat Preference: The panther occurs in a variety of wilderness habitats, avoiding those areas occupied by humans and their dogs. Because Florida has little true wilderness left, the panther has declined to the point of near extinction. The Everglades and Big Cypress Swamp, where the panther still occurs in low numbers, may actually be marginal as a preferred panther habitat, but this is the nearest thing to sizeable wilderness remaining in Florida.

Life History and Reproduction: Recent studies with radiotelemetry of marked panthers in southern Florida reveal that they range over vast areas. Males have much bigger home ranges than females, sometimes as large as 400 square miles. Females have home ranges only about one-fifth that of males. In many western states, cougars exhibit smaller home ranges than Florida panthers, possibly because the terrain is rougher and the food supply more abundant.

Panthers are secretive, solitary predators that are active mainly during the night and at dawn and dusk. They are terrestrial foragers, but swim quite well and climb trees with agility. The principal foods of the panther in Florida are the white-tailed deer and wild hog. They also take rabbits, rodents, armadillos, and raccoons, but apparently cannot thrive without an abundant supply of large-bodied prey. A panther catches its food by stalking it, then pouncing and biting the back of the neck or the throat. After eating its fill, the carcass is dragged into a thicket or other dense cover and concealed with leaves, sticks, and debris. A panther will return to this cache and feed for several days, until either the meat is consumed or it putrefies.

Little is known about the reproductive cycle of the Florida panther because of its rarity. However, based on recent studies in the wild and in captivity, we know that females are 2½ to 3 years old before they first breed, and thereafter they have a litter only once every 2-3 years. Breeding apparently can occur at any time of the year. Adults only tolerate one another during the brief breeding encounter, so males play no part in caring for their offspring. The gestation

Flesh-eating Mammals

period is between 82-96 days (average 90 days), and the litter size ranges from 1-6, averaging 2-3 young. The kittens weigh around one pound at birth, and are 12 inches long including the tail. They are covered with a soft, buffy fur spotted with black, they have brownish-black rings on the tail, and they are blind. Their eyes open at 7-10 days of age. Young panthers are weaned and start accompanying their mother on nightly hunting trips when 3-4 months old. The kittens gradually lose their spots and weigh 30-45 pounds at six months of age. They typically stay with their mother until they are 1½ to 2 years old.

The life span of panthers in the wild is unknown but seldom exceeds 12-15 years. In zoos they have lived a maximum of 25 years. The age of panthers can be estimated by tooth wear or by annual growth rings in the cementum of teeth.

Economic Importance and Remarks: The panther was voted the official state mammal of Florida in 1982 and is much revered by the public. It is fully protected throughout the state and listed as "endangered" by both the Florida Game and Fresh Water Fish Commission and the federal government.

In earlier times the panther culled and helped control Florida's deer populations, which regularly overpopulate. Man now performs this function during the annual hunting season, so the natural role of the big cat is largely gone. It remains today as an elegant remnant of our rich wildlife heritage and an impressive top carnivore in the food chain.

Panthers occasionally kill calves, colts, pigs, sheep, or goats on the farm or ranch. However, they are seldom habitual in this regard because of their aversion to humans and dogs.

The greatest cause of death in panthers continues to be the automobile. A sizeable number have been killed in recent years on the major highways in southwestern Florida, including Alligator Alley, State Highway 41, and State Highway 29. Portions of these highways have been elevated in critical areas to provide panther crossings.

Numerous sightings of "black panthers" are reported in Florida each year. These must represent misidentified large dogs, hogs, cattle, or other animals, because there have never been any dark or black-colored panthers collected anywhere in the United States.

The Florida race or subspecies of the cougar has a range that extends from Arkansas through the Deep South to Florida. It is presently identified by three rather superficial characteristics: a ridge of hair or cowlick down the center of the back; small white spots or flecking on the throat and chest areas; and a kink or sharp bend in the tail near the tip. Cougars from the western states do not show all three of these characteristics. In Florida today a sizeable number of captive nonnative cougars are kept as pets and in zoos, but there are only an estimated 30-50 native Florida panthers remaining in the wild. Thus, there is a good probability that some Florida sightings of the big cat in various parts of the state represent escaped or intentionally released cougars of nonnative origin. The only way to be sure which race is involved is to capture the animal and see if the three characteristics of the Florida race are present.

Another factor that could facilitate the survival of the remaining southwest

Florida panthers involves increasing the deer herd in that region. Many experts think that heavy hunting pressure, using large numbers of off-the-road vehicles each fall, has depressed the deer herd and harassed panthers by periodic human intrusions. During the hunting season each fall, I have observed large numbers of hunters invading the panther's prime habitat within the Fakahatchee Strand armed with a multitude of weapons, half-track vehicles, swamp buggies, airboats, three-wheel motorcycles, to pursue white-tailed deer. This annual invasion by an army of humans must be considered a major disruption to any panther's well-being, and it probably contributes to the significant automobile-caused mortalities.

FLORIDA DNR

panther, 59-98.4 in. (150-250 cm) overall, tail 19.6-31.1 in. (50-79 cm)

The panther has no serious natural enemies except man and domestic dogs. The latter frequently trail, harass, and tree them. Panthers can usually outdistance trailing dogs, but they often panic and climb a tree if pressed. Panthers probably do not have the stamina in long chases that dogs exhibit.

A recently emphasized mortality factor in Florida panthers is feline distemper. It can cause abortion of litters or death of juveniles, and was probably introduced to the panther population via domestic cats, foxes, or raccoons. In the remnant population of endangered Florida panthers present today, distemper could contribute significantly to a final decline of the race. Hopefully, they will withstand the disease and continue to reproduce successfully.

Since 1989, mercury poisoning has been identified as the probable cause for one panther death, and implicated in at least two others. The elevated mercury level in panthers in the southern Everglades is correlated with their diet, which is higher in raccoons than in deer or wild hogs, suggesting that raccoons are accumulating mercury through their diet. Besides being implicated in the death of adult panthers, mercury accumulation in females can lead to aborted, stillborn, or sickly young.

Biologists are also concerned about the apparent poor quality of the semen of Florida panthers. Males tested had low volume and low concentration of semen, poor sperm motility, and a very high proportion of abnormal sperm, all factors that should combine to reduce panther fertility.

Because of several adverse factors (including habitat loss, roadkills, harass-

Flesh-eating Mammals

ment by man and domestic dogs, disease, mercury poisoning, and infertility) the prognosis for the survival of the Florida panther in the wild is dim. It could easily be extinct in our state by the year 2000 if present trends continue to run their course. Amid much controversy, the Florida Game and Fresh Water Fish Commission began a captive breeding program in 1991. Young panthers are being taken to be bred in captivity with Texas cougars over the next several years, with hopes of eventually releasing offspring back into the wild within a decade or so. This will increase genetic diversity and hopefully improve the panther's chances for survival. Some environmental groups oppose this approach, but it may be the only viable alternative since the panther is rapidly approaching extinction in Florida.

ORDER PINNIPEDIA
Seals and Sea Lions

The pinnipeds include the fur seals, hair seals, and walruses, all of which are carnivorous marine mammals. Pinnipeds occur along most of the marine coasts of the world and some species ascend rivers or live in inland lakes. Seals and walruses are most abundant in polar and temperate waters, but a few species occur in the subtropics and tropics.

Pinnipeds have streamlined, fusiform or torpedo-shaped bodies and all four limbs are modified into flippers. The hands and feet are long and flattened, hence the name pinniped, which means wing-footed. Each limb has five broadly webbed, oar-like digits used for propulsion through the water. The external ears are reduced or absent and the nostrils are slit-like. The necks of seals and walruses are thickened and muscular, yet flexible in the water.

T. FRENCH

harbor seal, 5-6 ft. (1.5-1.8 m) overall

Seals and Sea Lions   135

Males are always a good deal larger than females, except in a few of the hair seals where the sexes are about equal in size. Pinnipeds have a thick layer of fat or blubber beneath the skin to provide insulation against cold water, and to serve as a reserve energy supply, as well as to provide buoyancy and padding to prevent serious injury. These marine carnivores are clumsy on land, but they are very impressive swimmers and divers in the water. Some seals can swim 15 miles per hour when pressed, dive to a depth of at least 2,000 feet, and remain submerged 45 minutes.

The distribution of pinnipeds is worldwide, but they are most numerous in polar and temperate waters. There are 31 species in the world, and only two species, both hair seals, venture into Florida waters. Also, one Caribbean species is now extinct.

Harbor Seal *(Phoca vitulina)*

Description: The harbor seal is small (5-6 feet long) and the color is variable, but it is usually yellowish gray, whitish gray, or dark grayish brown, often mottled with dark spots, blotches, or rings. The front flippers are small and the hind flippers always point backwards. The eyes are large, the nose whiskers are prominent, and there are no external ears.

The skull has four blade-like cheek teeth on each side of the upper and lower jaw, all of which are double rooted. The third upper cheek tooth is the largest.

Geographical Range: The harbor seal has been taken, rarely, along the Atlantic coast of Florida as far south as Ponce de Leon Inlet in Volusia County. The species occurs over a wide range along the shores of oceans in the northern hemisphere.

Habitat Preference: This seal, as the name suggests, inhabits harbors, bays, inlets, and estuarine areas along the coast. They spend a good deal of time resting on shore, and forage in shallow coastal waters, but sometimes they are also found well out at sea.

Life History and Reproduction: Harbor seals feed on a wide variety of shallow-water fishes and shellfish. They migrate seasonally up and down the marine coasts. Individuals are widely scattered during most of the summer months. In New England, they congregate in small herds of mixed ages and sexes by August. In September, mature adults swim to secluded inshore areas and mate in the water. Males do not maintain harems of females as do some species of seals. The winter is usually spent at sea, away from the mainland.

The gestation period is about 280 days, and one or two pups are born in the spring. The newborn seals are covered by a soft coat of white or yellowish-white fur. It is shed and replaced by a darker coat within a week or two. Young seals are precocial and can swim shortly after birth. They nurse for a few weeks, grow rapidly, and are soon foraging on their own for fishes. Young harbor seals become sexually active at 4-6 years of age. The maximum life expectancy is about 32 years. Killer whales, sharks, and polar bears are considered the seal's main predators besides man.

Economic Importance and Remarks: These seals are taken by Eskimos in arctic areas. They eat the meat, wear the hides, and even use the tendons for sewing garments together. The skins are sometimes sold commercially for leather and coat trimmings. However, because of their small size (maximum weight 300 pounds), hunting them is not a profitable business. This, of course, has no relevance in Florida waters where seals are rare visitors.

In some areas harbor seals are believed to compete seriously with commercial fishing interests. They are often subject to wanton killing because of this reputation. There is a record in Florida of a small harbor seal taking the baited hook of a fisherman who was surf fishing just south of Daytona Beach in June, 1968. The seal was pulled ashore, carefully unhooked, and released, apparently without serious injury from the experience.

Hooded Seal *(Cystophora cristata)*

Description: This seal is large (7-10 feet long), mottled gray and black, and males exhibit an elastic nose pouch. When inflated with air, this "hood" looks like a black rubber football extending from the nostrils to the forehead. The snout is wrinkled when the hood is deflated. Inflatable nose pouches are absent in females and immature males.

SEAWORLD

hooded seal, 7-10.5 ft. (2.1-3.2 m) overall

Seals and Sea Lions

137

The skull has only two pairs of upper incisors, one pair of lower incisors, and the cheek teeth are simple pegs.

Geographical Range: The hooded seal only rarely wanders south into Florida waters along the Atlantic coast. There are only three records spread over the last 15 years that extend from Fort Lauderdale north to Jacksonville Beach. This seal is most abundant in the North Atlantic off the coast of Canada and Greenland.

Habitat Preference: Hooded seals are animals of the open ocean and northern ice packs. They are highly migratory and usually occur in small groups. They are also deep divers, feeding mostly on clams, octopi, squid, shrimp, fish, and starfish.

Life History and Reproduction: Hooded seals are most gregarious during the breeding, migrating, and molting seasons. From March to June, they undertake long pelagic migrations from the birthing areas on the winter pack-ice off Labrador, northward to Greenland. In late summer they return southward to feed in waters off Newfoundland and Labrador.

In early spring, each female gives birth to a single pup that weighs about 50 pounds. The pups are nursed for only about two weeks and then abandoned by the mothers to fend for themselves. Adults mate immediately after the end of lactation, and breeding is monogamous. Therefore, the gestation period is about 11½ months long. Young seals grow very rapidly on the rich milk produced by their mothers. Young seals are not sexually mature until they are 4-6 years old. The maximum life expectancy exceeds 35 years. Sharks, polar bears, and killer whales are the primary predators of the hooded seal, in addition to man.

Economic Importance and Remarks: In arctic waters, hooded seals are extensively hunted for their pelts. The young seals or "blue-backs" have the most valuable and sought after fur. They are harvested in large numbers and are a significant economic factor in some northern countries.

Florida records of the hooded seal apparently represent lost and widely wandering individuals. No colonies or migratory groups of this seal have occurred in Florida waters in historic times.

ORDER SIRENIA
Manatees

The manatees or sea cows are a bizarre looking group of aquatic mammals found in coastal waters in tropical and subtropical areas. They are all massive, blimp-like vegetarians that sometimes occur in herds. They are also quite social and gentle creatures. The forelimbs are modified into paddle-like appendages, and the tail is stubby, muscular, and horizontally flattened into a broad spatulate flipper used for propulsion through the water. There are no hind limbs or dorsal fin present.

Manatees consume copious amounts of submerged and floating vegetation. They spend the winters inland in large spring-fed rivers and the warmer months in coastal marine waters. Sirenians can be solitary, live in pairs, or associate in larger social groups of various sizes.

Sirenians are considered the source of the legendary mermaid stories. Sailors returning from months or years at sea apparently let their imaginations run wild when they glimpsed the amorphous bodies of manatees in the water. The two mammary glands located in the chest area at the base of each front flipper for suckling the young no doubt contributed to the mermaid myth.

Sirenians occur along the coasts of warm seas and in the associated large rivers of southern Asia, northern Australia, eastern Africa, southern North America, and northern South America. In many areas of the world their populations have been decimated by man and his activities.

Manatees have no close relatives, but elephants and sirenians are believed to have evolved from a common ancestor. The cheek teeth of the two groups are very similar in their structure and replacement. They also share some other characteristics. Only one species of manatee lives in Florida waters, and there are only four living species of sirenians in the world.

Manatee *(Trichechus manatus)*

Description: This species, also called the West Indian manatee, is shaped like an overstuffed cigar, with a small, blunt head and no visible neck. The tail is broad and rounded; the forelimbs are short, stocky flippers; and hindlimbs are absent. The body is almost hairless and the thick, blubbery skin is dull gray to dusky gray in color. The snout is broad and square, and the lips are generously covered with short tactile bristles.

P. ROSE

manatee, 8-14 ft. (2.4-4.3 m) overall

The skull has a narrow, forward-projecting rostrum and the molar teeth wear off anteriorly and are replaced by the next ones in line posteriorly. The lower jaw is rather massive and curved slightly downward.

Geographical Range: Manatees occur throughout the marine coastal waters of Florida. In the winter months they reside in most of the large spring-fed rivers of both the east and west coasts of the state. In the United States, this species ranges from South Carolina along the south Atlantic coast and throughout the Gulf coast to the southern tip of Texas. It also occurs throughout most of the islands of the West Indies, the east coast of Mexico and Central America, and the north and east coasts of South America.

Habitat Preference: The West Indian manatee prefers shallow marine bays and estuaries during the warmer months of the year. When the ocean temperatures drop in the fall, manatees move into fresh water to spend the winter. They prefer the large spring-fed rivers because of the constant, relatively warm water temperatures during the winter months. They often congregate in large numbers near spring pools and in the channels downstream from the springs.

Life History and Reproduction: Manatees are intolerant of cold temperatures. Their metabolic rate is so low that they cannot maintain body heat when surrounding temperatures are below 65° F. In the winter, a long cold snap can result in the deaths of significant numbers due to colder than average water temperatures, pneumonia, and other respiratory ailments. During the winter, manatees congregate at warm water sources such as artesian springs and power plant discharges. They have a gentle disposition, are completely harmless to humans, and almost defenseless as well. Skin divers that swim among them are often ignored or at least tolerated with impunity. It is also not uncommon for them to come up to divers and solicit a back scratch.

In the winter, manatees usually gather in herds of 5-25 individuals to forage and socialize. Occasionally, larger congregations of 50 or more occur in especially favorable locations. Manatees can remain submerged for as long as 15 minutes, but normally they surface for a breath every 2-3 minutes.

When an adult female comes into heat, which can occur at any time during the year, several bulls follow her around and attempt to mate. Courtship activities include nuzzling and embracing a prospective mate, and actual copulation usually takes place in shallow water. The females are promiscuous, i.e., they mate with several pursuing males. Gestation is 12-13 months long, and a single calf (rarely two) is produced once every three to five years. More calves are born during spring and summer than at other times of the year. The pinkish babies weigh 30-60 pounds at birth and are about four feet long. The mother nudges her offspring to the surface to breathe immediately after birth, and holds it there for about an hour. After 4-5 hours, the baby can surface and breathe on its own without assistance. Calves nurse underwater at each of two mammary glands located in the mother's armpit regions. Young manatees start taking vegetation within a few months, but they remain with their mother for up to two years. Young females reach sexual maturity and start breeding at about 7 years of age.

Young males are seldom successful breeders even when sexually mature, because they must attain bulk and size to compete with the older bulls.

Adult manatees measure 8-14 feet long (but seldom exceed 12 feet), and weigh 600-2,600 pounds. The adult females are usually larger and heavier than the adult males. The maximum longevity of manatees in the wild is unknown, but it may approach 40-50 years; they have lived 35 years in zoos. There is presently no reliable method for determining the age of adult manatees. Man is the only predator of adult manatees, but sharks, alligators, and crocodiles may account for occasional mortality in the young.

Economic Importance and Remarks: Manatee meat was once considered a delicacy by early Indian cultures and pioneer Floridians. The hides made excellent leather, and oil derived from the blubber once was used for cooking and burned in lamps. The manatee is now protected as an endangered species by both the state and federal governments. The total population of manatees in Florida is estimated to be approximately 2,000 individuals, and its stability is not known. As with most endangered species, man is the major decimating factor that has reduced manatee populations. Boat propellers do the most damage by maiming and killing manatees. Many adults show the telltale scars of old or recent propeller injuries. In recent years, the state has launched a major campaign to post and enforce reduced boat speed limits in most manatee areas. More importantly, some areas near springs are now entirely closed to motor boats when manatees are present. Poaching, vandalism, and harassment by curious divers and swimmers are other causes of the manatee's demise influenced by man. The periodic outbreaks of red tide along the Gulf Coast of Florida are responsible for an undetermined number of manatee deaths.

Manatees are becoming more appreciated by the public for their unique aesthetic value to Florida. They are now major attractions in some areas, including Crystal River, Homossassa Springs, Manatee Springs, and Blue Springs, where tourists flock to enjoy the natural wonders of Florida's manatees and the waters they inhabit.

ORDER ARTIODACTYLA
Even-toed Hoofed Mammals

This group of mammals includes deer, elk, caribou, moose, pigs, cattle, antelopes, goats, llamas, camels, and sheep. The tips of the second and third toes on each foot support the weight of the body and are sheathed in large hooves. The other toes (called dewclaws) are reduced in size or absent. The limbs are elongate and some ankle and foot bones are fused to form a single lower leg or cannon bone.

A closely related group, the odd-toed hoofed mammals (order Perissodactyla), has no wild representatives in Florida, but includes our domestic horses, donkeys, mules, and asses, as well as tapirs and rhinoceroses. The odd-toed hoofed mammals bear the body weight either on one toe (the third) or on three toes (the second, third, and fourth).

Artiodactyls often have horns or antlers developed as outgrowths of the frontal bones. In the deer family they grow each year and are shed, but in the cattle family they are permanently growing structures that are not shed. All artiodactyls are herbivores, but they are variously adapted to feed on a wide variety of plant materials. Many of them have complex, multichambered stomachs (the first chamber is called a rumen), and will regurgitate food, chew it a second time, then swallow it again. The whole process is called rumination.

Species of artiodactyls occur throughout the world except Australia, New Zealand, and Antarctica. There were two species of native artiodactyls in Florida when the European explorers arrived. One of these, the bison or buffalo, has been extirpated; the other, the white-tailed deer, is still common. In addition, the Spaniards brought with them the domestic pig, which, when released, became a free-living wild species, the feral pig or wild boar, now widely established throughout Florida.

Wild Boar, Feral Pig *(Sus scrofa)*

Description: Wild pigs look much like domestic hogs except that they are lean and rangy, and have a narrower, longer skull with large, sharp tusks. The predominant pelage color of feral pigs is black, although spotted and mottled color patterns of black, brown, orange, russet, yellow, or white are also common. A hog population that I inventoried in central Florida consisted of 60 percent black individuals and 40 percent spotted. The pelage of feral pigs is coarser and denser than that of domestic hogs and presumably provides better protection against cold weather.

The skull is long and narrow with a downward-sloping forehead and snout. Males have enlarged sharp-edged, recurved canines in both upper and lower jaws that are formidable weapons. The tusks of females are small and inconspicuous by comparison. Cheek teeth are of the bunodont type, with low, rounded cusps.

Geographic Range: Wild hogs are not native to Florida but are said to have been first introduced by Hernando DeSoto in 1539, and later by many others. Feral populations now occur throughout much of the state. The range in the United States extends throughout the South from Virginia and Tennessee to Texas and Arkansas. Isolated populations also occur in California, Hawaii, Puerto Rico, and the Virgin Islands.

Habitat Preference: Wild hogs occupy a wide variety of plant communities in Florida but apparently prefer moist hardwood forests, swamp borders, mesic oak hammocks, and dense pine-palmetto flatwoods.

Life History and Reproduction: Wild hogs are omnivorous and forage extensively on food they pick up on the surface of the ground or just beneath the surface, found by rooting with their broad shovel-like noses. An area recently foraged by feral swine usually looks like an unevenly plowed field of dirt or mud.

Even-toed Hoofed Mammals

wild boar, 53.1-78.7 in. (135-200 cm) overall, tail 9.4-13 in. (24-33 cm)

They damage or eliminate many plants growing in the understory, eating large quantities of bulbs, roots, and tubers in the process. Hogs also love acorns, hickory nuts, pecans, seeds, mushrooms, fleshy fruits and berries. They also will consume all types of small animals including snakes, lizards, insects, grubs, arthropods, mice, baby birds, eggs, frogs, toads, worms, and even carrion. Wild pigs forage mainly from dusk until dawn, but occasionally they also are active during the daytime, especially in areas of heavy cover or on cloudy, overcast days.

Wild hogs breed throughout the year. When a female comes into estrus, she usually breeds repeatedly with the dominant boars in the area. After the dominant males have satisfied themselves, subordinate boars may then breed with the still receptive sow. Such breeding activities and fighting among the boars may extend over a two-day period. The gestation period is 112-114 days long and the litter size varies from 1-12 piglets, averaging about five. Baby pigs are precocial, born with their eyes open, fully haired, and able to walk and move about shortly after birth. The piglets grow rapidly and wean within a few weeks, but often remain with the female as a foraging family group for several months. Young sows can reach sexual maturity as young as three months of age. In central Florida, I collected one small sow that weighed only 50 pounds but her uterus bore three small embryos. Young boars reach puberty at about five months of age but rarely have an opportunity to breed until they are 12-18 months old, due to dominance by the older males.

Feral hogs characteristically travel in herds composed of several adult females and their offspring of various ages. Adult boars are usually solitary except at breeding time. Feral pigs often forage in groups, sometimes concentrating their

Even-toed Hoofed Mammals   143 activities in a fairly confined area. Movement within the home range is often linked to seasonal changes in the type of food available. Average home range size varies from 500-750 acres, depending on habitat quality and density of cover.

The age of young wild hogs can be determined by the sequence of tooth eruptions, and as they age, by tooth wear of the molars. The weight of the eye lens is also an accurate alternative method of determining the age of a dead animal. In the wild, feral hogs usually live a maximum of 10-15 years. In captivity, some have lived for 20 years.

Other than man and his dogs, feral hogs do not have many enemies. In the few areas where bears or panthers remain, hogs, along with deer, can be preyed upon by these carnivores. Young pigs are sometimes also taken by alligators, bobcats, and possibly coyotes.

Economic Importance and Remarks: Wild boars are a major big game animal in Florida. They provide, along with deer, a significant share of big game sport hunting in the South. Wild hog meat is a significant part of the diet of some rural Florida families. The heads of large boars with large tusks are often mounted and proudly displayed as trophy specimens. Florida property owners are allowed to harvest the feral hogs living on their land on a year-round basis.

Feral pigs seriously damage most types of groundcover while foraging. Some delicate and rare plants and animals can be completely decimated by foraging hogs. Particularly vulnerable are orchids, ferns, lilies, bog plants, bird eggs, amphibians, and small reptiles. Hogs also compete for mast (acorns, nuts, and seeds) with several species of desirable native wildlife including wild turkey, white-tailed deer, quail, and squirrels. Also, at the edges of many urbanizing areas, they cause damage to lawns, golf course greens and fairways, road shoulders, parks, and recreational areas. In regions where hogs have rooted extensively, runoff water has greater volume and lower overall quality than in adjacent areas with good groundcover.

Problem wild hogs can be readily trapped and removed using corral-type pens having trigger-release, swinging trapdoors, baited with rancid corn. Multiple catches of sows and young pigs are frequent in these traps, but wily old boars are often difficult to lure into the corral. Boars and smaller pigs are readily captured using trained "hog dogs" such as pit bulldogs and trailing hounds. Most trained dogs will lock their jaws on the ears of a cornered wild boar, or wherever they can secure a hold, and hang on until the hunter arrives to tie up or dispatch the pig. There is a high injury and mortality rate in hunting dogs from the slashing tusks of the boars.

White-tailed Deer (Odocoileus virginianus)

Description: White-tailed deer are moderately large, have long, slender legs, and a broad well-haired tail that flashes white on the underside. Antlers are present only in males (bucks), and are formed and shed each year. The pointed antler branches are called tines. Deer walk on the tips of the toes, which are sheathed in hooves. The upper parts of the white-tailed deer are grayish brown

Even-toed Hoofed Mammals

to russet brown, and the underparts and insides of the legs are white. They have a white eye ring, a white spot around the rostrum, and the cow-like ears are large.

The skull can be identified by the presence of bifurcating antlers or antler pedicles on the frontal bones in bucks. Both males and females lack upper incisor and canine teeth, and there is a gap in the bones (lacrimal opening) in front of the eye socket that measures at least one-half inch wide.

Geographical Range: White-tailed deer occur throughout the state of Florida, and include the small-bodied, short-legged Key deer of the lower Florida Keys. The range in the United States is nationwide, except portions of the arid southwestern states and western mountain areas. The species also ranges through Mexico and much of Central America and northern South America. In the eastern two-thirds of the United States, it is usually the only species of deer present.

Habitat Preference: White-tailed deer occur at least sparingly in most nonaquatic habitats in Florida. They are probably most abundant in various forest edge habitats, where they can find both good cover and ample forage.

Life History and Reproduction: White-tailed deer are mainly browsing mammals, which means they feed upon the twigs, leaves, and tender shoots of many trees and shrubs. They forage mainly from dusk to dawn and bed down in a thicket or clump of dense grass during the daytime. On cloudy, overcast days or when they are hungry, deer may also forage during daylight hours. In the fall, acorns are an important food; they also eat fruits, berries, and mushrooms when available.

Individual home ranges of white-tailed deer are not as large as might be expected. Bucks have larger home ranges, averaging 1 to 1½ square miles; those of does average ½ to ¾ square mile. During the mating season, bucks may cover an even larger area in search of females. Deer have several scent glands located on the legs, near the hooves. These glands are important in marking scent posts and trails, which aid deer in locating each other. They have a keen sense of smell, as well as good hearing and excellent eyesight.

The breeding season for white-tails is long in Florida, extending from September to early March. Most of the does are impregnated in the fall; those not breeding are usually young does of the previous year which are late in reaching sexual maturity or have foraged on poor range. Each doe is in heat only for about 24 hours, and should she not encounter a buck during this period, she will recycle each lunar month (every 28 days) for 4-5 times until bred. The gestation period is 6½ to 7 months long and averages 202 days. The litter size is 1-3 fawns, but the average is two. Young females breeding for the first time usually produce a single offspring. On poor deer range, even older females are likely to produce one fawn each year instead of the normal two. At birth, a fawn weighs 3-7 pounds. They are precocial, with eyes open, and they are able to run about shortly after birth. Fawns are well camouflaged by their color of pale white or creamy spots on a cinnamon brown background. They hide motionless in thick vegetation while the mother is away foraging. They also have almost no scent, which make them very difficult for predators to locate.

white-tailed deer, 55.1-80.7 in. (140-205 cm) overall, tail 7.9-13.8 in. (20-35 cm)

When the fawns are 3-4 weeks old they begin to follow the doe about and start eating some solid food. Fawns are usually weaned when 3-4 months old, and the spots fade at that time, giving them a uniform brown coloration on the upper parts. Young deer usually continue to accompany their mother until they are old enough to breed. Some young females breed at 6-8 months of age, but most does and all bucks are about 1½ years old before they are part of the breeding population.

In the wild, the majority of white-tails do not survive to old age, especially if they are hunted. Most deer harvested in Florida are between 1½ to 3½ years old. A few deer (especially does that aren't hunted) will survive in the wild about 15 years. The maximum longevity in a zoo is about 25 years. The oldest bucks do not possess the largest antlers. Antler size peaks during the prime of breeding life (usually 6-10 years old), after which the antlers of aging males decline in size. Deer age classes are determined by analyzing the sequence of tooth replacement and by measuring tooth wear.

Economic Importance and Remarks: The white-tailed deer is the primary big game mammal throughout most of the eastern United States. State wildlife departments have historically put more emphasis on its study and management than any other game species. Deer hunting is a major recreational business with strong economic impact in most rural, undeveloped areas of our state.

White-tailed deer sometimes cause agricultural damage by foraging heavily on field crops or gardens. They can usually be frightened away with noise-making devices or excluded with electrified fences.

Even-toed Hoofed Mammals

Young deer are sometimes kept as pets but this is against state wildlife regulations and can even be dangerous. If the fawn grows up to be a buck, there is particular risk from the antlers. Bucks in rut become extremely aggressive and joust with other males to determine dominance for breeding. There are recorded cases of owners of previously docile deer being attacked, injured, or even killed by their pets in rut. During rut, deer become very aggressive and combative due to the presence of certain sex hormones in their systems.

Antler growth and maturation in male deer is controlled largely by the male hormone, testosterone. Antlers grow from skin-covered buds on the frontal bones, richly supplied with blood vessels that transport calcium, phosphorus, and other building materials for antler formation. As antlers grow longer and branch, they are always covered with soft, fuzzy skin called velvet. By early fall, antler growth is complete and the blood supply to the velvet is cut off because of hormonal changes. The velvet dies and sluffs off, leaving the hard bone-like antlers we are accustomed to seeing. Bucks vigorously rub and polish the antlers on shrubs and saplings, usually leaving evidence in the form of broken branches and stripped bark. Antlers remain functional throughout the fall and winter months. In the late winter or early spring, a portion of the bony core of the antler is resorbed near the antler base, causing a weak zone called the abscission layer. The antlers then break off because of the weakened zone, usually one at a time, and this completes the annual cycle. Bucks are then antlerless for 6-8 weeks before the buds on the frontal bone begin to grow again.

Most of the races of white-tailed deer found in Florida are small compared to populations farther north. The extreme example is the short-legged, small-bodied Key deer living on Big Pine Key and adjacent islands. This race is adapted to living in the thick tropical brushlands characteristic of that area, where smaller body size and shorter legs are an advantage. The Florida Keys form of the eastern white-tailed deer is officially listed as "endangered" by the federal government and state of Florida. It has declined in numbers in recent years for three reasons: increased roadkills on the busy Overseas Highway to Key West and other roads; increased poaching by certain residents of the area; decreasing habitat availability as new homes, vacation resorts, and businesses are built in the Lower Keys.

The largest white-tailed deer living in Florida are found in the panhandle counties. Nearly all those bucks approaching "Boone-and-Crocket" class have been taken along the northern tier of counties.

Deer do not regulate their own population numbers, and they gradually increase in density to the point of damaging and reducing the carrying capacity of their habitat or range. Large carnivores such as the panther or wolf at one time probably helped offset this innate tendency of deer to overpopulate, but they are now rare or absent, so there is no regulator of deer populations except man. The carefully controlled harvest of surplus animals in the deer population is desirable and necessary for the future health of the species. The major problem is securing accurate data on the annual production of new deer each year so a significant overharvest or underharvest of the breeding stock does not occur.

Packs of stray dogs sometimes run, harass, or even kill white-tailed deer. Free-running dogs should be eliminated from deer habitat to ensure the well-being and survival of white-tails. In Florida, bobcats, coyotes, and bears take a few fawns, and the panther, where it still exists, needs the white-tailed deer in large numbers to thrive.

Sambar Deer *(Cervus unicolor)*

Description: This introduced species is an elk-sized deer, several times larger than Florida's native white-tailed deer. The hair of the sambar deer is coarse and ranges from dark chocolate brown in winter to rusty chestnut brown in summer. Calves are brown and unspotted. They have a large muzzle, broad ears, and a black-tipped bushy tail that is about one foot long. Antlers are well developed and present only in males. The skull is marked by the presence of small canines in the upper jaw of most individuals.

Geographical Range: The sambar deer was introduced from India to St. Vincent Island, Franklin County, Florida in 1908 by the owner of the island. See map on page 205. The initial release consisted of only four animals, but they thrived and multiplied to several hundred animals within several decades. Individuals occasionally swim the short distance from St. Vincent Island to the

F.G.&F.W.F.C.

sambar deer, 78.7-102.4 in. (200-260 cm) overall, tail 7.9-14.2 in. (20-36 cm)

mainland, but these have been shot by hunters, preventing their establishment in the Florida Panhandle.

The range of the sambar deer in southeastern Asia includes India, Sri Lanka, Burma, South China, Taiwan, Thailand, Malaysia, Sumatra, Borneo, Celebes, and the Philippines.

Habitat Preference: Studies on St. Vincent Island reveal that sambar deer favor wetland habitats, particularly freshwater marshes and adjacent dense brush and trees. Most of the freshwater marshes occur on the eastern half of St. Vincent, and 80 percent of the sambar deer population occurs there.

Life History and Reproduction: Sambar deer on St. Vincent Island breed over a ten-month period from September to June. The peak of the rut occurs in midwinter (December-February). Females (or hinds) usually produce one calf per year, but twins are born on rare occasions. Stags are sexually mature at 1½ years, but the older dominant males

148   Even-toed Hoofed Mammals

do most of the breeding. Hinds do not become sexually active until 2½ years old. The gestation period is approximately eight months. Calves are born in the summer, fall, and winter.

Adults lived up to 12-15 years on St. Vincent when it was an unhunted population. The present population on the islands is estimated to be 150-200 individuals. Much of the diet of the sambar consists of aquatic plants.

Economic Importance and Remarks: Florida's sambar deer have been under federal jurisdiction since 1968 when the U.S. Fish and Wildlife Service took control of St. Vincent Island as a wildlife refuge. Initial federal plans were to remove these exotic deer from the refuge. However, they proved difficult to trap and local opposition to the plan was strong. It was eventually decided that the sambar population should be retained and managed as a game animal. A controlled harvest of sambar deer by public hunts was begun in 1987 to help keep the population at proper density.

ORDER CETACEA
Whales

The whales, dolphins, and porpoises are wholly aquatic mammals, found almost exclusively in salt water. There are two major subgroups of cetaceans with markedly different feeding mechanisms and physical characteristics. One group is the toothed whales, which possess varying numbers of well-developed cone-shaped teeth in the mouth. The other group is the baleen whales, which are completely toothless and obtain their food by filtering large quantities of water through their strainer-like mouthparts (called baleen plates), trapping the small marine organisms that they eat. The baleen whales are the largest creatures that have ever lived on the earth. The blue whale or sulphur-bottomed whale is the largest species of the group, sometimes attaining a length of 100 feet and a weight of 200 tons.

All cetaceans have a streamlined body shaped like a torpedo or cigar, adapted for moving through water with minimal resistance. Their hides are smooth, thick, and hair is virtually absent. Their tails are broad and flat, designed for propulsion with an up-and-down motion of the body torso. Whales have relatively large brains proportional to body size, and they appear to have a fairly high level of intelligence. They also have a well developed biological sonar or echolocation system. Whales emit sounds that bounce off objects in the water, and they navigate in response to the echoes returning to their ears.

There are 28 species of whales recorded from the marine waters surrounding Florida. The names dolphin and porpoise are applied to the smaller species of toothed whales.

Rough-toothed Dolphin *(Steno bredanensis)*

Description: The rough-toothed dolphin is small (6-8 feet long), has a purplish-black back, and yellowish-white to pinkish-white spots on the sides. The beak and underparts are white, tinged with rose or purple. The snout is long and slender and is not set off from the rest of the head by a groove or indentation. The flippers and tail flukes are dark.

The skull is very similar to the bottle-nosed dolphin's skull, but the rostrum is much longer and slimmer. The teeth all have rough vertical ridges and wrinkles on their outer surfaces, giving the species its common name. There are 20-27 teeth present in each side of the upper and lower jaws.

Geographical Range: The rough-toothed dolphin has been recorded rarely in Florida waters. It occurs in both the Atlantic Ocean and the Gulf of Mexico, but seldom is stranded or washed ashore. It also occurs in the Pacific Ocean, Indian Ocean, Mediterranean Sea, and Red Sea.

Habitat Preference: This species lives in warm temperate and tropical seas, usually far from shore, off the edge of the continental shelf.

Life History and Reproduction: The habits of this dolphin are virtually unknown, but a group of 16 individuals became stranded the night of 29 May 1961 near Rock Island in Taylor County, Florida, which indicates they are social and travel in groups. The reasons for the stranding of a sizeable herd are unknown. Examination of stomach contents revealed octopus beaks and marine algae.

Economic Importance and Remarks: This small pelagic species has no economic importance. It is only rarely encountered by man.

rough-toothed dolphin, 6-8 ft. (1.8-2.4 m) overall

Whales

Long-snouted Spinner Dolphin *(Stenella longirostris)*

Description: The long-snouted spinner dolphin is small (6-7 feet long), grayish black on the back grading to gray on the sides, and white on the belly. The pectoral fins are black, as are the lips of the beak.

The rostrum of the skull is extremely long and slender, more than twice the length of the cranial portion of the skull. There are 47-64 teeth present on each side of the upper and lower jaws.

Geographical Range: This dolphin species has been recorded occasionally in Florida waters. It occurs in both the Atlantic Ocean and the Gulf of Mexico but is infrequently stranded or washed ashore. It also occurs in the Indian Ocean and eastern Pacific Ocean.

Habitat Preference: This species lives in warm temperate and tropical seas and prefers the deeper, open areas of the ocean well away from shore.

Life History and Reproduction: The habits of the long-snouted spinner dolphin are poorly known, but there is some evidence from the species of fish and squid found in stomach contents that they feed at considerable depths (800 feet or more). They occur in herds of up to several hundred individuals. They are called spinner dolphins because of their habit of spinning or rotating around the long axis when jumping clear of the water. The reasons for this behavior are unknown. A stranding of 36 long-snouted spinner dolphins on 23 September 1961, at Dog Island, Franklin County, Florida, strongly indicates their social nature and tendency to travel in sizeable herds.

Economic Importance and Remarks: This species is frequently seen in the company of schools of tuna in the Pacific Ocean. Fishermen keep a lookout for these dolphins as an indication of where and when to set purse seines. As a result, many are accidentally drowned because of entanglement in tuna nets. Regulations and modification of the nets have recently been adopted to encourage escape of the helpful porpoises before drowning occurs.

J. S. LEATHERWOOD

long-snouted spinner dolphin, 6-7 ft. (1.8-2.1 m) overall

Long-snouted spinner dolphins appear to take a particular delight in riding the bow wave of ships; they often continue this behavior for considerable distances.

Short-snouted Spinner Dolphin *(Stenella clymene)*

Description: Also called the clymene dolphin (from the Greek *klymenos* meaning celebrated, perhaps in reference to its spectacular spinning behavior), this species is small (5 to 6½ feet long), the back is black to dark gray with lighter gray on the sides, and the belly is white. The pectoral fins are black and the beak has white on the top, a black tip and black lips.

The skull is similar to the long-snouted spinner dolphin, but the rostrum is slightly shorter and more stout. There are 38-49 teeth present on each side of the upper and lower jaws.

Geographical Range: The short-snouted spinner dolphin occurs in the Atlantic Ocean from New Jersey to the northern edge of South America. It has been taken in Florida on both the Atlantic and Gulf coasts.

Habitat Preference: This species lives in warm temperate and tropical seas and prefers the open ocean and deep coastal waters near islands.

Life History and Reproduction: Until recently, the short-snouted spinner dolphin was confused with the long-snouted spinner dolphin and clearly has similar habits. This species also spins while jumping clear of the water, although it does not jump as high above the surface nor are its maneuvers as complex as in the long-snouted spinner dolphin. Very few species of dolphin spin while breaching, and the purpose of the spinning movement is unknown. The diet of the short-snouted spinner dolphin is small fishes and squids.

Economic Importance and Remarks: This dolphin was only recently recognized as a separate species, and it apparently has little economic impact.

short-snouted spinner dolphin, 5-7 ft. (1.5-2.1 m) overall

Whales

striped dolphin, 6-9 ft. (1.8-2.7 m) overall

Striped Dolphin *(Stenella coeruleoalba)*

Description: The striped dolphin or Gray's dolphin is small (6-9 feet long), bluish black on the upper side, and white below. A narrow black stripe runs from the eye along the side to the anus, with two shorter stripes branching off and extending toward the base of the pectoral fin. The lips are black and each eye has a dark ring around it.

The skull has a rostrum that is almost 1½ times the length of the cranium, and there are 39-55 teeth present on each side of the upper and lower jaws.

Geographical Range: The striped dolphin has been recorded rarely in Florida waters. It occurs in the Atlantic Ocean and the Gulf of Mexico, but only occasionally is stranded or washed ashore. It occurs widely throughout the oceans of the world.

Habitat Preference: This species lives in warmer temperate and tropical seas, usually far from shore in the pelagic zone.

Life History and Reproduction: Little is known about the life habits of this beautiful dolphin. They often occur in large pods of several hundred individuals. They feed at mid-depths on squids, fishes, and crustaceans. They are sometimes observed riding the bow wave of ships.

Economic Importance and Remarks: This small pelagic species has some limited economic importance. Like the long-snouted spinner dolphins, they often travel with schools of tuna, and this association tells fishermen where to set purse seines. Many striped dolphins are accidentally drowned when trapped in the nets. Procedures have been adopted that help reduce these wasteful losses of the striped dolphin.

Whales

Atlantic Spotted Dolphin *(Stenella frontalis)*

Description: The Atlantic spotted dolphin is small (6-8 feet long), dark purplish gray heavily flecked with small spots of white on the upper side. The underside is whitish and densely spotted with dark gray. The lips are white blotched with gray, and there is a distinct transverse groove at the base of the beak. A light-colored line extends from the eyes to the base of each flipper.

The skull is similar to that of the striped dolphin but it has fewer teeth. There are 34-37 teeth present on each side in the upper and lower jaws.

Geographical Range: The Atlantic spotted dolphin is found in the Atlantic Ocean from North Carolina southward to the Caribbean Sea. It is moderately common in the Gulf of Mexico, mainly in offshore waters. This species also ranges in the tropical Atlantic southward to northern South America.

Habitat Preference: This dolphin lives in both warm temperate and tropical seas, preferring deep water (over 100 fathoms) at least five miles from shore.

Life History and Reproduction: The Atlantic spotted dolphin travels in social groups or pods of various sizes and forages well offshore in pelagic waters. Deep-sea fishermen often report seeing them in groups of a dozen or more, breaking the water in unison in graceful arcs. They sometimes frolic about ships or boats, and can swim at 12-15 knots. Their diet is primarily squids and fishes. Atlantic spotted dolphins occur in herds of up to several hundred individuals.

Copulation has been observed in July in the northern Gulf of Mexico off the Florida coast. Like most dolphins, the female gives birth to a single calf about nine months after mating. The baby usually swims alongside the mother, staying between the front flipper and the tail fluke, the two rising and sinking in unison.

Suckerfish up to two feet long sometimes attach to Atlantic spotted dolphins and are carried along like trailing streamers in the water. This is probably the basis for the erroneous tale, often repeated, that baby spotted dolphins are towed along grasping a front flipper or tail fluke.

Economic Importance and Remarks: This small deep-water dolphin has no known economic importance. It is common enough in offshore waters that its biology could be studied more intensively.

D. O'DELL

Atlantic spotted dolphin, 6-8 ft. (1.8-2.4 m) overall

Whales

pantropical dolphin, 5-7 ft. (1.5-2.1 m) overall

Pantropical Dolphin *(Stenella attenuata)*

Description: The pantropical dolphin is small (5-7 feet long), its back is dark gray fading to light gray on the sides and belly, and there are small light gray spots scattered throughout dorsally and small dark gray spots scattered throughout ventrally. There is a distinct beak with white or pinkish lips. The sides of the head are light gray, and there is a black circle around each eye. A broad, black stripe extends from the corner of the mouth to the base of the front flipper.

The rostrum is less than twice the length of the cranium; there are 35-47 teeth present on each side of the upper and lower jaws.

Geographical Range: The pantropical dolphin has been recorded sparingly in Florida waters. It occurs in both the Atlantic Ocean and the Gulf of Mexico, as far south as the Lesser Antilles.

Habitat Preference: This species lives in warm temperate and tropical waters, usually well offshore, but occasionally near coastal areas and islands.

Life History and Reproduction: These dolphins travel in small herds of 5-30 individuals and often ride the bow waves of ships. They feed on fishes, shrimps, and squids. Very little is known about their life history.

Economic Importance and Remarks: The pantropical dolphin has little or no economic importance. Specimens of this rare dolphin have been recorded for Florida mainly during and after severe oceanic storms.

Saddle-backed Dolphin *(Delphinus delphis)*

Description: The saddle-backed dolphin or common dolphin is small (6 to 8½ feet long), black on the upper side, and the sides are marked with hour-glass (or saddle-shaped) patterns of yellow or tan mixed with bands of white. The underparts are white and there are two narrow black lines that bifurcate on the side in the tail region and extend forward along the flank, one passing through the black front flipper. Each eye is surrounded by a black circle, from which a black line runs forward to the base of the beak.

Whales   155

saddle-backed dolphin, 6-8.5 ft. (1.8-2.6 cm) overall

The rostrum is about 1½ times the length of the cranium, and two long grooves run just inside the tooth rows on the roof of the mouth. There are 48-50 teeth present on each side of the upper and lower jaws.

Geographical Range: The saddle-backed dolphin occurs in both the Atlantic Ocean and Gulf of Mexico, off both coasts of Florida. It is seldom stranded or washed ashore on beaches. The species occurs widely throughout most of the oceans of the world.

Habitat Preference: This species lives in both temperate and tropical seas, usually well offshore over the outer continental shelf.

Life History and Reproduction: Groups of saddle-backed dolphins are often sighted during the summer months 70-100 miles off the coast of Florida. They are fast swimmers and have been clocked at speeds of up to 30 miles per hour. Although the common dolphin is an offshore pelagic species, it occasionally enters the mouths of large, deep rivers. It also migrates northward during the summer months, following schools of fish. These dolphins are social, occurring in groups of ten to a thousand or more. They feed almost exclusively on fishes and squids living near the surface. In captivity, saddle-backed dolphins are timid and much less aggressive than bottle-nosed dolphins. Females produce a single offspring per pregnancy, born from midwinter to summer after a gestation period of about nine months.

Economic Importance and Remarks: In those areas where saddle-backed dolphins are abundant, they no doubt have some impact on schools of small fishes and squids. Their impact is of minor economic importance.

These dolphins are bow-wave riders and often come to a boat from considerable distances. Once on the bow wave, they may ride for extended periods.

Fraser's Dolphin *(Lagenodelphis hosei)*

Description: Fraser's dolphin is small (6-8 feet long), robust in build, and has a very short beak. The body is dark gray on the back and tail, but white on the belly, with a pronounced, narrow, and dark lateral stripe running from the rostrum to the tail. Above that, there is a creamy-white band beginning on the head and running almost to the tail. A second creamy-white band lies below the lateral dark stripe, and parallel to it, separating the gray color of the side from the white belly. There is also a dark gray ring around each eye, and the rostrum and pectoral flippers are dark gray. There is also a thin dark line running from the base of each pectoral flipper forward to the corner of the mouth.

The rostrum is short and broad, and there are 40-44 teeth present on each side of the upper and lower jaws.

Geographical Range: Fraser's dolphin has been recorded in Florida in the Marquesas Keys in Monroe County, at the extreme southwestern tip of the state. In the world, the species is known only from a few scattered specimens taken in the tropical Pacific and Atlantic Oceans.

Habitat Preference: This dolphin normally occurs well out at sea in warm tropical waters.

Life History and Reproduction: So few specimens of Fraser's dolphin have been taken or observed that its biology is poorly known. They are fast, aggressive swimmers and appear to be deep divers. One specimen taken near the island of St. Vincent in the Lesser Antilles contained large red shrimp, fish otoliths (ear bones), squid beaks, and isopods.

The record of Fraser's dolphin in the Marquesas Keys occurred in the fall of 1981, and constitutes a mass stranding of at least 17 individuals and probably more. Only the skulls and skeletons remained by the time the discovery was made. This evidence verifies that Fraser's dolphin is gregarious and travels in sizeable herds.

Economic Importance and Remarks: Fraser's dolphin has no economic importance. There have been several records of this species in the Atlantic Ocean recently, where none existed before, a possible indication that it has become slightly more common than in the past.

T. WALKER

Fraser's dolphin, 6-8 ft. (1.8-2.4 m) overall

Whales

bottle-nosed dolphin, 8-12 ft. (2.4-3.7 m) overall

Bottle-nosed Dolphin *(Tursiops truncatus)*

Description: The bottle-nosed dolphin is small (8-12 feet long), purplish gray to light gray on the upper side, and whitish on the underside back to the anus. The front flippers are dark gray.

The rostrum of the skull is short, about the same length as the cranium. There are only 20-26 teeth present on each side of the upper and lower jaws.

Geographical Range: The bottle-nosed dolphin is abundant in the coastal and inshore marine waters throughout Florida. In the Atlantic, it occurs from Massachusetts southward through the Caribbean and Gulf of Mexico to South America. Bottle-nosed dolphins are found in coastal areas throughout most of the oceans and seas of the world.

Habitat Preference: This species prefers the shallow-water coastal and estuarine areas along our shores. It is found in largest numbers near passes connecting larger bays with the ocean and is also present in back bays having lower salinity. It is the only whale commonly seen in Florida's inshore waters. Bottle-nosed dolphin are frequently observed just beyond the surf in the open ocean but are seldom found beyond the 100 fathom line.

Life History and Reproduction: More is known about the life habits of this small whale than about any other cetacean. It is abundant inshore and very adaptable to life in an oceanarium, so it can be studied readily. This is the species most commonly trained to perform the interesting acrobatic feats that so successfully hold the spectator's interest. A bottle-nosed dolphin was also used to portray *Flipper* of television and movie fame. Some oceanaria, in addition to presenting public entertainment, have also conducted research on the biology of these dolphins.

Whales

Breeding activity peaks in March and April. The adult males fight viciously for breeding dominance and acquire numerous battle scars. Posturing on the part of a male is the initial feature of courting behavior, which includes rubbing, stroking, nuzzling, mouthing, snapping the jaws shut, and barking. The male frequently positions himself vertically in front of the female with his body held in an S-shaped curve. The pair also swims about near each other, with their bodies in contact. Copulation occurs when the female rolls over on her side, presenting her lower surface to the male. The act lasts for only 10 seconds or less but is usually repeated several times.

The gestation period is about 12 months and one calf is produced every other year, beginning when a female is about six years old. Births occur from February to May and the single baby dolphin emerges tailfirst. A newborn bottle-nosed dolphin weighs about 30 pounds, is approximately 3½ feet long, and is precocial, able to move about and fend for itself. Each infant swims well from the moment of birth and immediately surfaces to breathe. If the newborn hesitates in any way, the mother will push it up to the surface to take its first breath. Babies start suckling milk almost immediately from one of two mammary glands. During the first month of life, the calf stays very close to its mother, but gradually it gains confidence and moves about some on its own. Weaning, however, does not occur until the young are about 1½ years old.

The groups (or pods) of bottle-nosed dolphins have a definite social hierarchy in the males, with dominance being closely associated with large body size. Jaw-snapping is one of the main forms of antagonistic behavior employed. The females do not appear to compete in or form part of the hierarchy.

The diet consists of various common fish species, including mullet, sheepshead, pinfish, pufferfish, speckled trout, black drum, eels, catfish, flounder, croaker, and sand trout. They also sometimes eat shrimp, crabs, and squids.

Bottle-nosed dolphins have a wide range of vocalizations. Some of these are used in a system of echolocation or biological sonar. Dolphins not only locate objects by sound, but they also can discriminate between objects of different shape and size.

Dolphins will sometimes cooperate to support an unfortunate individual at the surface to permit it to breathe when in trouble. Usually two dolphins place their heads beneath the front fins of the injured or sick companion and buoy it to the surface to breathe. The swimming speed of the bottle-nosed dolphin has often been exaggerated. Actual measurements in captivity of a frightened, rapidly swimming dolphin, have recorded maximum speeds of only 12 miles per hour.

In captivity, bottle-nosed dolphins are very playful and demonstrate intelligence. They can be trained to perform fairly complicated tasks. In recent years the U.S. Navy has successfully trained them to retrieve various objects from considerable depths, including divers in trouble and bombs.

Economic Importance and Remarks: The bottle-nosed dolphin is an important asset to various oceanaria because of its trained dolphin acts. This species is regarded highly for its aesthetic value and intelligence.

Bottle-nosed dolphins sometimes become entangled in and damage shrimp or fishing nets set in coastal and near-offshore areas. They also eat some shrimp and crabs that also are harvested by man.

Other than humans, bottle-nosed dolphins have no natural enemies except sharks. Some of the larger, more aggressive species of sharks occasionally attack, kill, and eat bottle-nosed dolphins. Dolphins sometimes defend themselves quite successfully by ramming the attacking shark in the gill region. It is not uncommon to find dolphins with healed or partially healed shark bites.

During the whaling era in the United States, the bottle-nosed dolphin supported a fishery based out of Cape Hatteras, North Carolina. The meat was marketed in eastern cities and the oil was used for lamps. All dolphins are now protected by state law from wanton killing, as well as by federal law (The Marine Mammal Protection Act).

False Killer Whale *(Pseudorca crassidens)*

Description: The false killer whale is medium-sized (12-20 feet long), uniformly black over the entire body, and sometimes is marked with white on the lips. There is no beak, and the head is narrow and bulbous. The flippers have a broad hump near the middle of the front margin. The false killer whale has a much shorter and more curved dorsal fin than the killer whale.

The rostrum is short, stout, and broad. There are only 8-11 teeth present on each side of the upper and lower jaws.

Geographical Range: The false killer whale has been recorded occasionally along both of Florida's coasts and is known mainly from infrequent mass strandings on the beach. It occurs throughout most of the oceans of the world.

Habitat Preference: This species lives in warm temperate, subtropical, and tropical seas, usually in deep water far from land.

Life History and Reproduction: False killer whales are social animals that usually live in large pods. On 11 January 1970, a total of 150-175 individuals stranded and died along the Atlantic coast between Vero Beach in Indian River County and Ft. Pierce in St. Lucie County. Most of these animals were 12-15 feet long, with males averaging 2-3 feet longer than females. The sex ratio was about equal, and one calf, 4½ feet long, was reported among the group. A female was autopsied and showed evidence of having recently given birth. Other mass strandings have occurred in Florida from time to time, but far fewer animals were involved. Large pelagic fishes and squids have been found in the stomachs of beached false killer whales.

Breeding apparently can occur year-round. Dissections of pregnant females stranded around the world in various months of the year have revealed fetuses of different sizes and stages of development. The young are 5½ to 6½ feet long at birth.

Economic Importance and Remarks: False killer whales sometimes steal fish from both commercial fishing and sport fishing lines. In some open ocean areas where they are abundant, there may be some impact on the numbers of large pelagic fish species.

Killer Whale *(Orcinus orca)*

Description: The killer whale is the largest member of its family (length 20-30 feet). The upper parts are black except for a prominent white patch behind each eye and a light gray or white saddle behind the tall dorsal fin. In adult females and juveniles, the dorsal fin is somewhat curved backward (falcate), but it is very tall and straight in adult males. The underparts are white, light tan, or pale yellow. The underside of the tail flukes is white, but the front fins and large dorsal fin are entirely black. Males are larger than females.

The rostrum is broad—at its base the width is more than one-half the length. There are 10-14 large teeth present in each side of the upper and lower jaws. The teeth are robust, long, and large in diameter at the base (up to one inch across).

Geographical Range: The killer whale occurs sparingly off the Atlantic and Gulf coasts of Florida, but they are seldom stranded or washed ashore. It has a widespread distribution in most of the oceans of the world. A group of six killer whales were videotaped 40 miles south of Pensacola in July, 1989. They ranged in size from 6 to 20 feet long.

Habitat Preference: This species prefers to forage near the surface in cool to cold coastal marine waters. It occasionally enters large rivers and ventures into subtropical and tropical waters, but it is most abundant in the Arctic and Antarctic.

Life History and Reproduction: Killer whales have an amazing range of temperature tolerance, occurring from polar seas to tropical waters at the equator. They forage in small packs or pods of 5-50 animals and have a reputation of being ferocious in their feeding habits. The packs travel in close association and sometimes simultaneously attack prey much larger than themselves, such as a baleen whale. Killer whales have been known to slash, tear, and wound baleen whales mortally during an attack. They are impressive predators that can swim extremely fast, reaching top speeds of over 30 miles per hour. Killer whales feed on a wide range of species including seals, other whales, large fishes, squids, sea turtles, and marine birds. The approach of a pack of killer whales usually panics most marine vertebrates in the vicinity. When the killer whale observes a bird or seal near the edge of an arctic ice pack, it sometimes dives deeply and rushes to the surface, breaking ice up to two feet thick and knocking the prey into the water.

Killer whales are very social animals, traveling, hunting, resting, feeding, and playing together in a pod, apparently for their entire lives. Different pods occupying the same general range sometimes (usually in summer and fall) join for a few days to form "superpods" of over 150 individuals.

Killer whales reach sexual maturity when they are about 12 years old. Mating occurs in the spring and summer in the Pacific Northwest, but in warmer waters breeding has been reported during the end of the year. The gestation period is long, averaging about 16 months. A single offspring about 6-8 feet long is produced no more often than once every third year. Some females breed less

Whales

false killer whale, 8-12 ft. (2.4-3.7 m) overall

killer whale, 20-30 ft. (6.1-9.1 m) overall

Whales

frequently and produce a calf only once every 6-7 years. A few researchers believe that killer whales may live as long as 100 years, but this is not verified.

The first baby killer whale to be born and survive in captivity was produced at Sea World near Orlando, Florida, on 26 September 1985. It was a female, six feet long, and weighed about 350 pounds at birth. The baby was born head first, and was released rather explosively from the mother as she swam in labor rapidly about the tank in spiraling circles. In 2½ weeks the young killer whale had grown to 7½ feet long and weighed about 700 pounds, as a result of drinking up to 10 gallons of her mother's milk each day.

The social groups of killer whales appear to be centered around the adult females. Most pods are composed of older females and their offspring of various ages. Some females first observed as calves were still associated with their mother's pod ten years later, and this female family group type of association may go on for life. The males also form small pods, apparently of shorter duration.

Killer whales emit a series of clicks that are used in echolocation of food and objects in the water. They also make pulsed calls (that sound somewhat like the screeching of a rusty hinge) and whistles, both of which are used in social interactions.

Economic Importance and Remarks: Killer whales are a major showcase species used in the cetacean shows put on by nearly all of the large oceanaria in the United States. Almost everyone has seen or heard of the impressive jumps and trainer-whale interactions of a "Shamu" or a "Namu," "the Killer Whale." Considering the ferocious feeding actions of groups of wild killer whales in nature, it is remarkable how gentle and submissive captive individuals become. However, vicious attacks by one killer whale on another sometimes occur in captivity. In August, 1989, during a whale show at Sea World, one large adult female killed a second smaller female almost instantly in a single slashing charge. The killer whale remains a very impressive top carnivore that usually attacks in groups. They may not pose a threat to humans, but to a seal in the path of a foraging pod of killer whales it is an entirely different story. There are presently no reliable records of unprovoked attacks on humans, but swimming near groups of killer whales is not recommended. There are a few documented attacks of killer whales on small boats, but these are rare.

The long, blade-like dorsal fin of the killer whale when sighted in the water is sometimes mistakenly identified as that of a shark. This contributes to the paranoia and fear of killer whales. They are occasionally shot at, wounded, or killed by people in boats or on shore because of this confusion and fear, and because they sometimes eat salmon, tuna, and other commercially important fish species.

Pygmy Killer Whale *(Feresa attenuata)*

Description: The pygmy killer whale or slender blackfish is small (7-9 feet long), and the entire body is dark gray or black, except a small area of white in the anal region and along the lips (called a goatee). There is no beak and the head

pygmy killer whale, 7-9 ft. (2.1-2.7 m) overall

is blunt and rounded. The species closely resembles the false killer whale but is much smaller.

The skull has a short, broad rostrum with 9-11 teeth present on each side of the upper and lower jaws.

Geographical Range: The pygmy killer whale is only occasionally recorded in Florida waters. It occurs in both the Atlantic Ocean and Gulf of Mexico but is seldom stranded or washed ashore. It also occurs throughout the tropical Pacific and Indian oceans.

Habitat Preference: This species lives in warm tropical and subtropical seas, and it prefers pelagic areas well offshore.

Life History and Reproduction: In captivity, the pygmy killer whale has a reputation for being aggressive toward handlers and other species of marine mammals. It is probable that this vicious nature carries over into its feeding behavior as well. The diet consists of larger fishes, squids, seals, and possibly small porpoises.

A group of five pygmy killer whales stranded at Singer Island in Palm Beach County, Florida on May 3, 1971. This and other more recent strandings suggest it has a social nature and travels in small pods.

Economic Importance and Remarks: Little is known about the biology of the pygmy killer whale, but its economic impact is probably minor. It might affect stocks of marine fishes in some areas.

Risso's Dolphin or Grampus *(Grampus griseus)*

Description: Risso's dolphin or grampus is small (9-13 feet long), the body is slate gray with underparts and head slightly paler, and light-colored scratches or scars normally crisscross the torso. There is no beak, and the melon-like forehead is rounded and bulges. The dorsal fin, pectoral fins, and tail flukes are dark gray to blackish. The dorsal fin is high and recurved backward (falcate).

Risso's dolphin, 9-13 ft. (2.7-4 m) overall

The rostrum is very broad, short, and stout. There are only 2-7 teeth on each side of the lower jaw, and one or two vestigial teeth (or no teeth at all) are present on each side of the upper jaw.

Geographical Range: Risso's dolphin is known in Florida from occasional scattered specimens found stranded or beached on both the Atlantic and Gulf coasts. It is fairly numerous well off our coastlines, and it ranges through most of the oceans of the world.

Habitat Preference: This species lives in temperate and tropical seas, usually beyond the edge of the continental shelf, but occasionally near shore where the waters are deep.

Life History and Reproduction: Risso's dolphin typically occurs in small groups of less than a dozen, but occasionally several small groups in an area may associate seasonally. The diet consists mainly of squids and some fishes. The numerous scars and scratches found on adult grampuses are apparently produced by intraspecific fighting and by squids defending themselves. A pregnant female carrying a near full-term fetus was recorded in December, 1990, as a beached specimen.

One famous grampus lived for more than 20 years in an area at the mouth of a bay in New Zealand. It delighted residents by its habits of jumping and playing about incoming ships and guiding them into the mouth of the sound. This individual (which was fully protected by the New Zealand government) gave some hint to the longevity of the species, when it died of apparently natural causes after at least 20 years as an adult.

Economic Importance and Remarks: Risso's dolphins are occasionally trained and used in oceanarium shows in some areas of the world. They are intelligent and jump readily in conditioned routines. This species has little economic impact. They sometimes ride the bow waves of boats and they often breach.

Short-finned Pilot Whale *(Globicephala macrorhynchus)*

Description: The short-finned pilot whale or blackfish is medium-sized (13-23 feet long), entirely black above and below, and has a bulbous, globe-like head. Frequently, there is a patch of gray on the chin and on the belly. The pectoral fins are moderately short.

The rostrum is extremely broad and short and there are 7-11 conical teeth located on each side of the upper and lower jaws.

Geographical Range: This species is abundant in both the Atlantic Ocean and the Gulf of Mexico, and group strandings on Florida beaches occur fairly often. It occurs widely in most of the world's oceans.

Habitat Preference: Short-finned pilot whales live in both temperate and tropical seas, usually seaward from the outer edges of the continental shelf, but they sometimes forage closer to shore.

Life History and Reproduction: This species is gregarious and usually is seen in herds varying in size from a few dozen to several hundred individuals. They show a decided tendency to follow a single leader, which probably explains many of the group strandings of pilot whales around the world. Pilot whales are migratory, moving north in spring and summer months and back to warmer waters in the fall and winter. Their diet consists of squids, fishes, and cuttlefishes.

Pilot whales breed in tropical waters during the winter months. The gestation period is about 12 months, and a single calf is born to a mother whale about every third year. The babies are 8-9 feet long at birth, and they nurse for several months. Young females reach sexual maturity in 6-7 years, but males mature in 12-13 years. The species is polygamous, with the few old, large males breeding with most of the females. Older females stop bearing young at 38-40 years of age. The maximum life span of the pilot whale is estimated to be 50 years.

Economic Importance and Remarks: The short-finned pilot whale was once the mainstay of the Newfoundland whaling industry that harvested

short-finned pilot whale, 13-23 ft. (4-7 m) overall

Whales

several thousand each summer. The average yield of blubber oil per animal was about 40 gallons, with about two gallons of head oil. The meat of pilot whales has been used as feed on fox and mink farms.

In the islands of the Lesser Antilles, where the pilot whales winter, they are sometimes killed for both meat and oil. The natives have typically hunted them with harpoons in small open boats.

The pilot whales sometimes rest, hanging vertically in the water with their heads out, but they seldom jump out of the water or breach. When swimming, the members of the herd frequently line up side by side in long lines facing forward, and advance as a front. This behavior could be related to stalking prey or perhaps is merely a social interaction.

Harbor Porpoise *(Phocoena phocoena)*

Description: The harbor porpoise is the smallest cetacean in Florida waters (4-5 feet long). The chunky body has a small, rounded head without a beak. The back is dark brown to gray, fading to light brown or light gray on the sides. The belly is white and the dorsal fin is small, dark, and triangular.

The rostrum is short, broad, and rounded at the tip. There are 26-28 teeth on each side of the upper and lower jaws.

Geographical Range: This species is recorded rarely along the Atlantic coast of Florida. It occurs along the eastern coast of North America from the Arctic south to Florida. It also occurs along the Atlantic coast of Europe and in the Pacific Ocean from Alaska to California.

SMITHSONIAN INSTITUTION

harbor porpoise, 4-5 ft. (1.4-1.5 m) overall

Whales

Habitat Preference: The harbor porpoise is usually found inshore in shallow waters and occasionally offshore out to the 100 fathom line. They also frequent bays, harbors, inlets, and the mouths of large rivers. They are found primarily in arctic and temperate waters.

Life History and Reproduction: The harbor porpoise sometimes travels in pairs or small groups and at other times has been recorded in schools of almost 100 individuals. They are less playful than many other species of small dolphins. They seldom jump out of the water and do not ride the bow waves of boats. They usually swim just beneath the surface of the water, rising to breathe around 3-4 times per minute. Harbor porpoises have also been trapped in fish nets at depths to 250 feet. Their principal foods are squids, herring, cod, mackerel, whiting, and other fishes.

Mating takes place in the late spring and early summer. The gestation period is about 11 months, and a single calf is born tailfirst and is approximately half as long as its mother.

Economic Importance and Remarks: At one time a harbor porpoise fishery existed in European waters. The meat was sold at markets and the oil was used in lamps. Eskimo and coastal Indian populations living off arctic waters still occasionally eat harbor porpoises, but the species has no economic importance in more temperate waters.

Pygmy Sperm Whale *(Kogia breviceps)*

Description: The pygmy sperm whale is small (8-12 feet long), the back is dark steel gray grading to lighter gray on the sides, and the underparts are dull white. The head is bluntly rounded and the lower jaw is small and terminates well behind the tip of the snout. The dorsal fin is small and only slightly curved backward.

The skull is short, broad, and triangular when seen from above. There are 12-16 conical teeth on each side of the lower jaw, but none in the upper jaw.

Geographical Range: The pygmy sperm whale is fairly common off both the Atlantic and Gulf coasts of Florida. Individual strandings have been increasing in recent years. It ranges through most of the world's oceans but is apparently rare in the South Atlantic.

Habitat Preference: This species lives in warmer seas in deep offshore waters, but it comes closer to shore during the calving season.

Life History and Reproduction: Pygmy sperm whales are migratory, moving northward in the summer and returning to warmer tropical waters in the fall. The diet consists of pelagic squids, cuttlefishes, shrimp, and some fishes that live near the surface.

Calves are born in the wintering areas, but breeding occurs the preceding spring or early summer. The gestation period is about nine months long, and an adult female produces one calf every two years. A 10 foot long female is recorded to have given birth to a 5.75 foot long calf that weighed 176 pounds. The duration of nursing is unknown, but the calf stays with its mother for about one year.

Economic Importance and Remarks: There is little or no economic
importance for this small whale. There is a small spermaceti reservoir located
in the head that contains sperm whale oil, a highly valued substance.

The pygmy sperm whale has an interesting defense mechanism. When
startled, it releases a dark cloud of reddish-brown fluid feces into the water from
the anus. This cloud is apparently intended to confuse predators while the whale
escapes. Octopuses and squids release their ink clouds for a similar purpose.

Dwarf Sperm Whale *(Kogia simus)*

Description: The dwarf sperm whale is small (6-9 feet long), dark steel gray
above with lighter gray on the sides, and the belly is dull white with some gray
splotches along the margins. This species is a slightly smaller version of the
pygmy sperm whale, and both were thought to be the same species. However,
the dorsal fin of the dwarf sperm whale is about twice the size of the dorsal fin
of the pygmy sperm whale and is more curved.

The skull is short, broad, and triangular when viewed from above, and is
smaller in overall size than the skull of the pygmy sperm whale. There are only
8-11 conical teeth on each side of the lower jaw, and sometimes there are 1-
3 pairs of teeth present in the upper jaw.

Geographical Range: The dwarf sperm whale occurs in small numbers off
both the Atlantic and Gulf coasts of Florida. It ranges throughout most of the
world's oceans.

Habitat Preference: The species lives in deep offshore waters of
temperate and tropical seas, but comes closer to shore during the calving season.

Life History and Reproduction: This species was only recently
recognized as a clearly separate form from the pygmy sperm whale, and its life
habits are poorly known. It is migratory, moving north to cooler waters in the
spring and summer and returning to warm tropical oceans for the winter
months. Dwarf sperm whales occur in small groups of 2-10 individuals. The
gestation period is believed to be about nine months, and the calving season
extends over a 4-5 month period during the winter. At birth, the calves are 3-
4 feet long.

Their diet consists of fishes, squids, cuttlefishes, crabs, and shrimp. This
whale appears to feed at considerable depths at the edge of the continental shelf.
This is indicated by the stomach contents of beached individuals. Their prey
species live only on or near the ocean bottom at a depth of 800 feet or more
below the surface.

The name "rat porpoise" is sometimes used for this species because of its rat-
like nose and face.

Economic Importance and Remarks: This small whale has no
economic impact. Like the pygmy sperm whale, the dwarf sperm whale ejects
a dark reddish-brown fluid from the anus when alarmed that apparently aids its
escape from predators.

pygmy sperm whale, 8-12 ft. (2.4-3.7 m) overall

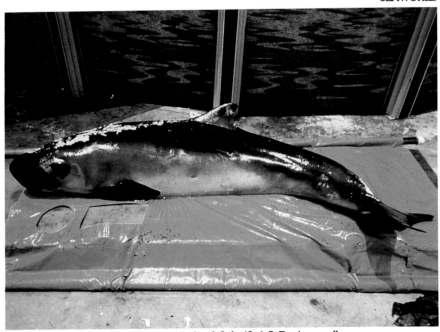

dwarf sperm whale, 6-9 ft. (2.4-3.7 m) overall

Whales

giant sperm whale, 40-70 ft. (12.2-21.3 m) overall

Giant Sperm Whale *(Physeter macrocephalus)*

Description: The giant sperm whale is the largest of the toothed whales, and the males are nearly twice as big as the females. The length of adult males ranges from 40-69 feet and adult females range from only 30-39 feet in length. Males can weigh 40-60 tons. The most striking feature of the giant sperm whale is the enormous square head, one-quarter to one-third of the total length, combined with a long slender lower jaw full of large conical teeth. The body color is dark brownish gray or dark bluish gray, and much of the skin looks corrugated or shriveled. There are scattered areas of white in the anal area and on the upper and lower jaws. The single blowhole is located well to the left of the midline and far forward on the head. Sperm whales have a distinct dorsal hump about two-thirds of the way back.

The skull is massive and out of proportion to the rest of the body size. There are 16-30 large cone-shaped teeth (each 6-8 inches long) on each side of the lower jaw, and occasionally a few small, nonfunctional teeth are present in the upper jaw.

Geographical Range: This giant whale occurs sparingly off both the Atlantic and Gulf coasts of Florida. It is widely distributed throughout the oceans of the world.

Habitat Preference: Giant sperm whales prefer to live in deep ocean waters off the edge of the continental shelf. They can tolerate both icy arctic waters and warm tropical seas.

Life History and Reproduction: The gigantic head of this species is a specialization that aids in diving to great depths in the ocean. When diving, they descend almost vertically, headfirst, and regulate buoyancy by varying the

Whales

amounts of air and fluids in the massive head. They feed at great depths exceeding 1,200 feet, and the diet is mainly squids (including the famous giant squid), cuttlefishes, octopuses, and fishes such as barracuda, sharks, skates, albacore, and angelfish. Giant sperm whales often bear the scars of battle with giant squids (sucker marks and beak bites). The maximum depth to which they are known to dive is well over one mile, and they have remained submerged for much more than an hour. After long dives, they may remain on the surface and blow for 10-15 minutes to recover from the oxygen debt. Their usual swimming speed is four knots, but when pressed they can attain 12 knots.

Females reach sexual maturity when they are about 28 feet long and eight years old. Most matings occur in the spring, and the gestation period is almost 16 months. A single calf, or rarely two, is produced, measuring 14-15 feet long and weighing about one ton. Immediately after birth the mother and nearby adults lift the newborn calf gently to the surface to breathe. Baby whales nurse at either of two teats located in deep, longitudinal grooves on each side of the vaginal opening. Each calf nurses for about two years, then is weaned when around 20 feet long. Adult females breed only once every 3-5 years. Sometimes females breed while they are still nursing, which is unusual in whales.

Giant sperm whales are gregarious and polygamous, and usually travel in pods of 15-20 individuals. They also may be found singly or in groups of up to 40 whales. Males migrate to cold temperate waters during summer months, but the cows and calves stay behind in warm tropical waters. Adult males sometimes wander far northward or southward into polar seas, then return to warm waters to spend the winter and to breed. The harem is the basic social unit of sperm whales. It consists of adult cows (usually nursing and/or pregnant), young cows, young bulls, and an old bull, the "harem master." This large bull patrols the perimeter of his herd, guarding against raids from other harem masters or bachelor bulls.

Giant sperm whales have well developed echolocation or sonar systems that permit them to locate and catch prey in the totally dark ocean depths several thousand feet below the surface. They emit a series of regular clicks at varying speeds and wavelengths that bounce off objects and return to their sensitive ears. Sperm whales forage mainly at night in hunting groups that sweep through a favorable area far below the surface. The younger whales do not participate in the long foraging dives, instead remaining at the surface with an adult female from the harem who is apparently designated as the babysitter. When sperm whales breathe, they make a characteristic spray or blow at a low, slanted angle.

Economic Importance and Remarks: A gummy substance called ambergris is expelled from the large intestine of the giant sperm whale. It is produced only by this species. After exposure to air and sunlight, the ambergris hardens into a semi-solid, orange-yellow substance with a sweet, earthy smell. It was once thought to have medicinal properties but is now used primarily in the manufacture of perfumes.

A large cavity in the forehead of the giant sperm whale contains spermaceti, a waxy, oily material that is used as a high-grade lubricant, as a base for face creams and salves, and for several other purposes. Early whalers erroneously thought the oil was sperm and named the species accordingly. The teeth of sperm whales are a favored material for ivory picture carvings or scrimshaw. Such artifacts are very expensive, especially if they are antiques from early whaling days.

The giant sperm whale once supported a great whaling industry in the United States and various countries around the world. Prior to overharvesting by the whaling ships, these giant whales were abundant throughout the Gulf of Mexico and Atlantic Ocean. They are now officially protected and classified as endangered by the State of Florida and the federal government.

One of the most interesting stories, based partly on facts, to evolve around the whaling era is the epic book, *Moby Dick,* by Herman Melville. It is based on a ship captain's quest for a white giant sperm whale living in the Pacific Ocean during the mid-1800s. Such an albino specimen is said to have really existed, and it became the basis for one of the most famous sea adventures ever written.

Mass strandings of the giant sperm whale have been recorded on only a few occasions along the coasts of Florida. On 13 June 1908, about 30 individuals beached and died at Ponce de Leon Inlet near New Smyrna Beach in Volusia County. Before that, 16 sperm whales stranded in the winter of 1882 near the Cape Canaveral Lighthouse. Another mass stranding consisted of 15 individuals that came through St. Augustine Inlet in St. Johns County on 22 November 1980 and stranded in various locations on sandbars, oyster bars, and salt marshes. Five adolescent sperm whales beached themselves on South Hutchinson Island in St Lucie County in late April 1990, and only one swam back out to sea and may have survived. The four that died each measured about 30 feet long. Individual giant sperm whales also beach occasionally in Florida, but mass strandings are much less common.

Goose-beaked Whale *(Ziphius cavirostris)*

Description: The goose-beaked whale or Cuvier's beaked whale is medium- sized (16-25 feet long), the body color is dark grayish brown or rust brown sometimes with scattered light spots occurring throughout, and the entire head and jaws are creamy white. The dorsal fin is small and located back toward the tail fluke. The head is small and drawn out anteriorly into a beak, with the lower jaw protruding forward beyond the tip of the upper jaw.

The rostrum of the skull is long, narrow, pointed, and lacking functional teeth. The lower jaw of males has only two visible teeth located at the front tip of the mandible, but in females these usually do not erupt.

Geographical Range: The goose-beaked whale occurs occasionally off both the Atlantic and Gulf coasts of Florida. It is widely distributed throughout most of the oceans of the world.

Habitat Preference: This species occurs in both temperate and warm tropical seas, usually in the deepwater zones well away from land, but occasionally near shore.

goose-beaked whale, 16-25 ft. (4.9-7.6 m) overall

Life History and Reproduction: The life habits of the goose-beaked whale are poorly known because the species is sparsely distributed and wary of man and his boats. Groups of 10-30 individuals have been seen traveling, diving, and feeding together. They are fast, vigorous swimmers and can remain under water for periods of over 30 minutes. When beginning a deep dive, they raise the tail flukes above the surface and go down almost vertically. One adult female was found to have more than 1,300 deepwater squids (the preferred food) in her stomach. They also take deepwater fishes.

Males reach sexual maturity at a body length of about 18 feet and females first become pregnant at a body length of about 19 feet. The gestation period is approximately 12 months long, and an adult female produces a single offspring only once every third year. Goose-beaked whales can be aged by counting growth rings in the cementum of teeth. The maximum number of growth rings reported approaches 40, which presumably indicates the years of life expectancy.

Economic Importance and Remarks: There is little or no economic importance associated with the goose-beaked whale.

Dense-beaked Whale *(Mesoplodon densirostris)*

Description: The dense-beaked whale or Blainville's beaked whale is medium-sized (14-18 feet long), and the upper parts are black to dark gray, usually blotched with grayish white. The belly is white from the anal area forward to the tip of the lower jaws. The body is distinctly spindle shaped. The head is narrow and the lower jaws have a prominent rise at their junction with the skull.

174   Whales

The only teeth in the skull are a single large pair located on a prominence at the back of the lower jaws. In females the teeth usually do not erupt through the gums. The bones of the rostrum are extremely dense and heavy, about one-third more dense than elephant ivory.

Geographical Range: This species occurs occasionally off both the Atlantic and Gulf coasts of Florida. This rare species is found in most of the major oceans of the world.

Habitat Preference: Dense-beaked whales live well offshore in tropical and warm temperate seas.

Life History and Reproduction: Very little is known about the life habits of this species because it is rarely seen, being primarily a pelagic species, spending its life far out at sea. The stomach contents of stranded animals reveal that they feed on squids.

A subadult male that stranded on 16 June 1969 near Crescent Beach in St.

densed-beaked whale,
14-18 ft. (4.3-5.5 m) overall

Johns County, Florida, emitted a series of chirps and short whistles while still in the surf. The whale was weak, however, and died in captivity within 24 hours.

Economic Importance and Remarks: This species has little economic significance.

Antillean beaked whale, 12-22 ft. (3.7-6.7 m) overall

Antillean Beaked Whale *(Mesoplodon europaeus)*

Description: The Antillean beaked whale is medium-sized (12-22 feet long), the body color is dark grayish black, with white on the lips and anterior tip of the beak. The dorsal fin is small, curved backward, and located well toward the tail.

The rostrum is long, pointed, and very narrow. The only teeth in the skull are one pair found about one-third of the way back from the tip of the lower jaw. The teeth are laterally flattened and pointed at the tip.

Geographical Range: This whale occurs rarely off both the Atlantic and Gulf coasts of Florida. The species is found only in the western Atlantic Ocean from the latitude of New York south to northern South America.

Habitat Preference: The Antillean beaked whale appears to prefer the open sea in tropical and warm temperate waters.

Life History and Reproduction: The diet of this whale is almost exclusively squids. During the calving season, females come closer to shore than at other times. Little is known about their life habits.

Economic Importance and Remarks: This species appears to have little economic significance. It is rarely encountered by humans.

True's Beaked Whale *(Mesoplodon mirus)*

Description: True's beaked whale is medium-sized (14-18 feet long), the upper parts are dark gray to dull black, and the belly and lower sides are white to slate gray, often flecked with dark spots. The entire head and lips are dark gray to black.

The rostrum is long, very narrow, and pointed. The only teeth in the skull are a single pair located at the tip of the lower jaw, usually visible in the males, but not always erupted in females.

J. MEADE

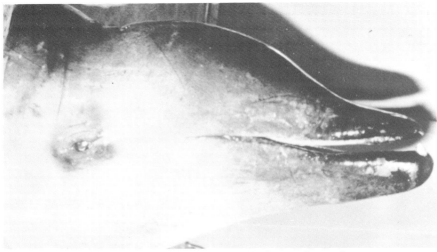

True's beaked whale, 14-18 ft. (4.3-5.5 m) overall

Whales

Geographical Range: True's beaked whale occurs rarely off the upper Atlantic coast of Florida. It lives in the western Atlantic Ocean from Nova Scotia to northeastern Florida.

Habitat Preference: This species prefers deep offshore areas in temperate seas.

Life History and Reproduction: This whale probably eats squids, like other species in the genus. It is seldom encountered by man, but specimens occasionally beach or wash ashore along the east coast of the United States.

Economic Importance and Remarks: True's beaked whale appears to have little economic significance.

Fin Whale *(Balaenoptera physalus)*

Description: The fin whale or finback whale is gigantic in size (60-80 feet long), and the largest mammal currently known to live in Florida waters. The color is blue black or brownish black above and white with long parallel folds or pleats on the belly. The posterior portion of the back is distinctly ridged, topped by a small backward-pointed dorsal fin. There is also an asymmetrical color pattern on the jaws. The right lower jaw area is white, while the left lower jaw is blue black. Large fin whales may reach a weight of 100 tons.

The rostrum of the huge skull is an elongated triangle, tapering to a distinct point when viewed from above. No teeth are present, but there are 350-400 baleen plates located in the mouth to strain and trap food. The plates vary in color from white to blue gray or purplish, streaked with white.

Geographical Range: The fin whale occurs sparingly off both the Atlantic and Gulf coasts of Florida. The species is widely distributed throughout all the oceans of the world and is one of the most common baleen whale species.

Habitat Preference: This whale prefers the waters of the open ocean but may come inshore when migrating. They tolerate both the warm water of the tropics and the frigid polar seas.

Life History and Reproduction: These giant whales sometimes travel in packs of 50 or more individuals, but small groups of only a few animals also occur. They can swim quite rapidly when pursued and have been clocked at speeds approaching 30 miles per hour.

Fin whales migrate to colder waters in the summertime and return to winter in warm waters. Movements of the pods for considerable distances along east-west routes have also been noted. Both mating and calving take place during the winter months. The gestation period is about one year, and one offspring is normally produced by each mother. Twins occur at a rate of roughly one pregnant female out of a hundred. The calves are 19-22 feet long at birth but grow at a tremendous rate. A baby fin whale drinks about 140 pounds of milk per day, and gains about 125 pounds of weight each 24-hour period. Whale milk contains 30-40 percent fat (compared to only 3-5 percent fat in cow milk). Young fin whales are weaned at about six months of age, when they are about 38-40 feet long. Sexual maturity occurs when the young whales reach about six years. The maximum life span is believed to be around 50 years.

fin whale, 60-80 ft. (18.3-24.4 m) overall

Fin whales feed on small sea creatures such as crustaceans, small swarming fishes, plankton, shrimp, copepods, and mollusks. They pass huge quantities of seawater through the baleen plates in the mouth and trap millions of organisms from the water. They are believed to forage more deeply than other baleen whales (to a depth of at least 750 feet). Fin whales do not show their tail flukes when beginning a dive.

Economic Importance and Remarks: The fin whale, because of its gigantic size and relative abundance in some areas, has historically been the second most important baleen whale harvested by the whaling industry, behind only the blue whale. Today, only Russia and Japan continue to support large commercial whaling operations. These countries harvest fin whales as one of their preferred species. There is a worldwide moratorium on taking any blue whales because of their low numbers; this puts more pressure on the fin whale. The whale oil yield from a large fin whale is around 50 barrels. The meat is sometimes used to feed furbearers such as foxes and mink that are raised on farms. The large bones are usually ground up to use as bone meal. Japanese fishermen also harvest large quantities of krill, which may have an adverse effect on the food supplies of the fin whale and other baleen whales.

Because of the fin whale's low population numbers, the United States government and the State of Florida both list it as officially "endangered."

Minke Whale *(Balaenoptera acutorostrata)*
Description: The minke whale or little piked whale is large (23-33 feet long), yet is the smallest baleen whale found off Florida. The body color is dark blue gray or black above, and the belly and undersides of the pectoral flippers are white. The front half of the belly is furrowed or pleated. This is the only baleen

minke whale, 23-33 ft. (7-10 m) overall

whale with a patch of white on the upper side of the pectoral flippers, and the baleen plates (numbering 230-350) are yellowish white. The dorsal fin is tall and directed backward.

The long, pointed rostrum has straight sides (rather than outwardly bowed as in its close relatives) when viewed from above.

Geographical Range: The minke whale is found sparingly off both the Atlantic and Gulf coasts of Florida. It ranges throughout most of the oceans of the world.

Habitat Preference: This whale prefers open seas, above the continental shelf, in both cold temperate and warm tropical seas. They sometimes enter bays, inlets, and estuaries in pursuit of food.

Life History and Reproduction: The minke whale migrates northward for the summer and returns to warmer waters to winter and breed. Its seasonal distribution from year to year is also highly dependent on krill—small fishes, shrimp, and other invertebrates. Individuals often show little fear of boats or ships, and can frequently be observed breaching or leaping free of the water's surface as they swim along.

Adult females give birth to a single calf on the average of once every 12-18 months after they reach maturity. The gestation period is about 10 months, and newborn calves are around nine feet long. Young minke whales wean at six months and reach sexual maturity at a length of about 21-23 feet, or two years of age.

Whales   179

Economic Importance and Remarks: Minke whales are rated approximately sixth in commercial value of the baleen whales taken by the remaining whaling industries in Russia and Japan. Norway resumed taking minke whales in the fall of 1992, in violation of an international treaty signed by Norway. Because minke whales are much smaller than the other great whales of the baleen group, their oil and blubber yield per individual is much smaller. Most experts feel the remnant whaling industry should die a natural and timely death because its profits are now marginal, and because the great whale stocks of the world are being further decimated needlessly in the process. Minke whales often have a curiosity about ships and will approach them closely. This makes them tempting targets for whalers despite their relatively small size.

Sei Whale *(Balaenoptera borealis)*

Description: The sei (pronounced *say*) whale or pollack whale is gigantic in size (42-62 feet long) but smaller than the fin whale. The color is bluish black on the back grading to dark steel gray on the sides and under the tail, and the pleated portion of the belly is grayish white. The undersides of the flukes and flippers are not white, but gray. The ventral pleats extend only a short distance posterior to the pectoral flipper. The dorsal fin is tall, pointed, and directed backward. The baleen plates number 320-400 and are black, fringed with grayish white.

The skull is much more massive than the skulls of Bryde's and minke whales, but smaller than that of the fin whale. An expert on whales must be consulted to make an accurate identification.

Geographical Range: The sei whale occurs rarely in the waters off the Atlantic and Gulf coasts of Florida. It ranges widely throughout most of the oceans of the world.

J. S. LEATHERWOOD

sei whale, 45-62 ft. (13.7-18.9 m) overall

Whales

Habitat Preference: This whale prefers the open waters of the temperate and subtropical oceans. It occasionally comes inshore to feed but normally is found far out at sea.

Life History and Reproduction: Sei whales feed on surface plankton, shrimp and other crustaceans, small schooling fishes, and small squids. They are skimmer feeders (at the surface) and usually do not dive deeply. Sei whales travel long distances, following the seasonal changes in location of food. They are usually found in groups of two to five but may congregate in larger numbers on a rich feeding ground.

The breeding cycle is apparently similar to that of the fin whale described previously. The gestation period is between 11 and 12 months. A pregnant female normally produces one offspring, but there is at least one record of twin calves. The calves are 15-16 feet long at birth and, like all baleen whales, they grow at a tremendous rate.

Economic Importance and Remarks: The commercial value of sei whales is ranked about fourth among baleen whales harvested by the remaining whaling countries in the world.

Because of its declining numbers, the United States government and the State of Florida both list the sei whale as "endangered."

Bryde's Whale *(Balaenoptera edeni)*

Description: Bryde's whale is very large (36-46 feet long), the upper parts are blue black, and the underside and front edges of the flippers are grayish white. The body is remarkably elongated and not as powerfully built as the sei whale or fin whale. This is also the only whale that has three longitudinal ridges located on top of the snout anterior to the blowholes. The dorsal fin is fairly large and directed backward, and the slate-gray baleen plates have a white or light gray front fringe. The pleats or belly folds extend back to near the anal area.

The skull is less robust and smaller than those of both the fin and sei whales, but is larger than the skull of the minke whale. There are 250-370 baleen plates in the mouth. A whale expert should be consulted for accurate identification.

Geographical Range: Bryde's whale occurs rarely in the waters off the Atlantic and Gulf coasts of Florida, and they range throughout most of the oceans of the world.

Habitat Preference: This species prefers the open waters of warm temperate and tropical seas. They sometimes come inshore to feed but more often are found far out at sea.

Life History and Reproduction: Bryde's whale has long been confused with the sei whale and was not recognized as a separate species until recently. For this reason, there is not much valid information on its biology. They are not surface skimmers, but are deep divers. Like the other baleen whales, they feed on small schooling fishes, crustaceans, and plankton. Surprisingly, they have been reported also to eat small sharks and penguins, obviously swallowing them whole since they have no teeth.

Whales   181

Bryde's whale, 36-46 ft. (11-14 m) overall

Economic Importance and Remarks: The commercial value of Bryde's whale is ranked approximately fifth among baleen whales harvested by the few remaining whaling countries in the world. Bryde's whales often are curious about ships and will approach them for a close inspection. This makes them easy targets for whalers.

In late November, 1988, a young Bryde's whale was found beached near Honeymoon Island in Pinellas County. It weighed 4,200 pounds and was 22 feet, 9 inches long. The ailing whale was taken to Sea World near Orlando and nursed back to health on a diet of squids and small fishes. The two-year old female was eventually returned to the Gulf of Mexico by the U.S. Coast Guard in January, 1989. This is believed to be the first baleen whale to be rescued near death and recover in captivity.

Humpback Whale *(Megaptera novaeangliae)*

Description: The humpback whale is gigantic (40-53 feet long), mostly black in color with the belly white or splotched with white. The pectoral flippers are extremely long (about 15 feet), nearly all white, and the front edges are scalloped. The tail flukes are marked with white in various patterns on the underside, and the rear edges also are scalloped. The top of the snout and border of the lower jaw have a series of raised fleshy knobs or protuberances scattered over the skin. The dorsal fin is quite small, directed backward, and positioned on a small hump two-thirds of the way back from the tip of the snout. The baleen plates (270-400 in number) are black with olive-black fringes anteriorly. Ventral pleats or folds extend from the throat to the midbelly region. A large humpback whale weighs 40-50 tons.

Whales

The rostrum is long, arched only slightly, and somewhat convex on the lateral edges.

Geographical Range: The humpback whale is found off both the Atlantic and Gulf coasts of Florida. It rarely becomes stranded inshore. It occurs widely in both the Atlantic and Pacific Oceans.

Habitat Preference: These large whales prefer to forage over the continental shelf or along island banks. They are also sometimes found far out at sea.

Life History and Reproduction: The humpback whale is gregarious and highly migratory, inhabiting cold northern and southern polar waters in the summer and then returning to warm tropical waters for the winter. For up to six months each year (during migration and while on the wintering grounds), humpback whales do not feed, but rely on vast stores of fat in the blubber and other body tissues to meet their energy demands. During the summer months they feed on enormous schools of prey in polar coastal areas and inlets. Populations of humpback whales concentrate in several distinct groups that are isolated from one another, and between which there is little exchange of individuals. There may be some mingling of northern hemisphere herds with southern hemisphere herds near the equator during the winter, but this is not certain.

The humpback whale's diet consists mainly of crustaceans and small schooling fishes. They are often observed to forage in groups and concentrate the food animals by forming "bubble curtains," created by releasing air bubbles while swimming in a wide circle well beneath the surface. The whales then rush upward in the center of the bubble column with mouths agape, gorging on

H. E. WINN

humpback whale, 40-53 ft. (12.2-16.2 m) overall

Whales

millions of small marine organisms. As many as 3-8 of these giant whales may breach simultaneously, lunge for the sky, and then crash thunderously back into the water with their pleated throats greatly distended with water and food. This bizarre and interesting feeding activity of baleen whales is called bubble netting.

Humpback whales mate in the wintering areas; the gestation period is 11-12 months. Adult males compete aggressively with one another to mate with receptive females. While mating, both male and female whales have been observed to administer alternate blows or slaps repeatedly to their partner. After the seasonal migration to forage, each pregnant female again returns to warm tropical waters where she gives birth to a single calf. On rare occasions, twins may be produced. Like most whales, the calves are born tailfirst and then lifted to the surface to begin breathing. A newborn baby humpback whale weighs about 3,000 pounds and is 13-15 feet long. In the early stages, each baby grows 100 pounds a day feeding on the mother's rich milk. The age of weaning is around 11 months. Female humpback whales become sexually mature when 7-8 years old, at a length of 37-40 feet. An adult female produces a calf only once every three years. The maximum life span is probably 50-70 years.

Economic Importance and Remarks: The humpback whale is a species highly prized by the whaling industry. The yield from a 40 footer is 40-45 barrels (about 8 tons) of oil, one-half ton of bone meal, and two tons of meat.

The stocks of the humpback whale have decreased to the point that they are listed as "endangered" by both the United States and the State of Florida. The only countries still killing them are Russia and Japan.

The variation in the white splotches on the tail flukes of this species are used by whale researchers to identify individuals. Photographs are taken of the tail flukes as they clear the water to begin a dive. Each whale has its own unique white markings, which serve as a "signature" wherever it is seen again. In this way, humpbacks observed in Iceland in the summer have been tracked in their migration to specific areas of the Caribbean in the winter.

Humpback whales are often heavily parasitized externally by amphipods called whale lice. Mature whales are also normally encrusted with barnacles, much like a ship's hull.

Right Whale *(Balaena glacialis)*

Description: The right whale is gigantic (40-53 feet long), the body is dark brown to black in color (somewhat mottled), and there are usually white areas in the midbelly region and on the chin. The head is enormous (one-fourth the body length), and the mouth is highly arched, curving upward in front of the eye on each side of the head. Both a dorsal fin and throat pleats are absent in this species. The top of the snout has a large, rough, horny projection that is light colored, called the "bonnet," located in front of the blowholes. Bonnets are hard protuberances representing the accumulation of cornified layers of skin, commonly infested with parasitic crustaceans (whale lice) and worms. Smaller callosities of this type also occur along the margins of the lower jaw (called "beards" and "lip patches"), and sometimes near the eyes ("eyebrows"). There are about 250 pairs of baleen plates which are very narrow, long (up to six feet), and black or dark brown in color. They hang like closely packed curtains from the top of the huge yawning mouth of the right whale. The pectoral flippers are short, broad, and rounded. Some right whales weigh 40-50 tons each.

The rostrum has a pronounced downward curving arch in it and is quite narrow and tapered to a point anteriorly.

Geographical Range: This large whale is found sparingly off both the Atlantic and Gulf coasts of Florida. It ranges widely throughout most of the oceans of the world.

Habitat Preference: Right whales are migratory and are found in both cold and warm temperate waters, but they avoid tropical seas near the equator. They often forage near shore in shallow water and sometimes enter large bays. These whales move north along the eastern Florida coast between early January and late March and then return the following fall.

Life History and Reproduction: This giant whale feeds on planktonic animal life, mainly copepods, shrimp, and mollusks. The whales use the skimming method of feeding, in which they swim through swarms of krill with yawning, open mouths and their heads above water to just behind the nostril openings. When a sufficient mouthful of food has been filtered from the water by the baleen plates, they dive, close their mouths, and swallow the food.

The name right whale was given by early whalers because this was the "right" or "correct" whale to harpoon. This was true for several reasons: they swam slowly (about 4 knots); they were abundant and easy to approach (being not at all wary of ships); they were buoyant and did not sink like other whales when killed; and, they yielded copious amounts of whale oil.

Despite their great size, right whales are surprisingly agile, and seem particularly to enjoy breaching almost completely out of the water.

Breeding takes place in the late summer or fall and gestation takes about 12 months. The young are born at the southern end of their north-south migration, in the Atlantic Ocean just off the general area of the Florida-Georgia state line. A calf is 15-16 feet long at birth and nurses for about one year. Young right whales reach sexual maturity in about six years, and an adult female produces an offspring once every three years. The maximum life span is around 40 years.

Economic Importance and Remarks: Unrestricted whale hunting during the 12th to 19th centuries nearly exterminated the right whale because the females and calves that frequented inshore waters made up most of the kills. Right whales are partially protected from exploitation by international agreements of the major nations. These magnificent giants are slowly increasing in numbers under this protection. The right whale is listed as "endangered" by both the federal government and the State of Florida.

Scientist who study the right whale have found that individual animals can be recognized by their unique patterns and shapes of bonnets and other callosities

Whales

right whale, 40-53 ft. (12.2-16.2 m) overall

located about the head and mouth. The whales are photographed at close range when their heads are visible, and their movements plotted as they are located and identified during migration.

Whale Profile Illustrations for Identification

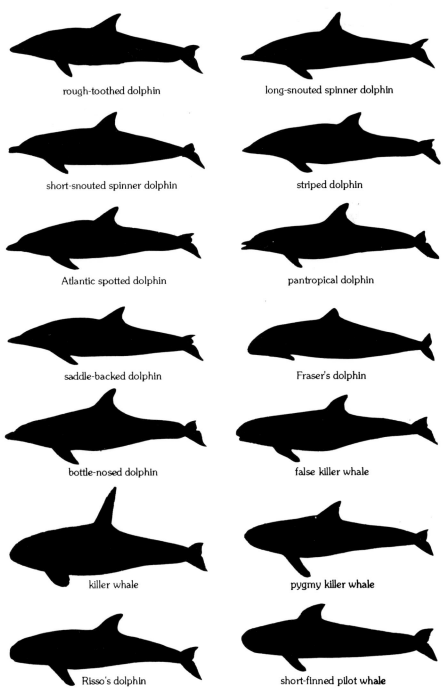

rough-toothed dolphin

long-snouted spinner dolphin

short-snouted spinner dolphin

striped dolphin

Atlantic spotted dolphin

pantropical dolphin

saddle-backed dolphin

Fraser's dolphin

bottle-nosed dolphin

false killer whale

killer whale

pygmy killer whale

Risso's dolphin

short-finned pilot whale

Whale Profile Illustrations for Identification

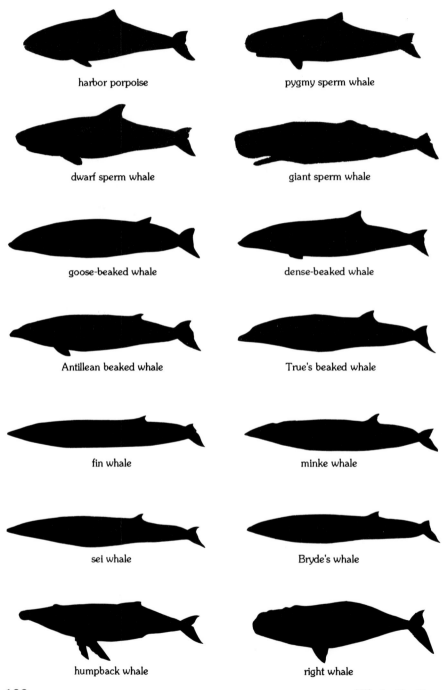

harbor porpoise

pygmy sperm whale

dwarf sperm whale

giant sperm whale

goose-beaked whale

dense-beaked whale

Antillean beaked whale

True's beaked whale

fin whale

minke whale

sei whale

Bryde's whale

humpback whale

right whale

Extirpated Florida Species

Red Wolf or Florida Black Wolf *(Canis rufus)*

The red wolf is very similar in color and general contours to the introduced coyote, but is slightly larger in overall body size. Some individuals, especially in Florida, were melanistic rather than tannish gray. They once ranged widely over the eastern half of the United States in the dense mature hardwood forests present when the first European settlers arrived. They apparently occurred throughout much of Florida but disappeared by the 1920s. Their demise was caused by four factors: the cutting of virgin timber stands and opening of the forests, i.e., habitat change; poisoning, trapping, and shooting of wolves by farmers and settlers; the red wolf hybridizing with coyotes; and competition from coyotes for both food and space. Recent DNA studies suggest that the red wolf is actually a hybrid between the coyote and the gray wolf and does not deserve its "endangered" classification nor should it be recognized as a separate species.

Elsewhere in the United States, the last remaining red wolves were captured in eastern Texas (1970s) and placed in a captive breeding program by the U.S. Fish and Wildlife Service. Offspring from this effort have been released in Great Smoky Mountain National Park (1990s) and on coastal islands in North Carolina (1980s). There is also a breeding red wolf pair in a compound on St. Vincent National Wildlife Refuge in Franklin County, Florida, and at the Tallahassee Museum of History and Natural Science in Leon County. Animals from these captive colonies will be used to reintroduce the red wolf to various suitable locations in the southern United States over the next few years.

Red wolves breed once each year, usually in February or March. The gestation period is 60-63 days, and 2-8 pups (average 4-5) are born in April or May. They use either excavated or natural dens for shelter and birthing. Both parents participate in caring for the young, and pups first leave the den at 5-6 weeks of age.

West Indian Monk Seal *(Monachus tropicalis)*

The West Indian monk seal was a tropical species that once occurred on islands and the Keys at the southern tip of Florida. They were docile, easily approached, and exploited by early sailors for meat, hides, and oil. The last one reported in Florida waters was taken near Key West in Monroe County in March, 1922. There were infrequent reports of isolated seals sighted on islands in the West Indies and along the coast of Mexico until about 1950, but West Indian seals are now apparently extinct, because none have been positively identified for more than 40 years. They are uniformly brown, tinged with gray at the tips of the hair. The color becomes lighter on the sides and yellowish white on the belly. They measure about 6-7 feet long, females being slightly smaller than males.

red wolf, 51.2-64.5 in. (130-165 cm) overall, tail 13.4-16.5 in. (34-42 cm)

Bison or Buffalo
(Bison bison)

When the first European explorers arrived, the American bison or buffalo occurred widely throughout the eastern United States and were especially abundant on the western plains. They were extensively slaughtered for meat and hides and disappeared in the East before 1800. Bison once occurred in northern Florida at least as far south as the Alachua County area and possibly farther south. They were eliminated from the state at an early date apparently due to overharvesting by settlers.

Interestingly, a small herd of bison was recently reintroduced to Florida and is presently maintained in semi-captive conditions (fenced pastures) at the

bison, 82.7-149.6 in. (210-380 cm) overall, tail 11.8-31.5 in. (30-80 cm

Extirpated Florida Species

Paynes Prairie State Preserve in Alachua County. These bison were brought east from a wildlife refuge in the western United States, and it remains to be seen if they will thrive satisfactorily and multiply in north-central Florida. This small herd does not, of course, represent a natural wild population of the species living in Florida.

Bison are large, shaggy, dark-brown members of the cattle family. They have a hump at the shoulders and black pointed horns that curve sharply upward and inward on a very broad skull. The bulls are considerably larger and more robust than cows. Calves are cinnamon brown, later changing to dark brown like the adults.

Species Possibly Present but Populations Not Yet Verified in Florida

	Possible Florida Range	Habitat Preference
Swamp Rabbit	W. Panhandle	Marshes, Wet Meadows
Common Muskrat	W. Panhandle	Marshes, Ponds
Blue or Sulphur-Bottomed Whale	Atlantic, Gulf	Marine
Melon-headed Whale	Atlantic, Gulf	Marine
Long-finned Pilot Whale	Atlantic, Gulf	Marine
North Sea Beaked Whale	Atlantic, Gulf	Marine
Jaguarundi	Statewide	Thickets, Brush

Swamp Rabbit *(Sylvilagus aquaticus)*

The swamp rabbit has been taken in the Mobile Bay area of Alabama and might be present in the extreme western Panhandle of Florida. It is larger than the widespread marsh rabbit but has similar habitat preferences, including marshy wetland borders and swampy habitats. Any large cottontail rabbit found in moist areas at the western edge of the Panhandle should be examined carefully, because it might be a swamp rabbit.

Common Muskrat *(Ondatra zibethicus)*

The common muskrat is much larger than the round-tailed muskrat and its tail is laterally flattened rather than round. It has been taken in the Mobile Bay area of Alabama, and possibly occurs in some marshes, ponds, lakes, or streams at the extreme western edge of the Florida Panhandle. Any muskrats encountered in that area should be carefully examined for the presence of a flat rather than round tail. Common muskrats have thick, shiny, dark brown fur on the back, and are lighter in color on the belly.

Blue or Sulphur-bottomed Whale *(Balaenoptera musculus)*

The gigantic blue whale is the largest animal ever to live, measuring up to 100 feet long and weighing 200 tons. It occurs in the Atlantic Ocean and has been recorded in the western Gulf of Mexico. There has as yet been no valid record of this largest whale in Florida waters, but in time it will probably be recorded. This whale is light bluish-gray above, mottled with gray or grayish white; the belly is yellowish; baleen plates are black.

Melon-headed Whale *(Peponocephala electra)*

The melon-headed whale or many-toothed blackfish is small (6.5-9 feet long) and similar in shape to the false killer whale, but with a sharper snout. It ranges throughout the tropical Atlantic, Pacific, and Indian oceans in deep waters well offshore. This warmwater whale has been taken in some areas of the Caribbean and thus might be found in southern Florida and the Keys. The pelagic lifestyle of this species makes the occurrence of beached specimens rare.

Long-finned Pilot Whale *(Globicephala melaena)*

The long-finned pilot whale is slightly larger than the closely related short-finned pilot whale. The pectoral fins are quite long (up to one-fifth of the body length). The species ranges throughout the major oceans of the world, primarily in temperate waters. This pilot whale has been recorded as far south as North Carolina and there are some questionable reports from Georgia. It normally inhabits offshore waters but may move into inshore waters and even bays during the summer months. The long-finned pilot whale could turn up along the Atlantic coast of Florida.

North Sea Beaked Whale *(Mesoplodon bidens)*

This arctic species is considered the most northerly of the beaked whales. Until recently, it had been recorded no farther south than Cape Cod in New England. It was therefore very surprising that, on 17 October 1984, a single specimen stranded in St. Joseph's Bay, Gulf County, Florida. It was a subadult male measuring 14.75 feet long. Since there are no other records of the North Sea beaked whale south of New England, this undoubtedly represents a very lost, widely wandering individual. It is not likely that a population of this cold-water whale occurs in Florida waters. It will remain on the "possibly present" list until other specimens are recorded.

This whale is dark charcoal gray on the back, with white spots scattered overall. Young animals are unspotted and lighter colored on the belly. The mouth contains only a single pair of teeth located midway between the tip of the lower jaw and the back corner of the mouth. This species sometimes reaches a length of almost 17 feet.

Jaguarundi *(Felis yagouaroundi)*

This is a small tropical cat with a long neck and weasel-like head. It has been sighted in many parts of Florida, but no specimen has ever been taken to prove its presence. It somewhat resembles a house cat and occurs in two color phases, bluish gray or reddish yellow, that are uniform over the entire body. The tail is nearly as long as the head and body combined, and the legs are short. The range of the jaguarundi extends from southern Arizona and Texas to South America. If it has been introduced to Florida, a specimen of this elusive creature will eventually be taken. It prefers to live in dense thickets and brushy areas.

Acknowledgements and Photo Credits

Many friends and colleagues assisted in the preparation of this book over the years—many without even realizing how helpful they were in sharing information and knowledge. These include Richard McGuire, Graham Hickman, Albert Maida, Stephen Adams, Georgene Carson, David Caldwell, Edwin Komarek, Roy Komarek, Clinton Conaway, Tom Stombaugh, Llewellyn Ehrhart, Don Wood, John Waters, Robert Baker, James Stevenson, Chris Belden, Ben Gregory, Nicholas Holler, Knox Jones, Daniel O'Dell, Edward Asper, Michael Smith, Durbin Tabb, Darren Williams, Dean Martin, William Hunsucker, Victor Heller, Wilson Baker, and Jeffery Gore.

I am also grateful to the following people who helped secure or provided photographs of mammal species to illustrate this book: Roger Barbour, Merlin Tuttle, James Parnell, Richard LaVal, Thomas Simmons, Thomas French, Barry Mansell, Robert Herd, David Decker, John Waters, Paul Lefebvre, Edward Taylor, James Brady, Karl Maslowski, Marion Boronell, Paul Rose, James Mead, Daniel O'Dell, Trey Walker, Stephen Leatherwood, David Caldwell, Howard Winn, Charles Carley, Gilbert Twiest, Phillip August, Charles Woods, Reginald Barrett, Lang Elliott, James Lackey, Eileen Taylor, Warren Parker, and Al Baker.

Those agencies or institutions that also graciously provided pictures of mammals are as follows: U.S. Fish and Wildlife Service; Florida Game and Fresh Water Fish Commission; Florida Department of Natural Resources; American Society of Mammalogists; Sea World, Inc.; Smithsonian Institute; New England Aquarium; Marineland, Inc.; University of South Florida.

A special thanks is also accorded those persons who reviewed and proofread parts or all of the book manuscript, including James Wolfe, Stephen Humphrey, David Cook, Bradley Gruver, and Albert Baker. Funds for the writing of this manuscript were provided under contract with the Florida Game and Fresh Water Fish Commission's Nongame Wildlife Program.

CHECKLIST OF FLORIDA MAMMALS

Species	Florida Range	Habitat Preference	Relative Abun- dance
ORDER MARSUPIALIA			
POUCHED MAMMALS			
Family Didelphidae, Opossums			
Virginia opossum	Statewide	most habitats	A
ORDER INSECTIVORA			
INSECTIVORES			
Family Soricidae, Shrews			
southeastern shrew	N 2/3	wet forests	R+
southern short-tailed shrew	Statewide*	forests	C+
least shrew	Statewide*	fields	C
Family Talpidae, Moles			
eastern mole	Statewide*	most habitats	A
star-nosed mole	N 1/3	moist soil	U
ORDER CHIROPTERA			
BATS			
Family Vespertillionidae,			
Twilight Bats			
little brown bat	N border	caves, buildings	R
gray bat	N Panhandle	caves	R+
Keen's bat	N Panhandle	caves	R
southeastern bat	N 2/3	caves, buildings	A
Indiana bat	N Panhandle	caves	R+
silver-haired bat	Panhandle	trees	R
eastern pipistrelle	Statewide*	caves, trees	C
Rafinesque's big-eared bat	Statewide++	trees, cabins	U
big brown bat	Statewide*	caves, trees	R
hoary bat	N 1/3	trees	C
red bat	N 2/3	trees	C
Seminole bat	Statewide*	trees	C
yellow bat	Statewide*	forests	A
evening bat	Statewide*	trees, buildings	C
Family Molossidae,			
Free-tailed Bats			
Brazilian free-tailed bat	Statewide*	buildings, trees	C
Wagner's mastiff bat	S 1/4	buildings, trees	R
little mastiff bat	Fla. Keys	buildings, trees	U
Family Phyllostomidae,			
Fruit Bats			
Antillean Fruit Bat	Lower Keys	hammocks	U
ORDER EDENTATA			
SLOTHS, ANTEATERS, AND			
ARMADILLOS			
Family Dasypodidae, Armadillos			
nine-banded armadillo**	Statewide*	most habitats	A

Species	Florida Range	Habitat Preference	Relative Abundance
ORDER LAGOMORPHA			
RABBITS AND JACKRABBITS			
Family Leporidae,			
Rabbits and Hares			
eastern cottontail	Statewide*	fields	A
marsh rabbit	Statewide	marshes, wet meadows	A+
black-tailed jackrabbit**	Dade County	fields	R
ORDER RODENTIA			
GNAWING MAMMALS			
Family Sciuridae, Squirrels			
eastern chipmunk	NW Panhandle	mesic forests	R+
eastern gray squirrel	Statewide	all forests	A
fox squirrel	Statewide*	open pine, cypress	C+
Mexican red-bellied squirrel**	Elliott Key	tropical forest	C
southern flying squirrel	Statewide*	oak forests	A
Family Geomyidae,			
Pocket Gophers			
southeastern pocket gopher	N 2/3	uplands areas	A+
Family Castoridae, Beaver			
beaver	N 1/3	streams, lakes	C
Family Cricetidae,			
New World Rats, Mice, & Voles			
eastern woodrat	N 2/3, Key Largo	mature forests	C+
hispid cotton rat	Statewide	fields, brush	A
eastern harvest mouse	N 2/3	fields	U
marsh rice rat	Statewide*	marshes	C+
Florida mouse	S 2/3*	dry oak-pine forests	C+
beach or oldfield mouse	N 2/3	coastal dunes, old fields	C+
cotton mouse	Statewide	forests	A+
golden mouse	N 2/3	forests	C
pine vole	N 1/3	upland forests	C
meadow vole	Levy County	salt marshes	R+
round-tailed muskrat	Peninsula*	marshes, lakeshores	C
Family Muridae,			
Old World Rats & Mice			
house mouse**	Statewide	cosmopolitan	C
black or roof rat**	Statewide	cosmopolitan	A
Norway rat**	Statewide	slums, wharfs	C
Family Myocastoridae,			
Nutrias and Hutias			
nutria**	Statewide*	marshes, lakes, streams	C
ORDER CARNIVORA			
FLESH-EATING MAMMALS			
Family Ursidae, Bears			
black bear	Statewide*	all habitats	R+
Family Procyonidae, Raccoons			
raccoon	Statewide	all habitats	A

Checklist of Florida Mammals

Species	Florida Range	Habitat Preference	Relative Abun-dance
Family Mustelidae, Weasels & Skunks			
mink	N coasts, Everglades	marshes	R+
long-tailed weasel	Statewide*	most habitats	R
striped skunk	Statewide*	most habitats	C
eastern spotted skunk	Statewide*	fields, open forests	C
river otter	Statewide*	streams, lakes	C
Family Canidae, Dogs, Foxes, and Coyotes			
gray fox	Statewide*	most habitats	C
red fox	Statewide*	uplands	C
coyote**	Statewide	fields, prairies	R
Family Felidae, Cats			
bobcat	Statewide	most habitats	C
panther or cougar	S 1/3*	most habitats	R+
ORDER PINNIPEDIA SEALS AND SEA LIONS			
Family Phocidae, Hair Seals			
harbor seal	Atlantic	coastal marine	R
hooded seal	Atlantic	coastal marine	R
ORDER SIRENIA MANATEES			
Family Trichechidae, Manatees			
manatee	Statewide	rivers, coastal marine	R+
ORDER ARTIODACTYLA EVEN-TOED HOOFED MAMMALS			
Family Suidae, Pigs			
wild boar or feral pig**	Statewide*	most habitats	A
Family Cervidae, Deer			
white-tailed deer	Statewide	all habitats	A+
sambar deer**	St. Vincent Island	wetland borders	C
ORDER CETACEA WHALES			
Family Delphinidae, Dolphins and Porpoises			
rough-toothed dolphin	Atlantic, Gulf	marine	R
long-snouted spinner dolphin	Atlantic, Gulf	marine	R
short-snouted spinner dolphin	Atlantic, Gulf	marine	R
striped dolphin	Atlantic, Gulf	marine	R
Atlantic spotted dolphin	Atlantic, Gulf	marine	C
pantropical dolphin	Atlantic, Gulf	marine	R
saddle-backed dolphin	Atlantic, Gulf	marine	C
Fraser's dolphin	Atlantic, Gulf	marine	R
bottle-nosed dolphin	Atlantic, Gulf	marine	A
false killer whale	Atlantic, Gulf	marine	R
killer whale	Atlantic, Gulf	marine	R
pygmy killer whale	Atlantic, Gulf	marine	R
Risso's dolphin or grampus	Atlantic, Gulf	marine	R
short-finned pilot whale	Atlantic, Gulf	marine	A

Checklist of Florida Mammals

Species	Florida Range	Habitat Preference	Relative Abundance
Family Phocoenidae, Porpoises			
harbor porpoise	Atlantic	marine	R
Family Kogiidae, Pygmy Sperm Whales			
pygmy sperm whale	Atlantic, Gulf	marine	R
dwarf sperm whale	Atlantic, Gulf	marine	R
Family Physeteridae, Sperm Whales			
giant sperm whale	Atlantic, Gulf	marine	R+
Family Ziphiidae, Beaked Whales			
goose-beaked whale	Atlantic, Gulf	marine	R
dense-beaked whale	Atlantic, Gulf	marine	R
Antillean beaked whale	Atlantic, Gulf	marine	R
True's beaked whale	Atlantic, Gulf	marine	R
Family Balaenopteridae, Fin Whales			
fin whale	Atlantic, Gulf	marine	R+
minke whale	Atlantic, Gulf	marine	R
sei whale	Atlantic, Gulf	marine	R+
Bryde's whale	Atlantic, Gulf	marine	R
humpback whale	Atlantic, Gulf	marine	R+
Family Balaenidae, Right Whales			
right whale	Atlantic, Gulf	marine	R+
EXTIRPATED NATIVE SPECIES			
red wolf or Florida black wolf	Statewide	mature forests	
West Indian monk seal	Atlantic, Gulf	coastal marine	
bison or buffalo	N 1/3	uplands	

KEY TO SYMBOLS

A = Abundant in Florida
C = Common in Florida
R = Rare in Florida
U = Unknown abundance in Florida
+ = Some populations are endangered, threatened, or species of special concern in Florida
++ = Absent from extreme southern tip and Florida Keys
* = Absent from Florida Keys
** = Nonnative established species (exotic species)

Florida Distribution Maps

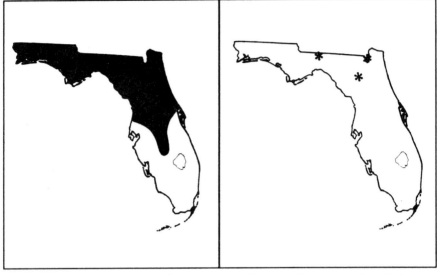

Distribution of southeastern shrew (pg. 19) in Florida.

Distribution of star-nosed mole (pg. 27) in Florida and vicinity.

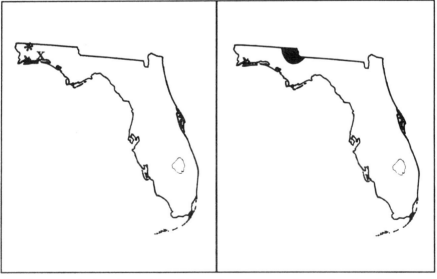

Distribution of silver-haired bat (✳), (pg. 37), and little brown bat (X), (pg. 29), in Florida.

Distribution of gray bat (pg 31), Keen's bat (pg. 33), and Indiana bat (pg. 36) in Florida.

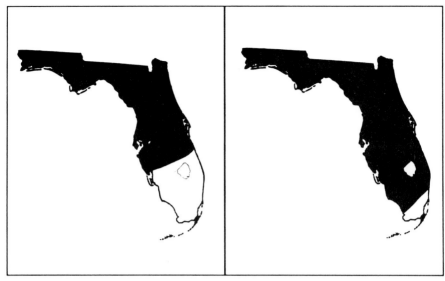

Distribution of southeastern bat (pg. 34) in Florida.

Distribution of Rafinesque's big-eared bat (pg. 39) in Florida.

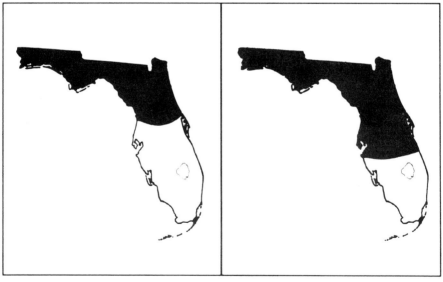

Distribution of hoary bat (pg. 41) in Florida.

Distribution of red bat (pg. 43) in Florida.

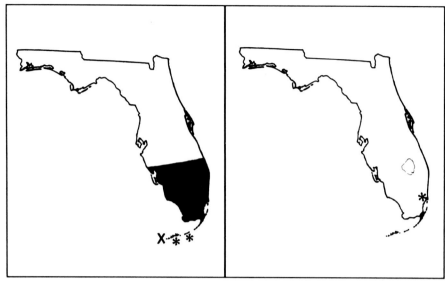

Distribution of Wagner's mastiff bat (pg. 49), little mastiff bat (✱), (pg. 51), and Antillean fruit bat (X), (pg. 52) in Florida.

Distribution of black-tailed jackrabbit (pg. 60) in Florida.

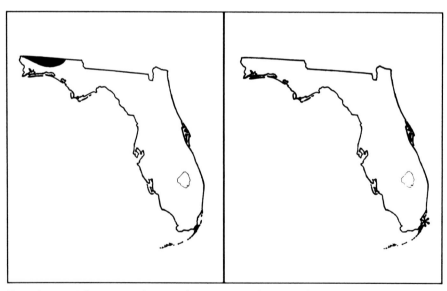

Distribution of eastern chipmunk (pg. 62) in Florida.

Distribution of Mexican red-bellied squirrel (pg. 68) in Florida.

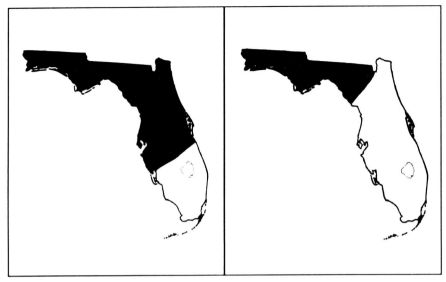

Distribution of southeastern pocket gopher (pg. 73) in Florida.

Distribution of beaver (pg. 76) in Florida.

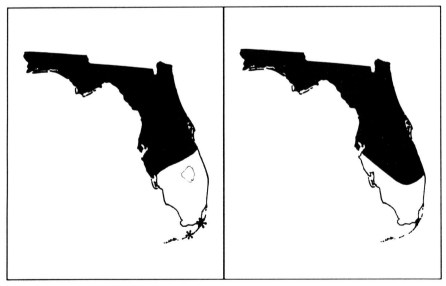

Distribution of eastern woodrat (pg. 80) in Florida.

Distribution of eastern harvest mouse (pg. 83) in Florida.

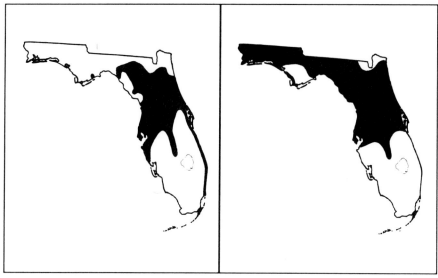

Distribution of Florida mouse (pg. 87) in Florida.

Distribution of beach or oldfield mouse (pg. 89) in Florida.

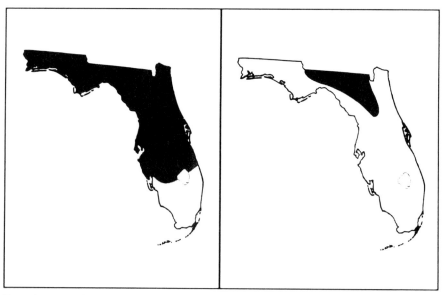

Distribution of golden mouse (pg. 93) in Florida.

Distribution of pine vole (pg. 95) in Florida.

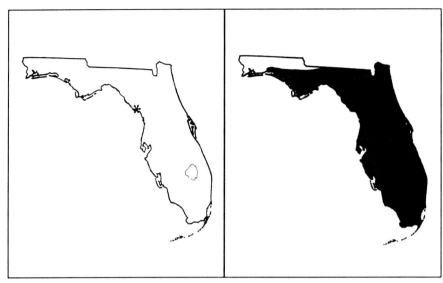

Distribution of meadow vole
(pg. 97) in Florida.

Distribution of round-tailed muskrat
(pg. 99) in Florida.

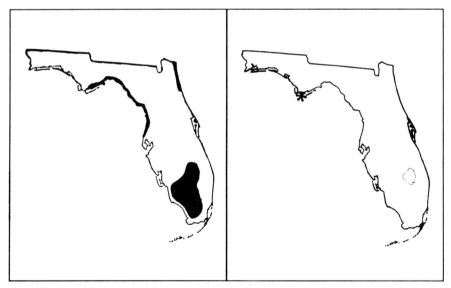

Distribution of mink (pg. 114)
in Florida.

Distribution of sambar deer (pg. 148)
in Florida.

The Study of Mammals

A wide variety of methods are used to study mammals and gain new insight into their natural history. The simplest approach, but not always feasible, is direct observation of the animals. Unfortunately, most mammals (in contrast to the ever-popular birds) are rather secretive and difficult to find or keep in view (about two-thirds of them are nocturnal). Therefore, we usually turn to certain indirect methods of obtaining data on mammals. Signs of animal habitation provide one of the most useful sources for study. These include tracks, nests, fecal droppings, tooth marks, food caches, feeding remnants, burrows or dens, scent posts, and runways or trails. A knowledgeable observer can often use such signs to determine the kind of mammal leaving the sign and gain considerable natural history information about the animals themselves.

The footprints or tracks that mammals leave are usually most easily identified if the substrate is mud, moist sand, or fresh snow. In many species, tail markings are also found with the tracks. Each species leaves its own unique signature such as the number and shapes of toes, claw imprints, palm prints, distance between the tracks, tail marks, and other signs. The tracks of many larger mammals are usually the easiest to identify and interpret. Those of smaller mammals are the most difficult to identify as to species because several forms may leave almost identical tracks.

The fecal droppings (or scat) of mammals also are very useful in identifying them to species, especially in combination with tracks and other signs. The size, color, shape, and contents of scat often have clear, species-specific characteristics. The droppings of larger mammals, such as artiodactyls and carnivores, are frequently the most distinctive, while those of small species such as shrews or mice are similar to one another. Careful dissection of scats can usually provide very accurate information about the feeding habits of species, both what was eaten as well as the relative quantities of each food item consumed.

For the naturalist who may wish to pursue the subject of mammal tracks, scat, and sign identification more actively, the following book is very helpful:

O. J. Murie. 1974. *A Field Guide to Animal Tracks.* Houghton Mifflin Co., Boston, Mass.

The home sites of many common mammal species are also easily recognized. There they spend much of their time rearing young, avoiding predators, and resting or sleeping. Burrowing and tree-dwelling species usually construct nests of grasses, leaves, sticks, fur, or other suitable materials. Aquatic mammals either build bulky nests in and over the water or live in deep bank burrows, whose entrances are frequently concealed below the water surface. Well worn trails often extend from terrestrial mammal nest and burrow entrances to feeding sites. Bats, woodrats, and several other nocturnal species often roost in caves, rock crevices, hollow trees, and old buildings.

Some mammals produce excavations that are evidence of their presence. Pocket gophers and moles bring dirt to the surface to form earth mounds. Rabbits and hares make shallow depressions (or forms) on the ground's surface for resting and birthing sites. Tunnel entrances of burrowing species may be either vertical or dug at an acute angle and can either be plugged or left open, according to the species of mammal involved.

In addition to fecal droppings, other signs can indicate feeding activities in mammals. Deer tend to browse on the twigs and leaves of trees and shrubs, sometimes pruning them rather severely. Rodents often leave shells of seeds that they have eaten or grass cuttings in runways. Several species also cache uneaten food items as a hedge against leaner times in the future. The items stored include tubers, roots, bulbs, grasses, seeds, fungi, fruits, nuts, and arthropods.

In general, the indirect types of evidence of mammal presence are almost boundless and await discovery by the trained eye and clever mind of the observer.

Many mammals must be trapped or collected for study. For most, this is the only way they can be seen at all. They must be brought into the laboratory for certain types of investigations, or may be marked for individual identification and released for field study. Mammals are captured in a wide variety of sizes and kinds of traps, nets, and snares. It is not unusual for a special kind of trap to be designed for only one type of mammal, as is the case with mole traps or pocket gopher traps.

Many state and federal laws or regulations control the capture, possession, transport, and deposition of various mammal species. At the state level, the Florida Game and Fresh Water Fish Commission is primarily empowered to enforce these regulations. At the federal level this responsibility falls mainly upon the U.S. Fish and Wildlife Service.

Marking mammals that are to be released back into the field for various ecological or population studies is accomplished through several different methods. The procedure may be as simple as toe or ear clipping to give each mammal a number or unique mark that can always be recognized and identified. Other marking methods include colored fur dyes, numbered or colored metal tags, fur clipping, branding, tattooing, radio transmitters, implanted radioisotopes, ingested food dyes, and related methods. The proper marking method must be carefully tailored to the scientific objective of the mammal study to be undertaken.

Finally, the keeping of detailed and accurate field notes and data sheets is a vital ingredient of any study of mammals. All collected specimens, to have any scientific importance, must be accompanied by recorded data on the precise locality, date of capture, physical characteristics and measurements, method of collection, sex and age, reproductive status, and name of the collector.

In these ways, much interesting and important information on the life histories of our Florida mammal species can be obtained.

Preservation of Mammal Specimens

Occasionally private mammal collections are made and maintained by individuals interested in mammals, but most studies today are conducted by specialists. Mammal collections are usually maintained by public or private institutions, because of the expense and special long-term curatorial problems. There are, however, many valuable contributions regarding the behavior patterns and geographical distribution of mammals that can be made by nonprofessionals and by the public in general. Such contributions are made through careful direct observations of mammals, coupled with accurate note taking and recording of the information.

Mammals are normally preserved in museums as study skins with the skulls or skeletons. Because the preparation of a series of study skins of mammals is a highly involved process and requires special skills, training, and experience, the layperson would be well advised to collect mammals with a camera.

For the reader who is specifically interested in learning the techniques for preparing museum specimens, I would recommend the following reference found in many libraries:

Hall, E. R. 1981. *The Mammals of North America*. John Wiley & Sons, New York, N.Y. 1181 pages.

To prevent decomposition of a mammal until it can be prepared as a museum skin or autopsied for other purposes, it should be properly labeled, then placed in a plastic bag, and kept frozen until prepared.

For the person who obtains a specimen that needs identification by a specialist and lacks freezer space, smaller species may be preserved in 70-90% alcohol or in 5-10% formaldehyde. An incision made in the abdominal wall of the mammal will speed penetration of the chemical and result in better preservation. Larger species should be refrigerated or frozen, if possible, until they can be examined by a mammalogist or wildlife biologist.

Selected References

For the student of natural history whose interests are stimulated by this book, a selected list of reference sources has been compiled to provide additional information on mammals.

General References:

Allen, T.B., ed. 1979. *Wild Animals of North America*. National Geographic Society. Washington, DC.

American Society of Mammalogists. 1969-present. *Mammalian Species*. American Society of Mammalogists, Allen Press, Inc., Lawrence, KS.

Anderson, S., and J. K. Jones, Jr. 1984. *Orders and Families of Recent Mammals of the World*. John Wiley and Sons, New York, NY.

Barbour, R. W., and W. H. Davis. 1969. *Bats of America*. University Press of Kentucky, Lexington, KY.

Brown, L. N. 1991. *Sea Mammals, Atlantic, Gulf, and Caribbean*. Windward Publishing, Miami, FL.

Chapman, J. A., and G. A. Feldhamer, eds. 1982. *Wild Mammals of North America: Biology, Management, and Economics*. The Johns Hopkins University Press, Baltimore, MD.

Current Mammalogy. 1987-present. An annual published by Plenum Press, New York, NY.

Davis, D. E., and F. B. Golley. 1963. *Principles in Mammalogy*. Reinhold Publishing Corporation. New York.

Gunderson, H. L. 1976. *Mammalogy*. McGraw-Hill Book Company, New York, NY.

Hall, E. R. 1981. *The Mammals of North America*. 2nd edition. John Wiley and Sons, New York, NY. Vols. 1-2.

Harrison, R. and M. Bryden, eds. 1988. *Whales, Dolphins and Porpoises*. Facts on File, Inc., New York, NY.

Honacki, J. H., K. E. Kinman, and J. W. Koeppl. 1982. *Mammal Species of the World: A Taxonomic and Geographic Reference*. Allen Press, Inc., Lawrence, KS.

Jones, J. K., Jr., R. S. Hoffman, D. W. Rice, C. Jones, R. J. Baker, and M. D. Engstrom. 1992. *Revised Checklist of North American Mammals North of Mexico, 1991*. Occasional Papers, The Museum, Texas Tech University, Number 146.

Journal of Mammalogy. 1919-present. A quarterly published by The American Society of Mammalogists.

Journal of Wildlife Management. 1937-present. A quarterly published by The Wildlife Society.

MacDonald, D., ed. 1984. *The Encyclopedia of Mammals*. Facts on File, Inc., New York, NY.

Minasian, S. M., K. C. Balcomb, and L. Foster. 1984. *The World's Whales*. Smithsonian Books, Washington, DC.

Nowak, R. M., and J. L. Paradiso. 1983. *Walker's Mammals of the World*. 4th edition. The Johns Hopkins University Press, Baltimore, MD.

Vaughan, T. A. 1986. *Mammalogy*. 3rd edition. W. B. Saunders Co., Philadelphia, PA.

Field Guides:

Boschung, H. T., J. D. Williams, D. W. Gotshall, D. K. Caldwell, and M. C. Caldwell. 1983. *The Audubon Society Field Guide to North American Fishes, Whales, and Dolphins*. Alfred A. Knopf, Publishers, New York.

Burt, W. H., and R. P. Grossenheier. 1976. *A Field Guide to the Mammals*. 3rd edition. Houghton Mifflin Co., Boston, MA.

Glass, B. P. 1973. *A Key to the Skulls of North American Mammals*. Oklahoma State University, Stillwater, OK.

Murie, O. J. 1974. *A Field Guide to Animal Tracks*. 2nd edition. Houghton Mifflin Co., Boston, MA.

Smith, R. P. 1982. *Animal Tracks and Signs of North America*. Stackpole Books, Harrisburg, PA.

Whitaker, J. O., Jr. 1980. *The Audubon Society Field Guide to North American Mammals*. Alfred A. Knopf, Inc., New York, NY.

State and Regional Publications:

Ashton, R. E., ed. 1992. *Rare and Endangered Biota of Florida, Vol. 1. Mammals.* University Press of Florida, Gainesville, FL.

Brown, L. N. 1994. *A Checklist of Florida's Mammals.* Fla. Game & Fresh Water Fish Comm. Publ. (Nongame Wildlife Program).

Leatherwood, S., D. K. Caldwell, and H. E. Winn. 1976. *Whales, Dolphins, and Porpoises of the Western North Atlantic.* National Marine Fisheries Service, NOAA Technical Report, Circular 396.

Lowery, G. H. 1974. *The Mammals of Louisiana and Its Adjacent Waters.* Louisiana State University Press, Baton Rouge, LA.

Schwartz, C. W. and E. R. Schwartz. 1959. *The Wild Mammals of Missouri.* Univ. Missouri Press, Columbia, MO.

Sealander, J. A., and G. A. Heidt. 1990. *Arkansas Mammals.* University of Arkansas, Fayetteville, AR.

Stevenson, H. M. 1976. *Vertebrates of Florida: Identification and Distribution.* Univ. Press of Fla., Gainesville, FL.

Webster, W. D., J. F. Parnell, and W. E. Biggs. 1985. *Mammals of the Carolina, Virginia, and Maryland.* Univ. of North Carolina Press, Chapel Hill, NC.

Techniques Manuals:

Anderson, R. M. 1965. *Methods of Collecting and Preserving Vertebrate Animals.* 4th edition. Bulletin of the Natural Museum of Canada, Number 69, Biol. Ser. 18, Ottawa, Canada.

Hall, E. R. 1962. *Collecting and Preparing Study Specimens of Vertebrates.* Miscellaneous Publications Number 30, University of Kansas Museum of Natural History, Lawrence, KS.

Schemitz, S. D., ed. 1980. *Wildlife Management Techniques Manual, Fourth Ed. Revised.* The Wildlife Society, Washington, DC.

Selected References

211

Glossary of Biological Terms

aardwolf a type of canid or dog found in Africa that eats termites, insects, and carrion

abscission layer in deer, a weak layer that forms near the base of an antler to facilitate shedding

alar membrane the large gliding membrane that extends from front leg to back leg along the sides of flying squirrels

altricial describes young that are born naked, blind, and helpless; requiring prolonged parental care.

ambergris a commercially valuable secretion from the large intestine of sperm whales, used in making perfumes

annuli the yearly growth rings found in the teeth of carnivores and other mammals

antler a branched, horny ornament that grows annually on the head of a male deer and is shed at the end of the breeding season. While they are growing, antlers are covered with soft, vascular skin called velvet that later sluffs off.

anus the posterior opening of the digestive tract

arboreal adapted for living in trees

arthropods invertebrates that have jointed legs and an external skeleton

auditory bullae knobby prominences of bone on the skull that surround delicate middle and inner ear bones

baleen plate-like food strainers, in the mouths of large whales, that filter large amounts of water and trap small fishes, shrimp, and other invertebrates

bifurcate forked or split into two parts

blowhole nostril opening of a whale

blubber thick layer of fat beneath the skin of whales and pinnipeds

brackish marsh a marsh having diluted salt water

breaching a spectacular swimming maneuver of whales whereby they leap totally or partially above the surface and crash back into the water

brow ridge a prominent elevation or bump on the frontal bones of some mammal skulls

bunodont type of molar tooth with low cusps and flat grinding surface

cache a food hoard made by an animal for later use

calcar an elongated ankle bone that supports the trailing edge of the tail membrane of bats

canine tooth a type of tooth (located behind the incisors, usually long and cone shaped), adapted for grasping and piercing; one of the four basic types of teeth

cannon bone elongated leg bone in ungulates formed by fusion of foot and ankle bones that supports the animal's weight

carnassial tooth a type of cheek tooth in carnivores adapted for cutting or shearing flesh and bone

carnivorous feeding primarily on flesh or meat

castor gland the large scent gland, located at the base of the tail, in a beaver

cementum a bone-like layer surrounding the root of a tooth, that is often laminated, and used for determining the age of a mammal

centipede a flattened, elongate arthropod having one pair of legs per body segment and poison claws at the head end

class in taxonomy, a group of related orders such as Chiroptera, Rodentia, Lagomorpha, etc., that are placed together because of similarities

climax vegetation the final, self-perpetuating stage of plant succession

community a group of interacting organisms of various species, living in a common environment

coniferous cone-bearing trees such as pines and cypress

coy-dog the hybrid offspring of a coyote and a dog

cranium cavity of the skull which holds the brain

crepuscular being active at dust and dawn

cursorial a running type of locomotion

cuttlefish a squid-like marine mollusk eaten by whales

deciduous in plants, the yearly dropping of leaves at the end of each growing season; in animals, the milk teeth of young mammals that are replaced by permanent teeth as they grow and mature

delayed fertilization after copulation, fertilization of eggs is delayed over the winter, as in many bats. The sperm remain viable in the female reproductive tract until spring.

dentary the lower jaw bone containing teeth in mammals

diastoma a gap between teeth in the jaw, usually between the incisors and cheek teeth, because canines are absent

digitigrade adapted for walking on the tips of the toes

digits the toes or fingers of an appendage such as the foot and hand

diurnal active during the daytime

dolphin any small species of toothed whale; also, a species of marine fish

dorsal pertaining to the back or upper side of an animal

echolocation a means of locating objects by bouncing supersonic vocalizations off them, that are picked up by the ear, as in bats and whales

ecology the study of interrelationships between living organisms and their environment

endangered species a species at risk of becoming extinct

epiphyte a plant that grows upon another plant and obtains moisture and nutrients from the air

estuary a marine aquatic area where salt water and fresh water mix

evergreen a plant with foliage that remains green year-round

extinction the dying out or disappearance of an entire species

extirpation the disappearance of a species within a given geographical region or political subdivision (such as a state)

falcate hook-shaped or sickle-shaped, as the dorsal fin of some sharks and whales

fallow field an agricultural field that has not been farmed recently, but allowed to grow weeds, grass, vines, and brush

family in taxonomy, a group of related genera and species placed together because of similarities

fecundity the rate of reproduction

feral living under natural conditions or in the wild

flipper an appendage or limb with fully-webbed digits, that is adapted for aquatic locomotion

floodplain the area bordering a river that is subject to periodic flooding

forage to search for food

fossorial adapted for living under the ground, like the moles or pocket gopher

frontal bone the bone forming the top of the skull above the eyes in mammals

frugivorous feeding primarily on fruit

fusiform shaped like a cigar, tapering on both ends

gestation the duration of pregnancy for a species of mammal

genus a group of closely related species

guano bat or bird droppings deposited at their roosting sites

guard hairs the outer coat of coarse, longer hairs, covering the underfur of mammals

habitat the place where an organism is normally found living

hammock a stand of hardwood trees, usually of the broadleaf evergreen type

hedgehog a type of insectivore from Europe and Asia that is covered with spines and can roll up into a ball

herbivorous feeding primarily on plants or vegetation

hibernation a state of reduced metabolism and physical activity, usually occurring over winter

hierarchy the behavioral peck order of dominant animals in a population

hind a female deer or doe

hispid grizzled color pattern of the fur, resulting from a combination of brown, black, and light tan banding of the hairs

home range the area that a mammal is familiar with, where it carries on its normal daily activities

horn the hard sheath-like projection growing from the head of some members of the cattle family. Each horn has a bony core and is not shed annually.

hybrid offspring resulting from the interbreeding of two species

implantation the attachment of the tiny developing embryo to the wall of the mother's uterus

incisor a type of tooth, located at the front of the mouth, usually adapted for biting off pieces; one of the four basic types of teeth

induced estrus the presence of an adult male triggers ovulation in an adult female

insectivorous feeding primarily on insects and other invertebrates

interfemoral membrane the tail membrane of bats that stretches from one hind leg to the other and includes the tail

juvenile breeding occurrence of reproduction before the body has reached adult size

keeled calcar in some species of bats, the ankle bone supporting the tail membrane has a blade-like lateral flange

kit the young of certain mammals such as beavers, mink, raccoons, etc.

krill tiny oceanic crustaceans eaten by whales in huge quantities

labyrinthine having many complex chambers or tunnels

lacrimal referring to the tear gland of the eye

lactation secretion of milk by the mammary glands of a mammal with young

larva an immature, feeding stage of an insect or other invertebrate

Lepidoptera the order of insects that includes butterflies and moths

litter a group of offspring produced by a female at one birth

longevity the length of life of a species

marsupium the external pouch on the lower abdomen of marsupials that encloses the mammary glands and serves as an incubation chamber

mast seeds or nuts of trees such as oak, hickory, pecan, beech, etc., that are used as food by mammals and birds

maternity colony in certain bats, adult females that form unisexual colonies to give birth and care for the young

melanistic a black color phase of an animal

migration regular periodic, seasonal movements of a species from one part of its range to another

millipede an elongate arthropod having two pairs of legs per body segment and a round worm-like body

molar tooth one of the two types of cheek teeth (located at the back of the mouth), often large and adapted for grinding

molt the shedding and replacement of fur or hair

monogamous each male of a species mates with only one female

musk glands the strong-smelling scent glands present in certain animals such as shrews, skunks, and weasels

nocturnal active at night or in the dark

omnivorous feeding on both plant and animal material

order in taxonomy, a group consisting of related families of animals that are placed together because of similarities

os baculum the Latin name for the bone found in the penis of certain mammals such as carnivores, pinnipeds, and rodents

otolith an ear bone found in the inner ear of some animals, involved in balance and orientation

ovary the egg-producing organ located in the abdomen of female mammals

ovulation the release of an egg (ovum) or eggs (ova) from the ovary of the female

parietal bones skull bones located on top of the cranium

parturition the process of giving birth

pectoral located in the chest of midtrunk area, as the fins of whales or fish

pelage the hair or fur coat of a mammal

pelt the skin and fur or hair of a mammal that often has commercial value

pelvic located in the hip or lower trunk area as the appendages of certain animals

penis the male copulatory organ of an animal

placenta the vascular connection within the uterus between the developing embryo and its mother

plantigrade adapted for walking with the sole and heel of the foot touching the ground

pod a social group or herd of whales

polyestrous in a female mammal, having several reproductive cycles in a year

polygamous one sex of the species mates with multiple individuals of the other sex, rather than forming a strong pair bond with one mate

porpoise a small species of toothed whales

precocial describes young that are born fully furred, with eyes open, and able to move about, requiring little parental care

prehensile the ability of an appendage, such as the tail, to grasp or coil around objects

premolar tooth one of the two types of cheek teeth (located just behind the canines and in front of the molars), usually adapted for grinding or shearing

prey an animal that is killed and eaten for food by a predator

pseudorumination reingestion of soft fecal pellets by certain lagomorphs to pass the partially digested food through the digestive tract a second time

pupa a nonfeeding, resting stage of an insect which transforms into the adult stage

race a geographically and morphologically distinct subspecies or subgroup of a species

relict population a remnant population that has shrunk to a small size with time

rostrum a forward nose-like projection of the skull

rumen the first compartment of the complex stomach of some ungulates

rumination regurgitation, rechewing, and reswallowing of food by cattle as an aid to digestion

runway the worn, conspicuous pathway resulting from repeated use by some animals, such as rodents

rut the annual recurring state of sexual arousal; the time when breeding takes place

salamander a colloquial name used by some Floridians for the pocket gopher (a rodent); a rather slimy-skinned amphibian having a long tail and four limbs extending out at right angles to the body

saltatorial a hopping type of locomotion

scat the fecal droppings of a mammal

scavenger an animal that feed on the dead bodies of other animals

secondary succession the type of plant succession that occurs following a disruption, such as fire or plowing

sedentary inactive or settled in one place

semen the fluid produced by males which contains sperm

seral stage one of the community stages of plant succession, such as grassland or forest

sibling species a closely related species

sign an indirect evidence of the presence of an animal, such as tracks, hair, scent post, etc.

slug a shell-less, snail-like, terrestrial gastropod

solenodon a primitive shrew-like insectivore found in Cuba and Hispaniola

species a freely interbreeding group of animals that are reproductively isolated from other kinds of animals

species of special concern a species that is not yet threatened or endangered but its population numbers are declining and its overall status is of concern for the future

spermaceti the oil from the large cavity in the skull of sperm whales

subspecies a geographically and morphologically distinct race or subdivision of a species

succession over a period of time, the orderly replacement of communities on a given site, terminating in a climax community that is self-perpetuating

supraorbital process bony projection above the eye socket (orbit) on a mammal skull

supraorbital ridge prominent ridge of bone running anteriorly above the eye socket or orbit

tail fluke the dorsally flattened tail lobes of a whale or manatee

tenrec a type of shrew-like insectivore found in Madagascar

terrestrial adapted for living on dry land

territory an area defended by an animal or group of animals from other individuals or groups

testis the sperm-producing organ of male animals

threatened species a species whose numbers have declined to the point that they may eventually become endangered

tine a spike or prong of a deer antler

torpor a dormant or hibernating status

tragus a thin, leaf-like spike at the base of the ear opening of bats

underfur coat of dense fine hair, usually overlain by guard hairs, for insulation

understory vegetation and plants growing on the forest floor beneath the canopy of trees

unicusp single, cone-shaped tooth near the front of the mouth in shrews

uterus the organ of the female reproductive system within which embryos develop

vagina the female reproductive canal used for copulation and birth

ventral pertaining to the belly or underside of an animal

vertebrate an animal that has a vertebral column down the back protecting the delicate nervous system

vestigial the remnant of a structure that at one time was more developed and functional in a species

vibrissae long, stiff hairs or whiskers on the snout, that serve as touch receptors

wean to transfer the young mammal from mother's milk to other types of food

whale lice parasitic amphipods (crustaceans) found attached to the skin of whales

zygomatic arch the cheek bone of mammals

Index

Numbers in parentheses ( ) refer to photos or illustrations.